Solar Photovoltaics

Second, over the last two decades there has also been subtle but real evolution in the energy sector. We are no longer tied exclusively to power from our local utility or from gasoline or propane fired generators. Now, anyone can generate not just a few watts, but tens of kilowatts from the sun with affordable home solar systems at costs that are even less than power from the utility.

Home solar systems typically operate at voltages from 300 to 500 V dc. They are not only a very significant economical source of energy, but they can also be a great independent source of power in the field, or at home when the grid is down. This capability can marry nicely with the modern universal supply high-voltage dc inputs noted above.

Hybrid Vehicles

The third disruptive technology began in earnest with the Toyota Prius in the US in 2000. The gas/electric hybrid technology not only doubled vehicle gas mileage through energy efficiency, but also paved the way for the future of battery electric vehicles. It is now available from almost all major car manufacturers.

Of special interest to the ham or the DIY energy buff is the fact that hybrid vehicles typically include huge electric generators on the order of 50 kW or more. With more than 75 makes and models on the market in 2018, these mobile generators on wheels have great potential for emergency and backup power. Further, compared to rarely used standby generators, a hybrid vehicle is extremely reliable because we drive it regularly. Hybrid vehicle power is available not only at the home and ham radio station, but also can travel wherever we go.

This massive electrical generation capability is something that should be considered in any backup or emergency response plan. So far, only two manufacturers have demonstrated car-to-home interfaces and only in Japan; but it is a huge untapped resource that will eventually be marketed to the car owners everywhere once the demand evolves. Just like solar power systems, hybrids operate at a high voltage of between 200 to 400 V dc, which is compatible with more and more of our energy systems.

Electric Vehicles

The fourth big development, not generally recognized yet for its full potential, is the modern electric vehicle (EV). Now approaching a full decade of growth, this newest disruptive technology can also find great application when integrated into the ham's home energy system. In just 10 years since the introduction of Tesla Roadster in 2008 and followed by the Nissan Leaf and Chevy Volt in 2011, there are more than 46 full-size EVs on the market from almost every major manufacturer. And the major manufacturers have already announced another 212 makes and models that will be introduced over the next seven years, by 2025.

Electric vehicles increase the battery size compared to hybrids by a factor of 10 to 50 times. This is an enormous number of kilowatt-hours of battery capacity now available to anyone, and it has great potential for hams interested in emergency and backup power. When combined with only a dozen solar panels, an EV can provide indefinite daily average American transportation mileage (40 miles a day) every day forever without any dependence on gasoline or gas stations. And in just my lifetime, the number of people living in urban areas has doubled from 30% to near 60%, making local transportation (easily done with electric) the largest disruptive energy change to clean up our air.

Big Battery Storage

The fifth disruptive technology in this power and energy revolution is big battery energy storage. This is really just a spinoff from the drastic improvements in energy density of batteries developed for EVs, but the ability to generate and store vast amounts of energy at home is a game changer.

The modern EV battery has improved at least a factor of 25 or so in lower cost and higher energy density over my 56 years in ham radio. Tesla, the premier maker of modern EVs, also takes the same battery technology used in their premium vehicles and makes it available in a product called the Powerwall. This is really just an EV battery hung vertically on the wall in the garage, where it can provide tens of kilowatt-hours (kWh) of battery capacity for whole-house energy use. Combined with a solar system, this technology can give the radio amateur a backup energy supply or potential energy independence never before possible.

Energy Choices
for the Radio Amateur

Your Power Sources in the 21ST Century

Bob Bruninga, WB4APR

Production:
Michelle Bloom, WB1ENT
Sue Fagan, KB1OKW — Cover Art
Jodi Morin, KA1JPA
Dave Pingree, N1NAS
Maty Weinberg, KB1EIB

Copyright © 2019 by
The American Radio Relay League, Inc.

Copyright secured under the Pan-American Convention

International Copyright secured

All rights reserved. No part of this work may be reproduced in any form except by written permission of the publisher. All rights of translation are reserved.

Printed in USA

Quedan reservados todos los derechos

ISBN: 978-1-62595-103-8

First Edition
First Printing

We strive to produce books without errors. Sometimes mistakes do occur, however. When we become aware of problems in our books (other than obvious typographical errors), we post corrections on the ARRL website. If you think you have found an error, please check **www.arrl.org/notes** for corrections. If you don't find a correction there, please let us know by sending e-mail to **pubsfdbk@arrl.org**.

Contents

    Preface

    About the ARRL

1. Introduction and Background
2. The New World of Everyday Power (DC)
3. The Solar Power Revolution
4. Choosing Your Home Solar System
5. Solar DIY at Home and in the Field
6. New Energy Sources of Radio Frequency Interference (RFI)
7. Electrification of Transportation
8. Electric Vehicle DIY Projects
9. Conventional Backup and Emergency Power
10. High Voltage DC Emergency and Backup Power
11. The Powerwall and Grid Battery Storage for Home
12. Life's Major Energy Milestones
13. Making the Switch to Clean Renewable Energy — Examples
14. Amateur Satellites and Thermal Energy Balance
15. How Our Energy Use Shapes Our World Today
16. Conclusion

    Appendix — References and Bibliography

    About the Author

Preface

Five Disruptive Energy Technologies

In the half century since I got my Novice license in 1962, the most exciting and fun part of ham radio to me has been operating in the field and making preparations for providing power for emergency operations when the grid is down. With the strong principles of emergency radio operations and preparations for all manner of civil disasters and response, the main concern of any such preparations is to have power available when and where needed.

As more and more of our routine daily lives depend on technology, we sometimes take the availability of power to run all of our devices for granted. Over this same half century, there have been five subtle but disruptive revolutions in power and energy in our daily lives that can be of interest to the Amateur Radio operator or DIY handyman. This book will look at these in detail and explore how they all have the potential to act synergistically to change our approach to energy and power and keep us prepared for operating no matter what the future brings.

Power Supplies

First, there has been a subtle and evolutionary transition in electrical power supplies that has also brought significant new capabilities to amateur operations. Power supplies are no longer massive 60 Hz boat anchors that weigh 10 times as much as modern supplies. Today's lighter supplies enable portable and handheld operations unheard of in the 1960s.

These modern universal power supplies now operate over a range of input voltages from 100 to 240 V ac. As will be discussed in Chapter 2, a little-known and untapped capability is that these power supplies typically can also run from high-voltage dc input as well. This high-voltage dc input capability may seem like an insignificant side note, but its compatibility with the other four disruptive revolutions has enormous potential applications in our new world of energy and the topics covered in this book.

Putting It All Together

And that is the purpose of this book, to address these five new disruptive technologies that are now available to anyone and at costs that are now less than that of the traditional energy sources — coal, oil, natural gas, propane, and diesel. The common element that we will explore in all of these disruptive technologies is that they operate on electricity as their primary source of power, and therefore there are many commonalities. First, there are now numerous sources of clean, renewable energy to produce electricity without burning fossil fuels. Second, electricity is now something we can generate at home or anywhere else with solar panels, independent of any external supply chain after initial purchase. And third, these technologies typically operate at high dc voltages roughly in the range of 200 to 450 V dc, and not the 120/240 V, 60 Hz ac that we are so accustomed to.

We will explore ways that these ideas can be used independently or together, not only for the Amateur Radio hobby, but also as our own sources of emergency and backup power at home and in the field. It's a whole new world of power and energy, and we will cover a number of my attempts — both good and not so good — to take advantage of it.

Bob Bruninga, WB4APR
www.aprs.org
January 2019

About the ARRL

The seed for Amateur Radio was planted in the 1890s, when Guglielmo Marconi began his experiments in wireless telegraphy. Soon he was joined by dozens, then hundreds, of others who were enthusiastic about sending and receiving messages through the air — some with a commercial interest, but others solely out of a love for this new communications medium. The United States government began licensing Amateur Radio operators in 1912.

By 1914, there were thousands of Amateur Radio operators — hams — in the United States. Hiram Percy Maxim, a leading Hartford, Connecticut inventor and industrialist, saw the need for an organization to unify this fledgling group of radio experimenters. In May 1914 he founded the American Radio Relay League (ARRL) to meet that need.

ARRL is the national association for Amateur Radio in the US. Today, with approximately 158,000 members, ARRL numbers within its ranks the vast majority of active radio amateurs in the nation and has a proud history of achievement as the standard-bearer in amateur affairs. ARRL's underpinnings as Amateur Radio's witness, partner, and forum are defined by five pillars: Public Service, Advocacy, Education, Technology, and Membership. ARRL is also International Secretariat for the International Amateur Radio Union, which is made up of similar societies in 150 countries around the world.

ARRL's Mission Statement: To advance the art, science, and enjoyment of Amateur Radio.
ARRL's Vision Statement: As the national association for Amateur Radio in the United States, ARRL:

- Supports the awareness and growth of Amateur Radio worldwide;
- Advocates for meaningful access to radio spectrum;
- Strives for every member to get involved, get active, and get on the air;
- Encourages radio experimentation and, through its members, advances radio technology and education;
  and
- Organizes and trains volunteers to serve their communities by providing public service and emergency communications.

At ARRL headquarters in the Hartford, Connecticut suburb of Newington, the staff helps serve the needs of members. ARRL publishes the monthly journal *QST* and an interactive digital version of *QST*, as well as newsletters and many publications covering all aspects of Amateur Radio. Its headquarters station, W1AW, transmits bulletins of interest to radio amateurs and Morse code practice sessions. ARRL also coordinates an extensive field organization, which includes volunteers who provide technical information and other support services for radio amateurs as well as communications for public service activities. In addition, ARRL represents US radio amateurs to the Federal Communications Commission and other government agencies in the US and abroad.

Membership in ARRL means much more than receiving *QST* each month. In addition to the services already described, ARRL offers membership services on a personal level, such as the Technical Information Service, where members can get answers — by phone, e-mail, or the ARRL website — to all their technical and operating questions.

A bona fide interest in Amateur Radio is the only essential qualification of membership; an Amateur Radio license is not a prerequisite, although full voting membership is granted only to licensed radio amateurs in the US. Full ARRL membership gives you a voice in how the affairs of the organization are governed. ARRL policy is set by a Board of Directors (one from each of 15 Divisions). Each year, one-third of the ARRL Board of Directors stands for election by the full members they represent. The day-to-day operation of ARRL HQ is managed by a Chief Executive Officer and his/her staff.

Join ARRL Today! No matter what aspect of Amateur Radio attracts you, ARRL membership is relevant and important. There would be no Amateur Radio as we know it today were it not for ARRL. We would be happy to welcome you as a member! Join online at **www.arrl.org/join**. For more information about ARRL and answers to any questions you may have about Amateur Radio, write or call:

ARRL — The national association for Amateur Radio®
225 Main Street
Newington CT 06111-1400 USA
Tel: 860-594-0200
FAX: 860-594-0259
e-mail: **hq@arrl.org**
www.arrl.org

Chapter 1: Introduction and Background

In this book, I hope to show how the changes in technology that are bringing us cleaner, renewable energy can be advantageous to the ham radio operator both at home and in the field. Although we resist change and it might seem daunting at the large scale needed to ensure a bright, clean energy future, changing to cleaner energy is easy to do as individuals. It can actually cost less than continuing to rely on traditional energy sources, and it has great potential for emergency backup power.

In our daily lives, we routinely face milestones where we have to make significant energy decisions — for example, the hot water heater fails and needs to be replaced. With a little bit of homework, we can be prepared to make the right decision when one of our legacy energy systems becomes unreliable or wears out. Replacing it with electrical systems that can run on clean power will actually save money in the long run.

Overview

This first chapter will give a brief background of my experiences over half a century in ham radio and my use of energy in my hobby and my home. Chapter 2 will set the stage by discussing how so many of our electronic devices now run on universal power supplies that can use high-voltage dc input as well as ac, and how switching converters have virtually eliminated the heavy 60 Hz iron transformer.

Chapters 3 and 4 show how properly investing in solar panels and a grid-tie system can supply a typical home with energy at half the cost of commercial ac from the local utility company. Chapter 5 suggests ways to apply solar panels to a variety of do-it-yourself (DIY) projects. Along with this switch to high-voltage dc systems comes the potential for radio frequency interference (RFI), and as discussed in Chapter 6, that can be devastating to ham radio operation nearby.

Since our cars and trucks are the second biggest energy consumer in our lives, Chapters 7 and 8 consider how the electrification of vehicles by almost every major car manufacturer is revolutionizing transportation and also providing mobile and portable energy sources that can be tapped for ham radio use.

Backup and emergency power are covered in Chapters 9 and 10. The availability of very large batteries in electric vehicles (EVs) gives rise to low-cost battery storage systems in other applications, such as home energy storage. That topic is covered in Chapter 11.

Chapter 12 gets back to the original thesis that we are forced to make major energy decisions every few years anyway, and that we should be prepared to make a choice that is not only less destructive to our environment and air quality, but that will also save us money in the long run, and better position us for backup power. Chapter 13 explores my practical experience with my home and my church, which have gone solar. We are also switching to EVs for clean, renewable transportation at lower cost.

In Chapter 14, I note how my experience in amateur satellites and in the classroom has taught me how the critical details of the surface of a small satellite has a profound impact on the equilibrium temperature of that object in space. These same principles apply to something as small as an Amateur Radio cubesat satellite (typically about 4 inches in each dimension) and as large as the Earth. We should be concerned about how we are making changes to our surface (land use and atmosphere) that will have profound impacts on the average temperature of the Earth. And finally in Chapter 15, I discuss how these changes are important to stop the pollution of our atmosphere caused by burning fossil fuels when there are so many cleaner, renewable alternatives.

Ham Radio and Energy Background

Before delving into some of these topics, it might be interesting to go over some of my own personal random-walk voyage in Amateur Radio and energy.

From getting my Novice license in 1962 in middle school, my first project was inspired by an article in *QST* to rewind an old dc car generator for 60 Hz, 120 V ac output when driven from a lawnmower engine. It was clever and extremely simple. Just remove all the multi-pole windings and replace them with a single coil in the same slots, but in such a pattern to end up with a two-pole armature. One wire was connected to the metal armature and the other wrapped around all the segments of the commutator so that the brushes then acted as a slip ring to carry off the ac power with the other side being the frame. Then it was a simple matter to choose the right size pulley

Figure 1.1 — A typical 1960s era homebrew generator (left) powered many portable operations. On the right, my first electric car project at Georgia Tech in 1970.

and adjust the field coil to get 60 Hz at around 110 V most of the time.

This portable power source provided a couple of hundred watts and went with us on all our local scout camping trips. It powered all our toys, which at the time were our first ham radios — military surplus ARC-5 transmitters with two tubes and capable of 75 W on CW, perfect for the Novice licensee.

My First Electric Vehicle (EV)

Amateur Radio was more or less on hold through college at Georgia Tech, where in 1970 my senior Electrical Engineering project was to build an electric car from an old WWII surplus aircraft starter motor on an old VW chassis (**Figure 1.1**). The goal was to make it to California in the first MIT/Cal-Tech Clean Air Car Race. Our car made it to the Mississippi River (St. Louis) before it would just not go another mile. For details, see "My first EV, The Elect-Reck at Ga-Tech - 1970" available online at **aprs.org/EV-at-tech.html.**

As a side note, in that final semester, an older fraternity brother took me for a ride in his Ford Mustang to give me my first sight of mobile ham radio. Where his ash tray used to be was a small metal plate with an on/off switch, a green and red lamp, and a connector for a big "car 54 where-are-you" carbon mic. This was wired to a huge suitcase-sized surplus commercial FM radio in his trunk, with crystals for operation on the original 146.94 MHz Atlanta FM repeater. I was hooked.

Early Ham Radio

I had attended Georgia Tech through the Navy ROTC program. After graduating in 1970, my first duty station was the Navy Post Graduate School in Monterey California, and the radio club was able to score a bunch of

Motorola Dispatcher FM radios in 1971. These had transistor receivers, but used instant warm-up pencil tubes in the transmitter. You had to pause one second from PTT for the dc/dc switching supply to squeal-up the high voltage and for the filaments to light before transmitting.

I put one under the seat of my MGB sports car and another on the side of my Honda 250 motorcycle. By 1972, I was stationed in Hawaii, and the dashboard of the MGB now had an old telephone dial and a new, bigger UHF suitcase-size Motorola transceiver that fully filled the trunk.

The telephone dial had not worked for a week since I finished it, but on a hunch, I turned the audio tone drive level down instead of up and up and up and bingo, without the overdrive distortion, it worked! I remember making my first successful telephone call through the Diamond Head autopatch late at night. The pulse tone dialing was just a tone oscillator and pulse dial inspired by a *QST* article on the Wichita autopatch. These surplus commercial mobile radios didn't even have transistors that could operate at UHF, and so the first stage of the receiver was simply a diode to downconvert to VHF, but it still had 1 microvolt sensitivity.

The Bluebox

A final communications adventure in 1972 was collecting 12 microswitches and cobbling together a crude keypad wired to eight twin-T transistor oscillators to generate touch-tones. The fun part was retuning these oscillators to the different tones used by the telephone long distance operators. This was called a *blue box* (**en.wikipedia.org/wiki/Blue_box**) and allowed the user to place a toll free 800-number phone call and then press a button for 2600 Hz, which would drop the trunk line connection and then allow you to dial your own new long-distance number.

Of course, this was of practically no use to me since I lived on a ship and did not have a phone! Ma Bell eventually moved to new signaling systems that did not use in-band tones. And they could also find and prosecute blue box users by listening for 2600 Hz tones on subscriber lines.

My Attempts at Wind Power

While stationed in Japan in 1973, my energy highlight was the construction of a 1 kW wind generator by laminating 21 layers of plywood into a 10-foot diameter, ideally shaped propeller mounted to an old car rear axle and 24 V truck generator. It was designed with a tip-speed ratio of 8-to-1 for maximum efficiency as a two-bladed propeller. These are far more efficient than 1-to-1 eggbeaters and other vertical axis types.

I waited weeks for there to be enough wind, and one day during lunch

Figure 1.2 — My first attempt at 1.5 kW wind power and immediate failure.

Figure 1.3 — A 4 foot Airpax turbine installed on my roof just to prove how poor home wind is.

hour I decided to do an initial test in an approaching typhoon while our ship was in Sasebo, Japan. Since this was prior to building any kind of brake mechanism, the system lasted about 5 minutes after I mounted the blade before I jumped off the 10-foot tower about the same time the blade flew off and broke 2 feet off of one end.

It was a *wow* moment and sounded like the whop-whop of a helicopter. I decided that this kind of wind power was just too scary, but also just too rare to be of any practical value unless one lived on a beach somewhere. Generally most people do not have enough wind at home to be of any value whatsoever. Unless your hat blows off your head every day when you go outside, you don't have enough wind. But in the Navy, I did live near water, and so it was fun to try. The prop now hangs over the door in my living room (**Figure 1.2**).

After building another 21-layer prop, this time only 4 feet in diameter, I finally bought a commercial 4-foot wind turbine typical of those seen on sailboats. The plan was to cut off the top of my tallest tree and mount it up there, but I never got around to it. So I mounted it at roof height as shown in **Figure 1.3**. It probably turns a dozen times a year and actually generates power only during huge storms for an hour or so. Worthless.

High-Voltage DC is Now Everywhere

Safety

High-voltage dc is dangerous, just like 60 Hz high-voltage ac, but there are very significant differences that must be relearned. Back when I got my Novice license in 1962, almost all ham radio involved high-voltage dc for both transmitters and receivers. In fact, a common Cub Scout requirement for 9 year olds was to build a two-tube radio with a high-voltage 100 V battery, and there seemed to be not much concern over safety.

By the 1960s, transistors and other solid-state devices were on the rise, and voltages dropped lower and lower. Over the next 50 years, the amateur and DIY (do-it-yourself) use of high-voltage dc dropped drastically and so the general knowledge about high-voltage dc safety has also atrophied. But in the last decade now, the DIY hobbyist is starting to see a comeback with higher voltages in several areas that might be of interest to the energy experimenter. So it is useful to go over these safety differences between ac and dc and the big difference in controlling them.

First is the war of the currents between ac (Tesla and Westinghouse) and Edison's dc where Edison electrocuted horses and dogs with ac to show how much safer his dc system was. It takes about four times the current at dc to have the same effect on muscles and heart as ac, though the currents are still quite small.

The National Institute for Occupational Safety and Health states that the let-go currents are considered to be about 22 mA for ac and 88 mA for dc. On the other hand, the ac may jolt the muscles and have some chance of throwing you off the current whereas with dc the muscles just clinch and may not let you let go. Using Ohm's Law and a dry skin resistance of 100 kΩ, you can see that relatively high voltages can be survived. But wet skin or broken skin can be as low as 1 kΩ, and under those conditions just 22 V ac is above the let-go threshold. And once the skin begins to conduct, the resistance can go down to 500 Ω, and even 44 V dc is at the let-go threshold.

Figure 1.A — With dc, opening contacts does *not* interrupt the circuit, it only creates a white hot plasma that will burn everything around it — The box it is in and then your house.

The Arc-Flash

An arc-flash occurs whenever a dc circuit is opened up under load. At the instant the switch is opened, the multiple amps of electrons are perfectly happy to jump the microscopic gap as the switch begins to open (**Figure 1.A**). This causes a small arc that vaporizes the metal and any impurities in the air and provides a nice low-resistance path to continue to flow. As the gap opens wider, the white-hot plasma continues to provide a path, and this continues with no end until the gap is so great (an inch or more) that the intense heat causes air convection to eventually blow out the flame. Meanwhile everything near the plasma is melted and ruined.

There are three basic ways to extinguish the high-voltage dc arc. One passive method is in the mechanical structure of the switch that opens the contact an inch or more. The contacts are surrounded by materials that can withstand the plasma for several milliseconds and which funnel air convection to blow the arc upward until it blows out. Another method, shown in **Figure 1.B**, is a properly placed

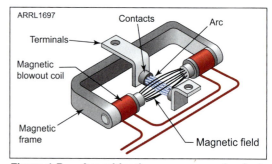

Figure 1.B — Arc mitigation can use mechanical or magnetic blowout structures or RC snubbers.

magnet that reacts against the magnetic field created by the heavy current flowing in the plasma to, again, blow the arc away (while still being able to survive the white-hot plasma for a fraction of a second). The final method is a simple RC snubber circuit.

RC Snubber Circuit

The RC snubber circuit places a capacitor across the contacts so that as the gap opens, the fully discharged capacitor will initially accept the current flow to bypass the switch contacts for a few milliseconds while the contacts can separate far enough that a plasma does not form. Thus, a simple capacitor does solve the dc disconnect failure of the switch, but then would destroy the same switch contacts the next time they close!

You will notice that when the switch is open, the full system voltage (maybe 500 V or more) appears across the capacitor, so it charges to full system voltage. When it closes, this very big voltage attempts to discharge through the contacts at infinite current and then destroys the contacts usually by welding them together. Not only does this ruin the switch, it also results in a high-voltage circuit *you cannot turn off*.

A solution is to put a resistor in series with the capacitor to limit this contact closure peak current to within the rating of the contacts. And this resistor has to survive that peak current for several milliseconds on each contact closure. Figuring out the correct values of the resistor and capacitor is very dependent on many variables and is considered more of an art than a science. See **Figure 1.C**.

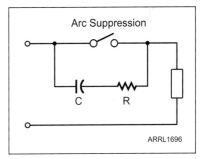

Figure 1.C — A simple properly designed RC snubber circuit can absorb the arc energy and save the contacts.

Notice also that for this to work, the capacitor has to be discharged when the contacts open to absorb the current. But to discharge the capacitor when the switch is closed to be ready for the next opening, there is the RC time constant of the two components. This means if the contacts are not closed for at least RC milliseconds, then the capacitor is not fully discharged and the snubber will not be ready for the next opening. I can envision someone rapidly toggling such a switch and not giving the RC circuit time to dissipate the first arc energy and so be ready for the next one. The plasma arc will form and you have the same disaster you were trying to avoid. I haven't seen anyone else really worried about this possible failure mode, but since the risk and consequences of failure can be catastrophic I am leery of depending on it, and always pause when cycling a dc switch.

On the other hand, ham radio has had nearly a century of experience with high-voltage transmitters and power supplies and the RC snubber on the high-voltage dc switch has been a matter of routine at power levels of a kilowatt or so. But in my thinking, all those power supplies and transmitters we built in past decades were all in metal enclosures. A little smoke and bang and fire inside a metal chassis was merely an inconvenience rather than a catastrophe.

Now almost everything is made of flammable plastic, and we have a new generation of operators who do not have this background and fundamental respect for high voltages, and so we have to be very careful in casually assuming that anything (think solar) acting at 500 V and higher with 7 to 9 A of white-hot potential plasma dissipating several kilowatts is easily protected against.

My First Production EV

The next project was my second electric car when I found an old abandoned Seabring Vanguard 1978 Electric City Car around 1983 and restored it to health for my 3 mile commute to the Naval Academy (**Figure 1.4**). These cars were considered the first production electric cars in the US and were slightly more than souped up golf carts, but they were street legal and could go 35 MPH. But then my job was moved down to Washington, DC, which was too far for that car.

Figure 1.4 — My 1978 Sebring Vanguard Electric City Car.

A few years later, my commute changed to a 30 mile round trip when I came back to the Naval Academy in 1990. That began a 28-year (and counting) crusade with the Naval Academy to let me pay the 50 cents a day for the electricity and privilege of plugging into a nearby 120 V ac outlet to charge the car battery at work to be able to make it home. After decades of letter writing to everyone from senators, congressmen, the vice president and president, as well as Chief of Naval Operations and admirals, I think I was finally successful in getting the US Department of Energy and Congress to include in the 2015 Congressional FAST act the provision that Federal agencies may in fact, do just that by law. Agencies may permit Federal employees to plug in to existing outlets for a payment of about $6 per bi-weekly pay period. Doing the math, that about equals the cost of daily charging at the national average 10 cent electric rate for the average government employee commute of 15 miles. A simple placard on the EV window would show that the employee has pre-paid for daily charging.

Yet still, after 28 years (and counting), that City Car is now in the weeds out back of my garage and as this was written in 2018, employees at the Naval Academy still cannot plug into any of the nine readily available standard 120 V ac outlets to trickle charge, in spite of a federal law encouraging it. My frustration with the lethargy-to-change, now several decades old, is part of the motivation for my recent energy evangelism and this book.

The First Amateur Radio BBS

Meanwhile, my other distraction at the time was amateur packet radio, which began with the AMRAD (Amateur Radio Research and Development) club in northern Virginia around 1978 or so. I built one of the first on-air and telephone-line packet bulletin board systems (BBS). This was at the same time as Ward Christensen's first telephone CBBS bulletin board system in Chicago that is credited as the start of modern online activity driving our lives to this day (**en.wikipedia.org/wiki/Bulletin_board_system**).

My system began on a Motorola AMI 6800 prototyping board and, by 1983 or so, evolved into a dual-port system based on the Commodore VIC-20 computer with a port on 145.01 MHz and on the 10.147.2 MHz HF packet frequency. I was able to get almost everyone in the AMRAD club on the air with modems that I found surplus at Dayton. These were telephone modem circuit cards built by Vadic.

At first I developed the modifications to use them at 170 Hz shift for RTTY, but then, when the AMRAD organization got the FCC to legalize ASCII on the ham bands, we began to use the modems as-is at 200 Hz shift. We put this on the HF port of the bulletin board and that established what became the worldwide 200 Hz shift amateur standard for HF packet radio.

The Automatic Packet Reporting System (APRS)

This dual-port system eventually morphed into a Commodore 64 (C64) and in the 1988 timeframe that morphed into the precursor to APRS that I called CETS for Connectionless Emergency Traffic System. This was first demonstrated at the 100-mile Old Dominion Run in northern Virginia, and then at the National Disaster Medical System (NDMS) exercise in Washington, DC, where we used CETS to transmit the 5-digit NDMS codes for tracking each casualty from triage to shelters.

With the advent of the IBM PC running at 8 MHz with 640 KB RAM and a 20 MB hard disk drive, in the 1990 time frame I began drawing maps so that we could see where packet stations were located in the growing EASTNET (East Coast Packet Network). I changed the name to the Automatic Packet Reporting System (APRS) to match my WB4APR call sign and made the first formal presentation of APRS in 1992 at the 11th ARRL Computer Networking Conference at Teaneck, New Jersey. (This annual conference is still going strong, and since 1996 has been the ARRL/TAPR Digital Communications Conference.)

There were no available online maps at the time, so over the next several years I spent hours every day manually entering the coordinates of every turn in every major highway in the US from highway maps into the original APRSdos map files. Then we advanced to the US Geological Survey DLG (Digital Line Graph) files and were able to automate this somewhat. Though the automatic process generated about 10,000 data points, most were redundant and I had to manually throw out points to get down to the desired 3 KB map file size for speedy loading.

Our first big event with it was in the 1993 Marine Corps Marathon for tracking the lead Humvee. I was given about 5 minutes to install it, and you can imagine my horror when I discovered the hood was aluminum and so the 2 meter magnetic mount antenna was quickly attached with a lot of 100 MPH duct tape. We were also an early responder with ham radio at the crash of an Amtrak train in Essex, Maryland, where we used APRS for sending shelter information for the Red Cross.

In 1996 or so the Sproul brothers (Mark, KB2ICI, and Keith, WU2Z) introduced MacAPRS and WinAPRS and were able to use the DLG maps directly. By about 1998, APRS was nationwide with over 20,000 users in the US and about the same number worldwide. **Figure 1.5** shows just a small portion of the activity today.

The intent of APRS was to be a universal single-channel nationwide contact channel for situational awareness of all the hams around you and what

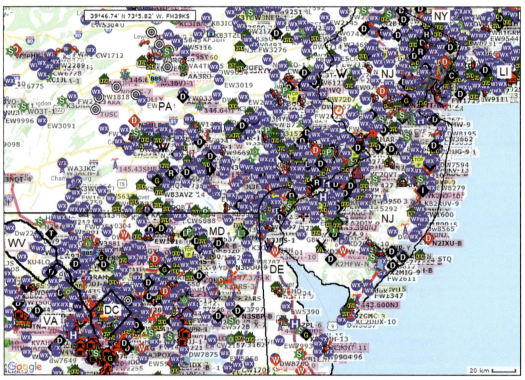

Figure 1.5 — APRS began in 1992 and grew to over 40,000 users worldwide. This map from APRS. FI shows just a portion of activity in Pennsylvania, Maryland, New Jersey, and Delaware.

Figure 1.6 — At (A), the messaging goal of APRS was to allow a single channel and global network for texting by call sign, seamlessly and transparently eventually among the dozens of independent ham radio texting modes. At (B), expansion of APRS symbol overlay characters to include some new energy symbols.

they were doing. Their latest status and position was always on the map, and from anywhere, to anywhere, hams could text message anyone by just call sign alone. At one time, I counted about 26 texting systems in ham radio ranging from CW to RTTY, to packet and APRS, and now smart phones; some of which are shown in **Figure 1.6A**. A lot of people thought the P in APRS was for position when in fact, it was always intended to be the Automatic Packet Reporting System to report everything about your activity in real time.

APRS Two-Way Communication and Voice Alert

This misinterpretation of APRS in the late 1990s as a *position* reporting system and the new availability of low-cost GPS was very frustrating to me and I consider it a lost decade in APRS development. Nobody was communicating via APRS; they were just transmitting their position. The plethora of transmit-only trackers and no one listening or even caring where you were prompted my "Tracker Manifesto" (**aprs.org/TrackerManifesto.html**). There was nothing more frustrating than driving down the interstate and seeing another APRS ham on your map coming your way, but then having no way to contact him.

This lead to a renewed push to remind everyone that APRS is a two-way, real-time, human-to-human communication system. All of the transmit-only and tracking misinterpretations were summarized on the APRS-Tactical web page (**aprs.org/APRS-tactical.html**). This lead to several additions to APRS in addition to a renewed emphasis on text messaging.

The first addition was *APRS Voice Alert*. This was the realization that every APRS ham in the country was driving around transmitting their position on a two-way radio (whether it was a one-way tracker, or full two-way APRS digital system), but with the audio turned off. What a waste of a receiver. We fixed that by asking all mobile operators to simply turn up the volume on the national APRS channel (144.39 MHz), but mute the speaker with a CTCSS tone of 100 Hz. This way, the speaker was quiet all the time, but at any time, anyone could call any other APRS operator in simplex range by simply setting CTCSS to 100 and making the call on voice. We called this Voice Alert. It works nationwide. It opened up a whole new dimension to APRS where any mobile operator could always be called no matter what they were doing with their other mobile radios.

Radar Detection

Then what we needed was a radar alert that another mobile APRS operator was in simplex range without having to look up positions on a map. Turns out, that APRS Voice Alert 100 Hz CTCSS speaker would not only open up on a voice call, it would also open up on the transmitted packet of any other Voice Alert radio that was in simplex range. At first this seemed to be a disadvantage, but it turned out to be the best thing that ever happened for mobile travelers.

About 99% of all packets on the air are not heard directly, but are relayed by the thousands of APRS digipeaters across the country. None of those packets relayed by digipeaters are accompanied by the CTCSS tone. But, every local direct packet from another mobile station does have the tone, and it is quite rare to ever be within a few miles of another APRS mobile operator. Therefore, you would never hear anything out of the speaker except when in range of another APRS mobile — and then only one ping per minute. This made Voice Alert also act as an automatic proximity detector.

This is an order of magnitude better than traveling on the national simplex frequency (146.52 MHz) because with Voice Alert, every APRS mobile is sending its 100 Hz PL "CQ" every minute. Even two APRS mobiles are traveling toward each other on the highway at a combined speed of over two miles a minute, you will still hear a few such pings and know someone is passing with their speaker on, and ready for a Voice Alert call.

APRS Frequency Format

The second major addition to APRS in 2004 was the addition of Frequency to the position format. This way, not only can you see where another ham is, but you can see what frequency his human-voice radio is tuned to. And unlike APRS Voice Alert that only works in simplex range, the Frequency format allowed someone to see where another operator was, and what frequency his voice radio was on. Then you could give a call via the local repeater on that channel. Prior to these changes, and with so many trackers on the road, it was very frustrating to be driving down the interstate or just monitoring local APRS activity and to see someone, but not be able to contact the live operator. See **Figure 1.7**.

Repeater Objects

The final change initiated in this timeframe was the provision to use the new position/frequency object format to have all local digipeaters not only provide their normal digipeating function but to also initiate local and direct object packets announcing the location and frequency for all local voice

Figure 1.7 — The APRS Frequency formats not only show local repeaters and users voice frequencies, but also the weekly net times as shown on the Kenwood TM-D700 display on the right when selected.

repeaters in the area. This way any visiting mobile would be instantly alerted to not only the location and frequencies of these recommended repeaters for mobiles, but the format also included the CTCSS tone requirements as well. The icing on the cake was when both Kenwood and Yaesu added automatic one-button tuning of the voice side of their dual-band APRS radios so that whenever the radio received a frequency packet either from a repeater object or the frequency/position of another operator, the radio could instantly TUNE or change frequency with the push of a single button to instantly establish human voice communication.

And lastly, these single local-repeater objects not only showed the location of the voice repeaters, but also their frequency offset, CTCSS tone, and other information such as weekly net times and monthly meeting times — all in a single packet transmitted once every 10 minutes suitable for display on the front panel of any visiting APRS mobile operator driving through the area. See **aprs.org/localinfo.html**.

APRS and Energy

Around the 2008 time frame, we greatly expanded the number of APRS symbols in a backward compatible way. Since every one of the approximate 190 initial symbols could have any of 36 overlay characters, we could define combinations of symbols and overlays to come up with thousands of possible symbols. An example of some of this expansion in symbols related to energy is shown in Figure 1.6B.

This allowed the ham to indicate power plant objects on the map during events, or show the type of power they are using at home or during portable operations. This included operations from solar, wind, or hydro power, as well as geothermal or backup power. It also expanded the car symbol to include a variety of new energy vehicles starting to be used by hams.

A Decade of Hybrids

After more than a decade of exponential growth of APRS and especially mobile operations, in 2007 I once again became interested in my original college project of an electric car. Hackers were beginning to realize the possibilities of modern EVs by converting Prius Hybrid systems to battery electric drive since they not only had a gas engine but also two large motor-generators and a high-voltage battery.

Finding drivable salvage Priuses for only a few thousand dollars was easy since commercial rebuilders were still afraid of working on their high-voltage systems. I first found a totaled black Prius with bashed-in driver door. I spent

Figure 1.8 — My family's fleet of recycled salvage Priuses were great DIY projects early on.

a weekend hammering and jacking out the damage and put a big white sign over the wrinkles. It ran fine, so I added 200 W of solar panels to the roof and 20 gel-cells in the trunk to absorb the power for added range (**Figure 1.8**).

My next salvage Prius was a white one with a roof that was crushed by a tree. To help with the jacking and hammering from the inside, I parked next to a utility pole and used a come-along and cable through the two back doors to lift the car by the roof. That constant 1200 pounds of force of the weight of the car plus impacts from the hammer slowly restored the original roof shape. I then covered the dinged moonscape of the roof with another 200 W of solar panels.

My most noticeable Prius recycle was a gold one that had been totaled from the rear. I just added a legal wood bumper and filled in what was left with plywood and a tailgate. Just Google "woodie prius" and you will find a dozen pictures posted by people who saw it on the road and took a picture, including a *before* shot.

A side story to the Woodie is a lesson in local law enforcement. Before I began the repairs, I thoroughly studied the Maryland vehicle regulations and planned to meet every one of them. When it was finished, I took it in for inspection, and the local inspection station refused to look at it and called in the head state inspector. He failed it on 17 counts. One claim that any unused window (such as my rear quarter driver side window on the white Prius that I had replaced with a black plywood panel) had to be replaced with all metal and solidly welded water tight. I pointed out there was no such rule in the law and his statement was "but that is just how we do it." In response I prepared a binder with "twenty seven 8 × 10 color glossy photos with circles and arrows and a paragraph on the back explaining each one" (as Arlo Guthrie said in *Alice's Restaurant*) and asked to meet with his boss. It almost seemed that they had never read the rules and just passed what they liked and failed what they didn't like. I met every rule. A week later the gas station inspector called and said to just come get the car. He grudgingly had signed the inspection.

Now 11 years later, these 13 and 14 year old cars are all still going strong with 220, 180 and 120 thousand miles respectively. They have never been in for repair and at the frustration of my wife, they just won't die and go away. You may have seen the black one as a fixture in the flea market at Dayton where the 200 W of solar power provides plenty of power in the field. With a trailer hitch, it is also my tow vehicle for my communications trailer and solar boat in the local area.

EV Battery Charging Lessons

The main lesson learned with the first conversion to EV driving was not to trickle-charge NiMH batteries beyond full. I rigged up a small trickle charger consisting of two diodes and two small capacitors to form a 120 V doubler to over 240 V dc, suitable for charging the Prius 208 V battery at 350 mA. It fit inside a modest size plastic wall transformer case like you might use to charge your cordless screwdriver. But looks are deceiving. I had only intended to top off the Prius battery for an hour. But several household projects later, about 8 hours or so, I heard popping noises, and ran out to see smoke and some flames coming from the battery. The battery is in a metal shield, but after removing the covers you can see in **Figure 1.9** that NiMH expands and heats up when overcharged. The metal rods that hold the stack together were sheared from the ends and could not contain the pressure. On the left of the cells is the battery management computer that was crushed as well.

Figure 1.9 — Do not overcharge a NiMH battery. Just 350 mA for 8 hours expanded the Prius cells and caught materials on fire!

The Prius battery is 28 modules of six plastic-enclosed cells each.

Each cell has about the capacity of a typical D cell. Fortunately, salvage Prius batteries were only $400 back then and so the fix was easy. But knowing that I did not have time to design a full fail-safe charging system that was over-voltage, over-current, over-pressure, and over-temperature safe, and that more members of the family might drive any given car at any given time, I disconnected all my hacks and have just driven the Prius for what it is. Now the 200 W of solar panels on the roof are just for powering ham radio gear and camping stuff when in the field. Not for charging the battery!

Prius Inn and Prius Hotel

Another advantage of driving recycled salvage cars is being able to hack them at will. My favorite projects on the Prius were for overnight accommodations as shown in **Figure 1.10**. The first one, called the Prius Inn, provides accommodation for one and has been seen in the flea market at

Figure 1.10 — Salvage Prius accomodations: The Prius Inn (right) and woodie Prius Hotel (below).

Dayton for a decade or so. The second one is called the Prius Hotel. That car not only folds down both seats for a double-wide bed, but also adds about 10 cubic feet of headroom, or storage when hauling #1 son to and from college. It's not generally designed for travel that way, but when stopped, the hatch lifts up, the tailgate goes down, and the wood side panels are slipped in place.

Economical Solar Power Arrives

In the background to my half-century ham radio hobby, I was also always fascinated by solar power. In elementary school in the 1950s, the science project next to mine had a few solar cells that were used to power a small transistor radio. But over the years, no matter how I looked at it, I just could not find any way that solar could possibly be cost effective when the basement stack of batteries would have to be replaced every few years.

When I first moved to my house in 1990, the utility was offering time-of-use electric rates of 2 cents at night and 10 cents during the day. I figured I'd drop my electric costs by 80% by filling my basement with a dozen old car batteries, charging them up at night, and then using the electricity during the day. That type of system is shown in **Figure 1.11A.** And that is when I discovered that even with that 5-to-1 price ratio in the cost for electricity, the batteries would only break even. The maintenance and replacement every five years would eat up every penny of any advantage to the cheap nighttime electricity. So I concluded that even if electricity were free, the cost of batteries and maintenance would never pay for itself. So how could adding expensive solar panels make any sense at all?

That all changed on the second Saturday in August 2010, when I finally woke up to the fact that the burgeoning solar industry was all grid-tie (GT) and had nothing to do with batteries, as shown in Figure 1.11B. Once you eliminate the battery problem, with grid-storage via a net meter, the economics of solar power are a hands-down winner. By 2010, solar was becoming cost competitive with normal utility power in almost every state in the US. By 2013, home solar amortized over 20 years was under half the cost of the utilities. My intense excitement that Saturday, however, was dashed the next day as I watched the shade move across my roof throughout the day. I had no usable sunlight!

But I did have sun down at the back of my lot and immediately began purchasing solar panels and propping them up in the backyard on 2×4s as shown in **Figure 1.12**. That led to a four year battle with the State of Maryland and local zoning that would not allow ground-mounted solar panels within 1000 feet of any tributary of the Chesapeake Bay. With a creek

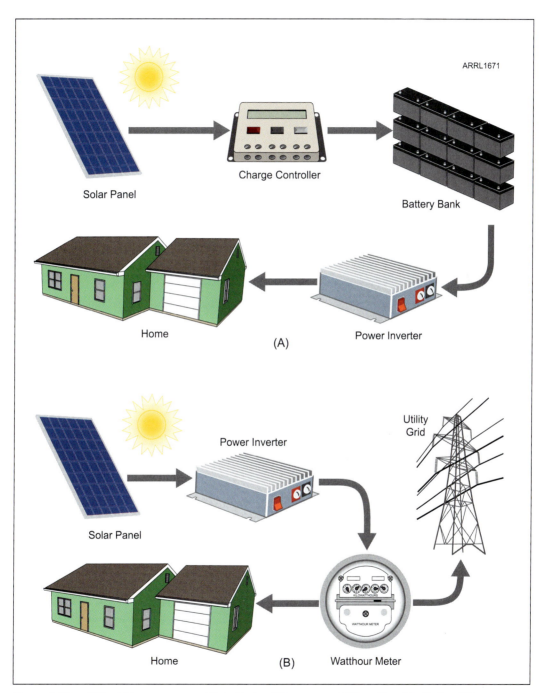

Figure 1.11 — Off-grid home power with batteries (A) versus grid tie without batteries (B).

Figure 1.12 — My initial 8 kW of panels in my backyard, propped up for initial testing.

Figure 1.13 — My 2012 DIY electric boat replaced the gas engine with a couple of trolling motors and a battery charged from solar.

out back, I was stuck. But eventually I became the first homeowner in Maryland to get a solar variance in the Chesapeake Critical Area to be able to connect those panels to the grid. My monthly electric bills went from as high as $400 per month in the winter to a typical low of $8 per month now, which is just the minimum service fee.

Meanwhile I was also fighting with the state about their prohibition of solar panels on piers. I wanted to build a floating solar array pier for more power, but the law was just outdated. It allowed anyone with a pier to put anything on it that was associated with the support of a gas burning, oil-leaking, energy consuming, noise generating, bay-polluting, air-fouling, fossil fuel boat, including a gas station to fuel it — but not solar panels to feed the house. (I tried arguing for feeding an electric boat (**Figure 1.13**), but they saw right through that.) Eventually, after my testimony to the Maryland Department of the Environment and the state legislature, they eventually removed the prohibition of solar on piers in 2013. I added another 3 kW array on the floating pier I made from 4×8 sheets of foam and a wooden deck as shown in **Figure 1.14**.

Figure 1.14 — Homemade floating solar pier supports about 3 kW of solar panels, with Bob Bruninga, WB4APR (the author, standing) and his son AJ, WA4APR, in the canoe.

Figure 1.15 — My solar arrays produce enough clean energy for a ground-source heat pump and heat pump hot water heater.

This was followed in 2014 with another significant change when we eliminated $3000 of annual heating oil costs by switching to a ground-source heat pump, and a heat pump hot water heater (**Figure 1.15**). This of course doubled my electric load and so I had to double the size of my arrays to make up the difference. With this major change, I could finally feel that I was no longer contributing to the destruction of the natural wonder of our neighboring state of West Virginia through massive

Figure 1.16 — Mountaintop removal coal mining in West Virginia. (Vivian Stockman, ohvec.org, photo)

mountain top mining for the typical average of 4 tons of coal per household per year (**Figure 1.16**). Heat pumps will be covered in more detail in Chapter 13.

My Second True EV (but the First of the Modern Era)

Figure 1.17 — My 2011 THINK City Car, acquired in 2015 in non-working condition and brought back to life.

Since the family Priuses still won't die, despite their never having been to the dealer or needing repairs in a decade and approaching 200,000 miles each, I just had to have a real EV. My first attempt was the acquisition of a non-working 2011 THINK City Car, practically brand new at auction (**Figure 1.17**). I took the risk since by this time, in 2015, the failure mode of these cars was well known. The failure mode was simply that if you quick-cycled the "start" key while the heater was left on, it would permanently kill the car. The problem caused by the quick cycling of the key was in the sequence of the three main power contactors.

In most hybrids and EVs, there is at least a three-click sequence as the high-voltage contactors first close the contactor in the negative battery lead and check for any shorts to ground on the + side. Then the system pulls in the + terminal contactor through a small capacitor pre-charge resistor to charge up any capacitors in the system and again check for any shorts to ground on the negative side before closing the final high-voltage contactor to bypass the pre-charge resistor after a few milliseconds. You can hear something like this three-click sequence in every hybrid or EV before full high-voltage power is available.

The problem in the THINK was that there was a few second dropout delay of one of those relays. If the key was quick-cycled while that one contactor was still on, then it allowed the full 4 kW heater load to attempt to pass though the small 5 W pre-charge resistor. This would explode that circuit board resistor in a huge, bright 400 V, 4 kW plasma on the main battery control board buried down in the 700 pound battery under the car. By the time this problem was well understood, the original manufacturer was bankrupt and there was not a single replacement control board in the supply system. To find a good board, I bought yet another THINK, and between the two boards, I got one to work. There are over 400 of these excellent modern EVs abandoned in the US and available at junk prices and needing this board.

These are really neat indestructible cars with all-plastic body panels that can never dent. All you have to do is come up with another control board! I keep hoping that one of the motor-controller manufacturers for ac motor golf carts will take pity on all these abandoned cars and show us all how to wire their new ac motor controllers into these cars.

Another use for these cars is to just buy one for the 16 kWh lithium battery for backup power for your house. In 2018, Maryland was the second state to offer 30% tax credit for the purchase of any large home battery system. The second car I bought was only $2400.

The Chevy Volt

After the distraction with merging the two dead THINK EVs into a single working vehicle in the 2015 time frame, I wanted something that did not look like a toy to be able to show others the current state of the art in modern electric vehicles. By 2016, the cost of three-year-old Chevrolet Volt EVs coming off lease was down to about $12,000 for a car with only 50,000 miles on it — and it looked like brand new. I bought one. At the same time, three-

Figure 1.18 — Finally after 35 years of playing with EVs, I finally got a real one.

year-old off-lease Nissan Leaf EVs were going for under $9,000 and most had low mileage.

My marriage survived the growing fleet of Priuses and EV projects when I was able to pawn one of them off to my daughter out of state, and the 1978 City car got shoved into the weeds behind the garage. So now, with the Volt, I finally had a real EV and wanted it to be visible. I was able to buy one of the last original full size VOLT decals in the country as shown in **Figure 1.18**. The vinyl lettering was black, which did not show up well on a deep maroon color, so I highlighted the edges of the decals with yellow electricians tape. The 50 mile Volt battery (16 kWh) has 10 times the energy of the Prius and has the potential to power even the largest Field Day site or power my house for a week in case of a power outage. The only problem is safely getting to that power. I'll discuss that in detail in Chapter 10.

2 The New World of Everyday Power (DC)

Wow, it seems hard to believe how much energy has changed during my half-century in ham radio, and yet, on the surface, how much of the change is evolutionary and hardly noticed. Every facet of ham radio and our lives in general requires energy. The question is whether we are prepared to embrace the change in energy and take full advantage of it in our hobby and homes, or if we are determined to avoid change until they pull the last 60 Hz boat anchor from our cold, dead hands.

I went through elementary school in the 1950s, followed by the heady days of science, electronics, and space. Now, at the age of 70 in 2018, I cannot believe that I have lived long enough to see this revolution in energy. The highlights are:

• the amortized cost of solar energy that is now less than half the price of electricity from the utility;

• the rise of the lightweight lithium batteries that are revolutionizing applications of portable Amateur Radio operations as well as power systems and tools; and

• the rise of electric vehicles (EVs) that are better, faster, cleaner, cheaper to buy, cheaper to operate, and cheaper to maintain than comparable gasoline cars when used in their best application, which is local travel and commuting.

We can get a hint of this change by simply looking at what has happened to power supplies and the death of heavy 60 Hz iron transformers. The classic supply of the past has always consisted of a transformer, rectifier, and filter. Both the transformer and filter were huge because of the amount of iron needed in the transformer and inductors, and the physical size of the large capacitors needed to smooth out the very low frequency at 50/60 Hz.

Although the old transformer/rectifier/filter configuration is still shown in the *ARRL Handbook*, the Power Sources chapter now presents a power supply in modern terms with a generic block diagram of energy source, power processing, and load. It then goes on to describe the variety of power processors: ac-to-ac transformers, dc-to-dc converters, ac-to-dc rectifiers, and dc-to-ac inverters. In the modern evolution of power supplies, we have traded heavy iron and large capacitors and simplicity for added inexpensive electronic complexity, but orders of magnitude smaller and lighter components.

Universal Supplies

The boat anchor power supply on the left in **Figure 2.1** is the most visible Amateur Radio example of this transformative change from the bulk and mass of 60 Hz linear power supplies just 20 years ago to the modern switching power supply that is only 10% of the weight and requires only 8% of the volume. Switching supplies now come with almost every modern piece of electronics. Not only are there obvious size and weight differences, but these new supplies are mostly in the category of "universal." That is, they are able to operate on any input voltage from 100 to 240 V ac.

The ability to operate on multiple international mains voltages used to be an expensive feature, but now it is more a factor of economic necessity. With global manufacturing and with markets around the world, it is more cost effective to just design one universal supply in every product than to have different designs for each country, such as the 100 V ac at 50 Hz in Japan, 220 V ac in Europe, and 120/240 V split-phase ac at 60 Hz in the US.

Figure 2.1 — From left to right: A 12 V, 9 A linear power supply; an 18 V, 8 A laptop supply; and a 12 V, 18 A PC supply.

In the past, the only way to accommodate these various ac voltages was to have a variety of taps on the heavy 50/60 Hz transformer primary, and input configuration straps or switches to select the right tap. There were several disadvantages to this approach. First, every transformer had to be 16% heavier for the greater amount of iron required to accommodate operation at 50 Hz as well as 60 Hz. Second, there was added cost and weight for the extra primary windings. Finally, there was the complexity of the input selection circuit and the danger of equipment failure if the consumer did not properly configure the input circuit for the right voltage.

All of these problems were solved with the complete elimination of 50/60 Hz iron and the advent of switching power supplies that could fully regulate the output voltage by simple feedback to modulation of the regulator. Of course a "transformer" is still used in most circuits for isolation and voltage step up/down, but the operating frequency of the switching circuits are more than three orders of magnitude higher in frequency — from tens of kHz to as high as 4 MHz, for example — compared to 60 Hz. That means that the transformer can have many fewer turns and weigh orders of magnitude less.

Since the switching converter needs dc on the input, all of these universal supplies initially rectify the incoming ac from the variety of mains voltages and apply that dc to the switching circuits. Then the regulation control has to have an operating range over the full range of output load, from virtually no-load to full-load, as well as additional range to accommodate the 100 to 240 V inputs. This wide operating range is easy to do for the modest power requirements of consumer devices such as a cell phone, LED light bulb, laptop, or TV. This wide range can then be accommodated without any input selection hardware. These are called universal supplies.

Universal High-Voltage DC Supplies as Well

Given the wide range of input voltages up to 240 V ac, it is easy to see that the input circuit of the dc-to-dc conversion module after the rectifier in any universal supply has to be designed for up to about 330 V dc, the peak ac line voltage (240 × 1.414) that results on the input capacitor. So now we have a supply that can not only work on any voltage from 100 to 240 V ac, but also work on any dc voltage from 140 to 330 V dc (the peak ac voltage) as a matter of routine.

I tested more than a dozen universal laptop and similar plug-in supplies in my lab, and every one of them not only worked fine on dc over the full range, but also continued to operate with input voltages as low as 70 or 60 V dc. These were short-term tests, and I can see how operating at rated output power at these low voltages would perhaps demand greater input current than the input diodes were designed to handle. So it's best not to overload the supply at low-voltage inputs.

Adding this wide dc input range to the ac input range makes these supplies truly universal. Coincidentally, they are very versatile to many of the other high dc voltages in this book and our new energy systems.

Dual Voltage 120/240 V Supplies

At higher power levels than routine electronics require, it is more efficient to design around just the high and low input voltage ranges, rather than to have the added challenge of designing for the entire wide input range found in a universal supply. This is why higher power systems may have a 120/240 V switch to preselect the input voltage.

A typical circuit that evolved in almost all desktop PCs is shown in **Figure 2.2**. Unlike switches for 50/60 Hz transformer taps, this input voltage select switch does not need to be multi-pole, but simply a single-pole, single-throw contact or a single jumper. When this switch or jumper is open, in the 240 V position, the input to the dc/dc electronics is simply the output of the full-wave bridge rectifier and operates at 330 V dc on the top of the filter capacitor. But when the switch or jumper is in the 120 V position, it bypasses

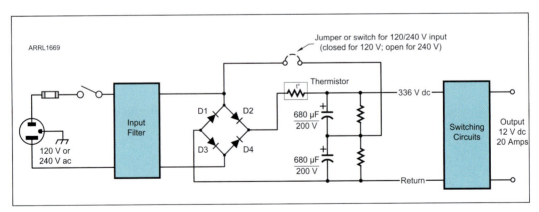

Figure 2.2 — Typical 120/240 V dual-voltage switching supply. A single jumper or switch converts the supply for use on 120 or 240 V ac. On 120 V, the capacitors and diodes act like a 60 Hz voltage doubler to raise the operating voltage to more than 300 V dc for the switching circuit. With the jumper removed, the 240 V ac is rectified to give more than 300 V dc. Notice that in either case, the +336 V dc is only +168 V to ground, and the return is at −168 V dc, and neither side can be grounded. The isolation is provided inside the switching electronics.

Figure 2.3 — Inside the Kenwood 12 V, 25 A power supply, there is a jumper for 120/240 V operation.

one side of the ac to the center tap of the two capacitors, and the resulting equivalent circuit conveniently configures the remaining two diodes and two capacitors into a 50/60 Hz full-wave voltage doubler circuit. As a doubler of the 120 V ac, the resulting dc on the top of the two capacitors is still the same 330 V dc as before, and the same peak 330 V dc as found in all universal supplies.

In the past, if a power supply had a 120/240 V input switch, that was a hint that it had a 60 Hz transformer with dual windings. But if the power supply does not have the heavy bulk of a 60 Hz transformer, then more than likely it is actually still a universal supply inside as shown in **Figure 2.3**. It likely has an internal switch or jumper for use in other countries. This is also common on most PC power supplies with a dual-voltage switch.

The only reason that the input voltage switch or jumper is there in these power supplies is so that the internal 120/240 V ac-input dc/dc switching supply can save the expense of having to have a 400 V input capacitor. With the switch or jumper in the 120 V position, the two 200 V capacitors and a pair of the full-wave bridge diodes form a 60 Hz, 120 V voltage doubler to the same 330 V as the full-wave rectified 240 V ac would be. With the switch or jumper in the 240 V position, the two 200 V capacitors are connected in series to serve as a single 400 V unit.

The advantage of this switched dual-input-voltage approach is that the manufacturer is able to save money on the rectifier input capacitor by being able to use two capacitors rated at only 200 V in either series for high input voltage, or as the two doubler capacitors in the low-voltage case.

Operating on DC Input — Cautions!

Now that we realize that all universal and dual-voltage modern supplies operate from rectified ac on the input to 330 V dc internally, then the only thing we need to remember to operate any of these supplies on dc input is to be sure any 120/240 V switch is in the 240 V position so that the dc goes directly to the dc switching input and does not go to the 200 V rated split capacitors except when the two are in series. Further, when operating from dc input, you must also be sure that there is no power switch in the input circuit, or it will fry in an arc-flash the first time it is opened (see the sidebar, "High-Voltage DC is Now Everywhere" in Chapter 1). The Power Sources chapter in *ARRL Handbook* also has some good general information on safely working around high voltages.

Distribution at High-Voltage DC

Just as Westinghouse (and Tesla) with their higher ac voltages won the late 19th century "War of the currents" (see **en.wikipedia.org/wiki/War_of_ the_currents**) against Edison's 110 V dc distribution due to the vastly lower losses at higher line voltage, there is the same significant reduction in losses when operating at higher dc voltages.

We can now translate dc voltages with dc/dc switching converters at lower cost and smaller size than if we were using ac line-voltage transformers. The lower loss at high voltage is because the loss in a given length of wire is proportional to $I^2 \times R$ (current squared times resistance). But I is inversely proportional to voltage, so operating at 330 V dc instead of 120 V dc is 1/3 the current, or only 1/9 the power loss when I is squared. The value in distribution then is almost a 9-to-1 reduction in the size (cost) of copper in the distribution wiring for the same loss.

This is such a huge benefit that modern data centers feeding hundreds or thousands of processors are being designed to operate at the rectified high-voltage dc directly to save wiring and distribution losses.[1] These systems are typically rated for normal operation from 260 to 400 V dc to accommodate a variety of input systems, but are nominally rated at 380 V dc where they can achieve 98% efficiency. Operating down to the low end of 260 V dc input only loses a bit at 96% efficiency.

Further, all voltage shifting is done with dc/dc converters instead of heavy transformers. For example, a modern 300 W dc/dc converter with 380 V dc input and operating at 97% efficiency only has to dissipate 9 W and can be smaller than the size of a matchbox, as shown in **Figure 2.4**. Compare this modern 300 W power supply with the 108 W vintage transformer-based supply, the 144 W laptop power supply and the 216 W PC supply shown in Figure 2.1.

Figure 2.4 — A modern 300 W high-voltage dc/dc converter is smaller than a matchbox.

High-Voltage DC Everywhere

And now, with high-voltage and high-power circuits on our roofs with solar, in our cars with hybrids and electric vehicles (EVs), and in our energy storage with high-voltage dc batteries, it's a new world of energy. That is the topic of this book. Once we realize that about 300 V dc is the new common internal operating voltage for almost all power supplies, it also opens up compatibility with entirely new sources of everyday power such as from solar and electric vehicles. This variability of dc power via switching power supplies is even extending into traditional old-iron appliances striving to improve overall efficiency. Examples are continuously variable compressors in refrigerators and heat pumps. Many of these advances and their application to the ham radio operator and DIY enthusiast are covered in Chapter 5.

This very wide supply input range opens up a whole new world of emergency power considerations. For example many electric cars have dozens of kWh of dc battery voltages in that range, and every hybrid has at least a 50,000 W generator built in at voltages from 200 to 360 V (and higher). The other very common high-voltage dc power available to the homeowner is from a home solar array. Many such arrays operate in series, with voltages from 300 to 550 V. If the dc voltage is above 360 V with no load, then it is a simple task to tap the series string at no higher than 360 V

---

[1]"High-voltage dc distribution is key to increased system efficiency and renewable-energy opportunities" Stephen Oliver, Vice President, VI Chip Product Line, Vicor Corp, **www.digikey.com/en/pdf/v/vicor/high-voltage-dc-distribution**.

so that you can have kilowatts of free 360 V dc power for all your modern power supplies. For example, with an array of 14 panels in series for 450 to 600 V dc maximum rating, it is possible to not just make a single tap at a 300 V point, but also to break the series string into two parallel strings at 225 to 300 V during power outages to provide twice as much current for your universal supplies (see **Figure 2.5**).

But the challenge is that most of the critical home systems such as sump pump, furnace, refrigerator, freezer, and so on — devices that you really need during a power outage — cannnot run on this dc power. This is covered in more detail in Chapter 10.

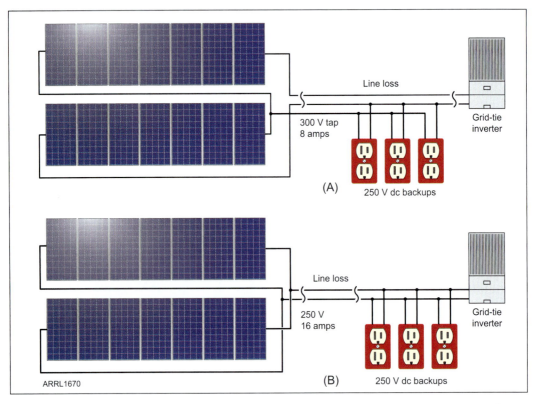

Figure 2.5 — Typical solar panels in series can be tapped at 300 V or lower to provide plenty of high-voltage dc for most modern universal power supplies directly during a power outage. At (A), 14 panels in series provide 500 V at 8 A, which reduces the line loss for a given wire size. The inverter is 94% efficient at 500 V. At (B), 14 panels in series/parallel provide 250 V at 16 A. This configuration adds 2% line loss, but the inverter is 96% efficient (+2%) at 250 V dc, for the same overall efficiency. With this configuration, almost any modern switching power supply can plug directly into 250 V dc.

3 The Solar Power Revolution

Before we look at solar, it might be a good idea to look at our overall US energy picture as shown in **Figure 3.1**. The sources of energy are shown on the left and our uses for that power are shown toward the right. There are a few big picture items to notice. First, notice that the top seven sources of energy on the left all predominantly go into electricity generation. Next, notice that the bottom biggest source, petroleum, goes predominantly into transportation.

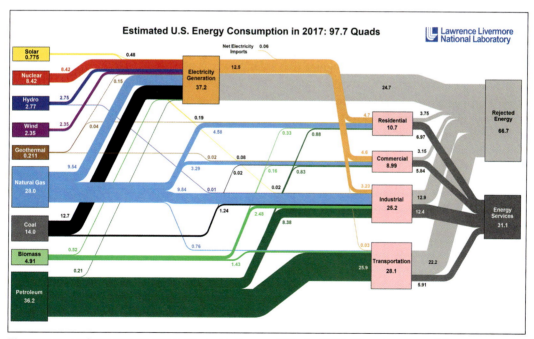

Figure 3.1 — US Energy Sources, Consumption, and Waste, 2017. (From Lawrence Livermore National Laboratory, flowcharts.llnl.gov/.)

The last big item to notice is the final split on the right of all these energy sources into the two categories of energy actually used versus the energy lost in the process. Following through from left to right, you can see that almost every one of these sources on the left that are based on burning fossil fuel pass through their applications but with nearly 2/3 of the energy lost as waste heat and only 1/3 providing useful energy on the right. This waste is not a consequence so much of human choices, but the byproduct of most fossil fuel generation systems. When we generate useful energy from burning fossil fuels, the predominant result is waste heat and unwanted emissions. This is even worse for the petroleum path, with over 3/4 of the fuel burned for transportation lost as waste heat and emissions (more on this later in Chapter 7).

Do not be misled by the apparent miniscule 1% of solar generation on the upper left. Compared to natural gas and coal, solar is growing almost 60% a year over the last decade (see **www.seia.org/solar-industry-research-data**) while coal has declined more than 32% over the same time period (see **research.stlouisfed.org/publications/economic-synopses/2017/10/06/the-decline-of-coal/**). Just since this chart was published, solar has doubled to 2%. If this rate of doubling every two years continues, in only 10 years, by 2028, it could go from 2% to 50% of our energy supply while virtually eliminating coal and half of petroleum.

Adding solar is now cheaper than building any other form of new energy plant including natural gas, and once built has no ongoing fuel costs. Further, it is important to recognize that solar power is not generated in central power plants but is mostly generated at the load. Not only does this eliminate most of the long-distance transmission losses, but most importantly, this source does not create the high level of waste generated by as fossil fuels because 95% of the solar energy converted to electricity is actually delivered to the load and only about 5% is lost. In addition, all the solar energy that is spilled or not directly converted to electricity is not a disaster, but is simply called a "nice day."

Solar Growth

Solar cells were invented at Bell Labs in 1954 when I was in 1st grade, and some of these 4% efficiency tiny cells flew on the earliest satellites in 1958. Costs were about $100 per watt. Efficiencies rose to about 11%, and by the 1970s after I graduated from college, scientists at Exxon had developed cells in the range of $20 per watt. Forty years later, by about 2013, the price of solar power had dropped 100-to-1, and efficiencies of this same simple silicon technology was around 18%. As costs began to approach parity with grid power, demand and economies of scale further drove price downward by about a factor of 10 in the last decade to about 50 cents per watt in 2018. By about 2010, the amortized cost of solar power about equaled the retail cost of electricity from the utility, and by 2013 it was half.

In 2018, solar electricity costs less than coal at wholesale, and even oil-rich countries in the Middle East, with vast oil reserves, were turning to solar for their energy because it is cheaper than burning their own oil that they can export at higher prices to everyone else. All of these panels use the same low-cost silicon cells that have been around since the 1950s, with some modest improvements in efficiency along the way. After almost 70 years of incremental improvements, this efficiency is now asymptotically approaching 20% or so and simply cannot go much higher.

Higher-Efficiency Technology

Waiting for higher-efficiency cells is a fool's errand. Since seeing my first solar cell in elementary school in the 1950s, I have been fascinated

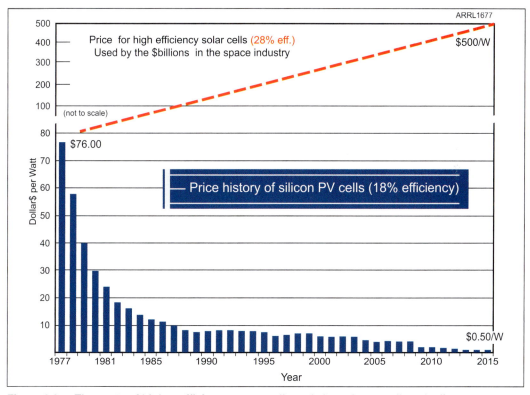

Figure 3.2 — The costs of higher-efficiency space cells and cheap home cells only diverges, and the difference is now 1000-to-1. (Based on data from Bloomberg New Energy and pv.energytrend.com.)

by the potential for solar power. From powering my first transistor radio, through to college in 1970, the space age brought fascinating advances in the technology. But, as the space sector demand drives higher solar cell efficiency, the cost only goes up. The cost of high-efficiency cells is now up to more than $500 per watt, while home solar cells are now down below 50 cents a watt. Yet, today with a 100-to-1 reduction in costs for simple silicon cells over the same time frame, we still hear people say they are waiting for newer, more efficient technology.

I have heard that excuse so much in almost every discussion of solar power that I was finally inspired to make the graph in **Figure 3.2**. While the cost of economical solar has dropped more than 100-to-1, the cost of more-efficient cells, which have always been with us, has only gone up over the same time frame! Today the cost of the most efficient cells is over 1000 times greater than the cost of simple home solar panels. For this 1000-to-1 difference in price, the space industry gains about a 2-to-1 power advantage. But in space, where satellites cost hundreds of millions of dollars each, a few million for the best solar panels is worth it. And this huge divergent price difference will never change because the space industry will always pay whatever it takes for higher efficiency on their multi-million-dollar satellites while home owners will only pay the absolute minimum.

This trend will continue. As the industry gains a percent or so for the most efficient cells, the space industry moves to that new technology and abandons last year's slightly less-efficient cells. So, with no demand and a 1000-to-1 price difference compared to home solar, there is no market and no potential to develop economies of scale for that slightly-less-efficient, year-old cell technology. See **Figure 3.3** to illustrate this three-order-of-magnitude difference in solar cell cost based on the 2-to-1 difference in efficiency just in my own experience. Pictured is my original 8 kW array, along with a small university class cubesat satellite with 8 W of solar cells that cost about the same as my big array — $20,000. At this point, the typical large 3.3 × 5.5 foot mass-produced panels cost less than the retail cost of a simple window of the same size from a home center, and the major cost of solar power is not the technology but the installation costs.

Grid Storage

The revolution in the economics of solar energy stems from the use of the electrical grid for energy storage instead of costly and high-maintenance battery storage. For off-grid isolated solar power systems, nearly $2 of every $3 invested is in the battery storage system and life-long maintenance, and only one-third of the investment is in generating power.

(A)

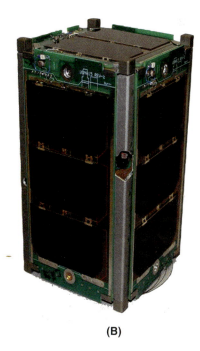

(B)

Figure 3.3 — Both the 8 kW home solar array and the 8 W set of high efficiency cells on a typical 4-inch university cubesat satellite cost about the same — $20,000 in 2018. (A typical cubesat is about 4 inches across on each side.)

When we eliminate the batteries, and "store" our daily excess in the grid, then $3 of every $3 invested goes to energy production at retail rates. Thus, it is the revolution of grid-tie solar and net metering that has tripled the value of home solar over the last decade, in addition to the 10-to-1 reduction in solar panel cost in the same time frame.

There are no moving parts, just the panels in the sun, and an inverter to switch the dc voltage into ac voltage for our home. The connection to our home grid is the same as simply adding another appliance. An electrician just connects the wires labeled Line1, Line2 and Ground through a circuit breaker in the distribution box. Simple it is, as shown in **Figures 3.4** and **3.5**.

Home Batteries — Maybe Later

Although the recent revolution in solar power economics is driven entirely by grid-tie net metering, which avoids the significant expense of batteries, the revolution in batteries is just now coming upon us. This topic will be covered in Chapter 11, where we will address the implications of this revolution on home solar and energy systems.

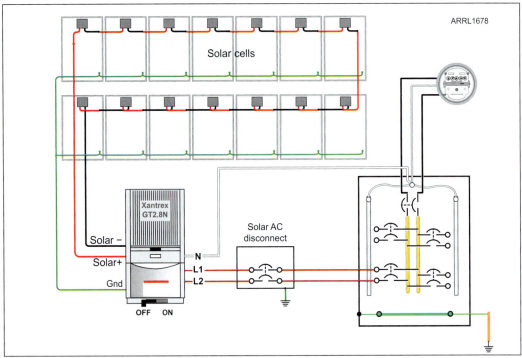

Figure 3.4 — Solar panels plug together in series for high voltage and low current to save wire size. They connect to an inverter, and then to a breaker in your panel.

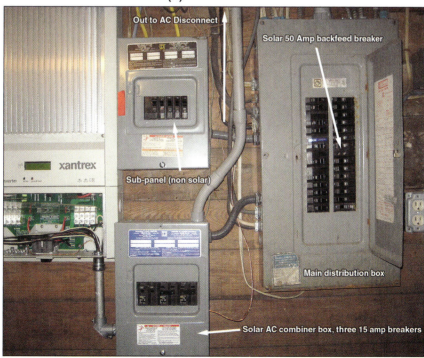

Figure 3.5 — At (A), my three grid-tie inverters with lower covers off. The left two are newer and have the black higher-rated dc disconnect switches. At (B), ac power from the three inverters is integrated into my home electrical distribution panel via a sub panel with three 15 A circuit breakers.

The Solar Power Revolution   3.7

Net Metering

Of course, the grid does not actually store the energy. It just shares our excess generation with someone else who needs it at the time. In fact, it probably does not even leave the neighborhood. Your neighbors just pay the utility for your power that the utility got from you for free, and then the utility gives it back to you when you need it at night.

The mechanism for this sharing is the *net meter*. When we draw power from the grid, our meter counts the kilowatt-hours (kWh), and at the end of the month we pay for the electricity we used. But with a solar net meter, when we generate excess electricity during the day, our meter can also run backward, subtracting from our kWh. At the end of the month, if we have used more than we generated, we pay the utility as usual. But if we generated more than we used (the meter reading is less than where it started at the beginning of the billing cycle), it shows a credit in kWh that we can use later. Since it is a 1-for-1 credit in kWh, we are getting the same retail value for the electricity we generated in excess as we have to pay when we consume it. Thus the term "net" meter.

Billing for Solar Power

The sun, as well as our lives, is on a daily and annual cycle. On a daily basis, we typically produce six times our average hourly power while the sun is up and store excess power for the other 20 hours of the day and for use on cloudy days. Solar panels will usually produce nearly twice as much energy during the long summer days as in the winter, and our heating and air conditioning loads vary drastically through the year. Therefore, the utilities only square up any net credit in our account on an annual basis. In the meantime, we pay those monthly bills showing net consumption, and we do not pay when we have a kWh credit (net retail value). Only at the end of a year, if our meter reading is farther back then where it started, will the utility actually pay for any net annual excess.

Net metering laws vary, and in some states the utility pays the retail price per kWh of annual excess, but others only pay the wholesale rate. This is fair. The idea of net metering is to let homeowners generate their own electricity at retail rates, but it was not intended to let them be greedy and build large power generating stations on their lots in the suburbs that produce more power than they need.

How Solar Cells Work

Solar power is very simple. Solar energy impinges on properly prepared silicon and bumps electrons to a higher energy state that can then be pulled off as current between the front and back of the cell. The voltage produced is about 0.5 V — maybe 0.55 V open circuit and 0.45 V at maximum current. This is why all solar systems require multiple cells connected in series to get the voltage up to a practical level.

Just counting the number of cells in series will tell you the voltage of the panel. Typical "12 V" panels have 36 cells with an open circuit voltage over 18 V and a maximum power point of about 16 V to be able to charge a 12 V battery to its fully charged state of 13.8 V. Similarly, "24 V" panels have 60 to 72 cells, and open circuit voltage more than 36 V with a peak power point around 30 V.

The typical 39 × 65 inch solar array panels that are being produced by the billions are 60 cell "30 V" panels that are driving the low cost of modern solar systems. In 2018, larger panels of 72 cells operating at more than 36 V are becoming available with power levels of 325 W or more.

The Solar Cell Current-vs-Voltage, or I-V Curve

Solar power differs in one respect from a battery or other power source in that it is current limited and its voltage will vary somewhat with the load. For this reason, the load needs to be matched to the immediate power available from the sun, which can vary over a 30-to-1 range depending on clouds and sun angle.

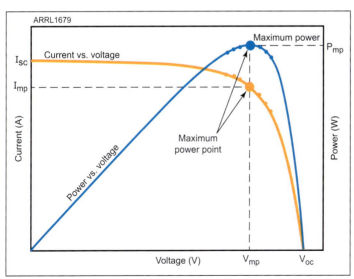

Figure 3.6 —Typical I-V curve for solar cell showing V_{oc}, I_{sc} and maximum power point (MPP). (Based on an illustration from www.ecmweb.com.)

The current-vs-voltage curve (called an I-V curve) shown in **Figure 3.6** makes this relationship clear. The key points on the curve are the V_{oc} (open-circuit voltage), I_{sc} (short-circuit current), and the maximum power point (or peak power point). Since power is the product of I and V, then the peak power point is always at the point where the rectangle under that point on the curve is the largest.

MPPT, or Maximum Power Point Tracking

All practical solar systems use MPPT (Maximum Power Point Tracking) to find the peak power point as it moves around with even the slightest variations in solar illumination. For any given I-V illumination curve, such as the one shown here, all the MPPT algorithm has to do is to measure the current power by multiplying I times V. Then it modifies the inverter load to draw slightly more current. Then it checks the power again. If the power product went up, then more current can be drawn. The MPPT algorithm continues this incremental adding of load until the I-V product becomes less. Then it backs up one step to that previously determined peak power point.

Similarly, whenever the current power product goes down, the MPPT algorithm will have the inverter reduce its current load slightly and then test the product. If the voltage goes up and the power product is greater, then the load was mismatched and it will continue reducing the load current to better match the new operating conditions. As before, it will continue to reduce current until there is no further increase in power product and then stay at the newly found peak power point. As you can see, these adjustments are moving back and forth along the I-V curve for that given exact level of

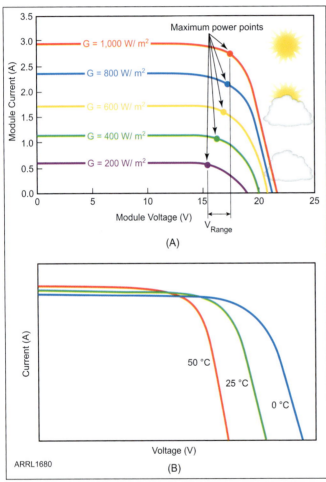

Figure 3.7 — At (A), as the solar illumination goes down the current goes down linearly, and the voltage points go down slightly. At (B), with increasing temperature, array current goes up, but voltage goes down by a greater amount. (Based on illustrations from www.ecmweb.com.)

illumination to always maximize the product of I and V. It continuously checks this algorithm so that it is always producing the optimum power as the solar input changes.

In **Figure 3.7A**, we can see how a change in illumination moves the I-V curve up and down. It is mostly a change in the current available with a small drop in open-circuit voltage. On an overcast day, it is common to still have an operating point that is 10 to 20 percent or more of the rating of the panel. During heavy overcast, the power can drop to almost nothing. For example, my 15 kW system during a heavy, dark rain is producing only 320 W into the grid, though still enough to operate some emergency equipment if needed. Typically the grid inverters just drop out and give up at below about 50 W each.

I even got curious about my power production during bright moonlight. Forget it. The light from a bright moon is about 0.1 lux compared to about 120,000 lux for the noontime sun. So the output for my 15 kW solar panel array could only be 15 mW, and at the system voltage of 500 V would only be a very un-useful 30 µA! And forget those silly indoor "solar cell gimmicks" advertised to recover power from indoor lighting. Most people are surprised that the light in a bright classroom is still only 0.3% of the power outside and would need a square foot 10 W panel just to generate 30 mW, just enough to light a few LEDs. There is no free lunch.

There is one more significant factor that affects solar cell performance, and that is temperature. As shown in Figure 3.7B, the current actually goes up with temperature, but the voltage goes down by a greater amount. The net result is that power output goes down with rising temperature. That is why solar panels are mounted a few inches off the roof, to allow some air cooling, and why you need to do your calculation for maximum open-circuit voltage calculations based on the lowest temperature in winter.

Estimating Solar Panel Performance

In order to fully understand all of the implications and ramifications of the variables in estimating real-world solar panel performance, you need to use some kind of evaluation system. The gold standard for these calculations is the online calculator called *PVwatts* maintained by the National Renewable Energy Laboratory (NREL). Google it since its exact URL may change.

This online tool will let you play solar panel designer like a pro, and it requires only a few keystrokes. In just a few moments you can compare the differences in location, azimuth direction, array tilt angle, tracking, electric utility cost, and just about everything that can affect solar production. The beautiful part of this tool is that it is not just theoretical. Each time you click "compute," it goes through the daily weather data for the last 10 years for that location and computes the exact solar incidence in about a second. It then prints out a month-by-month total production for the year in both kilowatt hours and dollars as shown in **Figure 3.8A**.

Use this tool for your area to evaluate the considerations in the next several sections. To make azimuth direction and tilt angle comparisons, just accept the default settings for your chosen location as shown in Figure 3.8B,

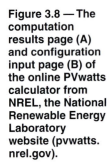

Figure 3.8 — The computation results page (A) and configuration input page (B) of the online PVwatts calculator from NREL, the National Renewable Energy Laboratory website (pvwatts.nrel.gov).

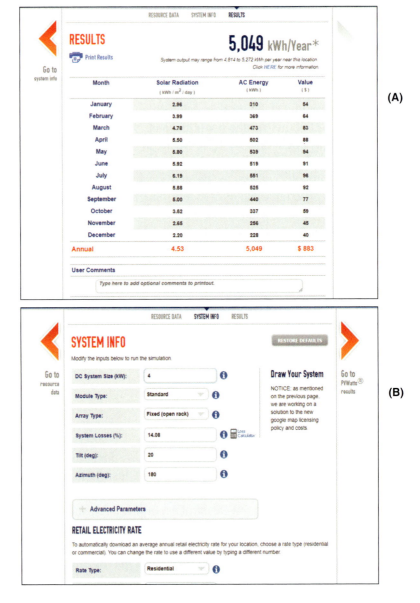

and you can use that for comparing all other possibilities.

Unfortunately, there is one default that is less than optimum. PVwatts assumes that the tilt angle is a typical 20° roof pitch instead of the ideal optimum, which is the same as your latitude (for example, 40° tilt angle for an array at 40° N latitude in Maryland). So you may want to change that parameter to make the tilt angle the same as your latitude, and that will generate the maximum possible annual output for the system. Then you can compare that value to the annual production of all other possible variables one at a time to see what is important and not so important in your particular situation.

Although weather and all other factors are taken into account with PVwatts, just remember that shade is not. You have to discount the PVwatts predictions by the percentage of the hours in the day that any of your panels are shaded, as discussed later in this chapter.

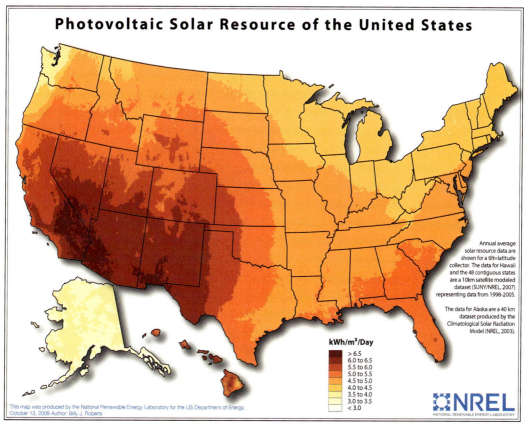

Figure 3.9 — Solar illuminance varies across the US, but so do electric rates and both are equally involved in calculating the value of solar in any given location. (From www.nrel.gov.)

Location, Location, Location (Not So Much)

We've all heard that location drives real estate desirability and values. At first blush, that would also seem to apply strongly to solar. Dry desert states in the southwestern US would seem to have much greater solar opportunity than those areas with more diverse climates, such as the northeast or Pacific northwest.

While **Figure 3.9** easily shows that to be true in solar illuminance, with Arizona having at least 30% more insolence than Maryland, it turns out that is not all of the story. The second most important location factor is the local cost of electricity. For example, an area with half the insolence of Arizona, but where electricity costs twice as much, will actually provide the same annual solar production value. State politics and incentives are the third major factor and can actually dominate the others.

Treat the PVwatts annual dollar estimates with a grain of salt. I do not trust their utility rate data base. It shows Maryland has a 10 cent rate when in fact, with all the add-ons, it is more like 14 cents per kWh. While there are clearly good solar locations and bad solar locations, the differences are not as great as many think, and you are kind of stuck with where you live anyway. You can easily make these comparisons using the PVwatts website.

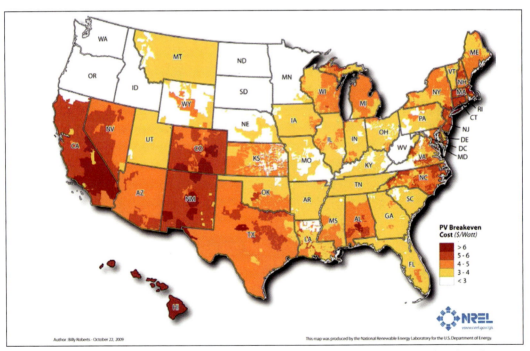

Figure 3.10 — When solar costs dropped below $3/W in 2015, every state is better than breakeven. (From www.nrel.gov.)

Figure 3.10 shows a breakeven map as of 2015. This map includes the cost of local electricity, the cost of labor, and any local state incentives, to show at what price residential solar power became breakeven. The high-solar-incident states shown in darker shades reached breakeven when costs were as high as $6/W. But when solar costs dropped below $3/W in 2015 it is easy to see that solar became cost effective in every state. As of this writing (before the tariffs imposed by President Trump in 2018), the cost in Maryland and Georgia, for example, was about $2.50/W with a contractor-installed system.

Panel Orientation

One of the most surprising results of grid-tie and net metering is the fact that the orientation of the array is not that important. This is in stark contrast to the thinking of most hams with some solar battery experience. They know that a solar panel must be pointed south at the tilt angle of the location's latitude to maximize solar production. And for remote sites that must provide power year-round and over several cloudy days at the lowest sun angle and shortest days of the year in December, the panels are even tipped 10 degrees lower to maximize power during those worst days while sacrificing energy in the summer when there is an excess because days are twice as long.

But grid-tie solar is economical power, and what counts is the total power generated over the year, not what is produced on any single solar day. Arrays for off-grid systems that are pointed south with optimum tilt for maximum power on the worst winter day are actually less than optimum for the summer when days are almost twice as long and the sun is 46 degrees higher in the sky.

As shown in **Figure 3.11**, at mid latitudes in the summer, the sun actually

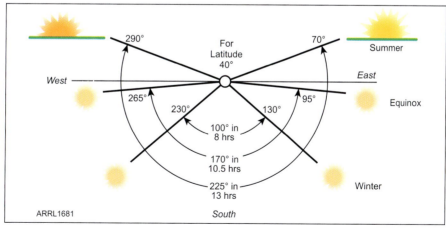

Figure 3.11 — In summer, the sun rises in the northeast and sets in the northwest at mid latitudes, for a day that is twice as long.

rises in the northeast and sets in the northwest and does not even fall on the south-facing array for several hours in the morning and late afternoon. In this case, an array at a lower tilt angle will maximize solar power in the summer when the days are twice as long. Roofs that are east and west facing will produce more in the summer than in the winter, and will thus produce more if the tilt angle is lower than the latitude angle for the south array. You can find the best tilt by using PVwatts.

Tilt Angle

For the array at my church that was to be located in the front lawn (**Figure 3.12**), we wanted to minimize the tilt angle to minimize the visual impact on the neighborhood. We used the PVwatts tools to compare total annual production at various tilt angles. To our surprise, the total annual production did not vary by more than 1% between the angles of 20 and 50 degrees as shown in **Figure 3.13** for our south-facing array.

Figure 3.12 — Tilt angle is not so important for grid tie. This array, which is the original array at my church, is at 25 degrees instead of 40 degrees to minimize the visual impact.

Azimuth Angle

Total annual power production is less dependent on azimuth angle as well. For off-grid/battery systems, the array must be optimized to south for maximum power on the worst winter days. But for grid-tie, the power collected on the worst day is insignificant. The total power produced over the year is what counts. As noted before, the mitigating effect over the year of the ideal south facing panel can be seen in Figure 3.11 when compared to summer sun. In the summer, during the first few hours of morning and in the late afternoon, sunlight does not even impinge on a south-facing panel.

Again, using the online PVwatts calculator, you can enter all possible azimuth angles and instantly get an estimate for annual power production. Doing the three examples in the **Figure 3.14** shows that the

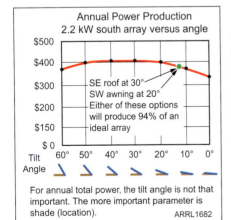

Figure 3.13 — Tilt angle makes little difference from about your latitude +10 to −20 degrees (for example, 20 to 50 degree tilt angle at 40 degrees latitude).

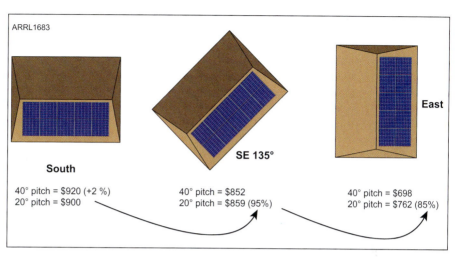

Figure 3.14 — There is only a 15% change in output when pointing east or west compared to south.

ideal south facing array tilt angle at 40 degree latitude is of course 40 degrees. But most roofs do not have that high a pitch. More modest roofs are about 20 degrees, but this only sacrifices about 1% at my 40 degree latitude. So we will take that as a baseline. Next we orient the house to the southeast and find that there is only a 5% annual loss. Taking it to the extreme of due east, the power produced is only 15% below that of the south-facing roof.

You can also try the ultimate extreme of just laying the panels flat on the ground and you will find that the array will still produce about 80% of the ideal south-facing array. In this case, azimuth doesn't matter at all because the orientation is everywhere at once. Of course, you never want to go less than about 15 degrees in any latitude because you must have enough tilt for snow, leaves, and dust to wash off.

The astute reader will notice something interesting about the east-facing array. That is, the house has *twice* the available roof area of the ideal south facing array! Looking at the additional options in **Figure 3.15**, adding the panels on the west-facing roof doubles the power, giving almost 170% of the power of the ideal south-facing array.

If that works, what about the northwest and even the north-facing roof? The northwest-facing roof is only 73% of ideal (even worse than flat), but added to the southeast array, this house can generate about 168% of the power of the ideal south-facing array.

Finally, let's look at the worst case, or panels on the north side of the

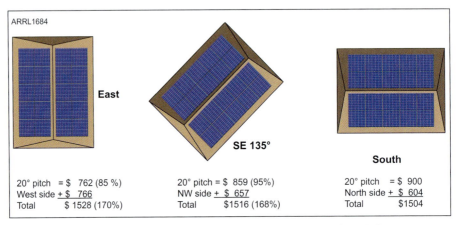

Figure 3.15 — Placing solar panels in opposite directions significantly improves output while being able to parallel the solar panels to use the same inverter.

house (with 20 degree pitch and at mid-US latitude). In this case, the north-facing array, which will produce practically nothing in the winter, will still contribute about 60% of ideal annually, and over the course of the year the whole house produces 160% of just the south-facing array.

When solar became economical and equaled the cost of utilities around 2012, solar panels still cost about $4 per watt and it was not cost effective to install these north-facing panels because of the poor efficiency during winter. By 2016, solar panel prices were six times lower at around 70 cents a watt, and even contractor-installed prices ($2.75/W) made these north-facing roof arrays practical. Of course the DIY handyman who pays no labor costs will see payback from these sub-optimum panels in only a few years.

There is another significant cost advantage of adding these opposite-direction east/west panels — they may not need another inverter. They can simply be wired in parallel with the original array since both arrays will not be receiving full direct sun at the same time.

Paralleling Different Facing Solar Panels

If you use the cosine rule, it is easy to see that the majority of a solar panel production is during the six hours when the sun traverses about 90 degrees across the sky centered on the panel (45 degrees either side of perpendicular). When the days are 12 hours long in the spring and fall and 16 hours long in the summer, it is obvious that there is more power available if you have more panels facing more of the path across the sky. To be clear, for a fixed array, the ideal south-facing array is always best. But as soon as you face the restrictions of property, existing roof angles, and shading issues, and no single array can get the full ideal south exposure for more than six hours a day, then there are other options to accommodate additional panels.

In my case, my best solar exposure was southeast, but when I needed more power for the heat pump, I added panels to the southwest. Because there were trees in the middle, the transition around 2 PM was rather abrupt. This way, I could simply wire the southwest panels in parallel with the southeast panels and use the same inverter. Even though the capacity of the inverter remains the same, the combined panels now produce twice the energy because they are in sunlight twice as long during the day. See **Figure 3.16**.

When paralleling arrays to a single inverter, do not worry about overpowering the inverter on those rare days in the winter (no leaves on the trees between my two arrays) when both see the sun at the same time. Remember, all of these inverters use MPPT (Maximum Power Point Tracking) algorithms to constantly adjust the inverter operating point to

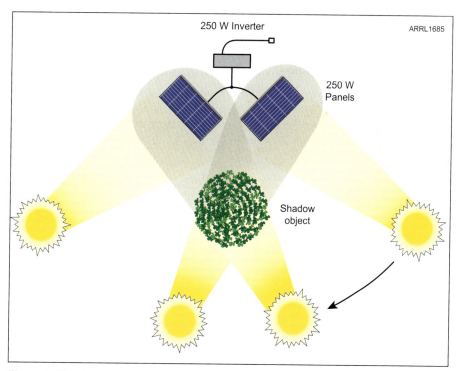

Figure 3.16 — In some arrangements on the author's property, it is possible to double energy production from the same inverter when the panels point in opposite directions or shading blocks morning or afternoon sun.

maximize the power. But by the same token, if there is more power coming in on the solar panel dc input, the MPPT algorithm will still only max out at the peak power rating of the inverter. For example, two paralleled arrays facing southeast and southwest with no trees in the middle will produce 1.4 times the power of one array at noon when the sun is 45 degrees on both. But this will only last for an hour or so, and the MPPT inverter will still only produce its rated power. But with the two arrays southeast and southwest, it will produce its maximum power twice as long.

Over-Rating the Inverter

As solar panels are now so cheap as to be cheaper than the cost of inverters, many installers now will often install panels as high as 20% over the rating of the inverter. This is because on the east coast, for example, when you consider clouds and haze, and less-than-optimum angles in the middle of the summer and winter, most arrays average perhaps no more than 80% of their rated power most of the time. So if the rating of the panels is made to be 120% of the rating of the inverter, and you have this average 80% due to all the other factors, you are actually able to keep the inverter more or less working closer to 100% of its rating. That saves perhaps 20% on the cost of the inverter.

Another significant advantage is that the DIY handyman can install additional panels at a fifth of the typical cost of contractor-installed solar. The DIY homeowner can almost double the output of existing inverters by pointing more panels in widely different directions. The net benefit is obvious.

This is the case for my house. My initial ground-mounted 8 kW system faces southeast because that was the only sunny spot in my yard. It was sized to provide all of our annual power. That was, until we replaced the old oil heat system with a heat pump. This reduced our $3000 annual oil costs and only added about $1200 to the electric load. To meet that new load and get back to net zero utility power, we added solar panels to our northwest roof and porch, as well as an array on the southwest-facing garage without more inverters.

Sun Tracking Arrays

Another question that is easily answered with the PVwatts web page is the benefit of tracking the arrays to follow the sun. Generally we see fewer tracking solutions these days because solar panels are so cheap. It is often easier and less costly just to put up more panels than to go with the added cost and complexity of motors and drive electronics that have to work for the next 20 years in all extremes of weather (**Figure 3.17**).

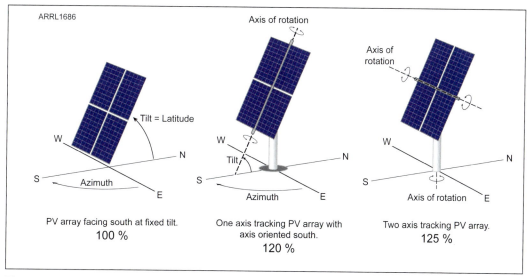

Figure 3.17 — With the cost of fixed panels so low there is little gained by multiplying complexity with sun tracking.

The PVwatts calculator allows you to select whether your array is fixed, or has one-axis or two-axis tracking, and then calculate the performance for your latitude and 10-year average weather. When you select the best system (two-axis tracking), that means the array moves in both azimuth and tilt angle every day to follow the sun across the sky. This gives the maximum possible power and can generate about 25% more power than a fixed array at my 40 degree latitude. The simpler single-axis tracking moves the array from east to west every day to follow the sun but does not adjust for the different tilt between summer and winter. This single axis tracking at my latitude can gain about 20% over the ideal south-facing fixed array.

A third method I tried to test is a three-time-per-year change in tilt between winter and summer optimum angles to account for the 46 degree difference in summer and winter sun elevation angles. As you recall, the cosine difference over 45 degrees is a factor of 0.707, or about 30%. I initially arranged my first ground mounted solar array to be able to adjust this way, but the analysis of this kind of adjustment is not available on PVwatts. So to find out what this approach would do, I came up with a way to get the data anyway. First, I set the array to the optimum tilt for my latitude and let PVwatts calculate the production. I wrote down the spring and fall months of March, April, September, and October. Then I set the tilt to 60 degrees to optimize for winter and let PVwatts calculate the monthly production for the four winter months, November through February Then I finished with the panels set for the best summer angle of 20 degree tilt and let PVwatts calculate the production for May through August. Then the sum of all 12 values would indicate the advantage to changing the tilt angle three times during the year. Turns out, the benefit was only 5% compared to just leaving them at 40 degrees all year. Surely not worth the effort.

Shading Considerations

It is important to understand the drastic effect of shade on solar panels. Since all the cells are in series, then a single cell shaded to 50% power (current) will theoretically reduce the output of the entire panel to that 50% current. In addition, imagine that a single cell is completely shaded (zero current) and there are 14 panels in series to 475 V producing 3 kW. That shaded cell could see –475 V of reverse voltage across it and a potential of 7 A, which would totally destroy the cell.

Since solar cells can only tolerate about 10 V of reverse voltage, as a result, all of the 0.5 V cells in any panel must be bypassed in groups of 20 cells by a diode to carry any reverse voltage. So in a typical 60-cell panel, the cells are actually arranged in three sub groups each with their own diode, and the diode has to be rated at the full array current (typically 9 A for a 270 W panel).

As shown in **Figure 3.18**, shading any single cell reduces the entire

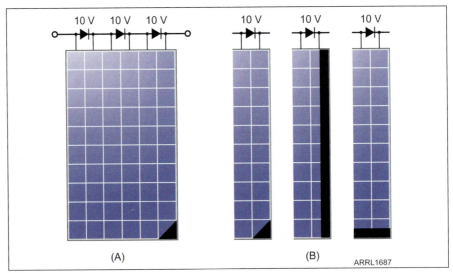

Figure 3.18 — Single-cell shading affects the entire 20 cell subsection of any solar panel. At (A) is a typical panel with one cell shaded. At (B), shading one cell will have the same effect as shading all the cells in one row of a subsection, or shading the bottom two cells of that subsection, or shading any other cells in that subsection.

20-cell section by the same amount. The three individual sub-sections on the right are all reduced by 50% because at least one cell is shaded by 50%. Since these three sections are internal to the panel, this kind of shadow degradation for one big leaf covering one cell in a full-string array of 14 panels and 42 sections is then just a 1/42, or 2% loss. But unlike common lore, this also applies to just a single panel of three sections connected to a microinverter. In that case, that microinverter power is reduced by 33%, but if you have 14 microinverters, then the overall power reduction is the same overall 2%. Chapter 4 discusses the different types of inverters in more detail.

Vertical or Horizontal Placement

Also be aware of the subtle difference in vertical or horizontal shading. Looking at the right-most example, if there is a shadow across the lower edge of a vertical panel, then all three sub sections are all reduced. But if the shadow comes in from the left or right, only one section is lost at a time. So if your shade has its biggest effects in the morning and afternoon due to the movement of the sun, then vertical placement of the panels is best. But if the predominant shadow comes up from below, then the panels should be turned horizontal so that only one section of the panel is impacted at a time. Of course, when morning and afternoon shadows appear, the sun is usually far off axis and the effect will only last for a few minutes, and so this detail may not be worth changing the orientation if it has other aesthetic considerations.

Shading Calculations

Finally, all of the annual power production calculations such as those from PVwatts assume your arrays have no shading issues and see the sun all day long. This is not the case for most of us on the east coast, with trees and other structures, and so most solar contractors will take a picture of your sky from the view of your solar panel location and use special software to predict the losses due to shading. The sun's path across the sky can be predicted by any amateur satellite tracking program, or you can use a plotting aid such as the one shown in **Figure 3.19**.

Plotting the angles and location of all your shade trees has been greatly simplified with a clever $260 device called a Solar Pathfinder

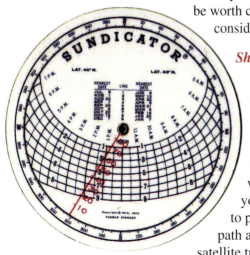

Figure 3.19 — A Sundicator tool by Thomas Spencer can show the sun angle for typical 40 degree latitude as the sun path across the sky for day of the year. Each tool represents a specific latitude (in this case, 40 degrees).

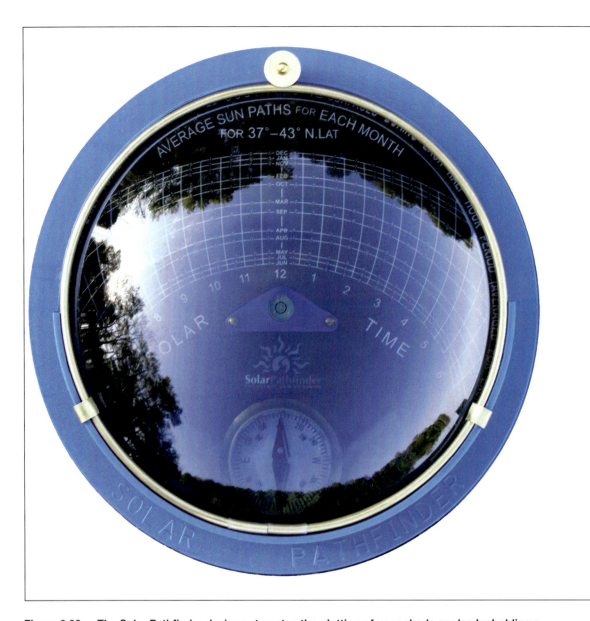

Figure 3.20 — The Solar Pathfinder device automates the plotting of your shade angles by holding a camera over the hemispherical reflective dome. The compass assures proper alignment to south. A photograph of the Solar Pathfinder dome shows the tree line. [Courtesy Solar Pathfinder]

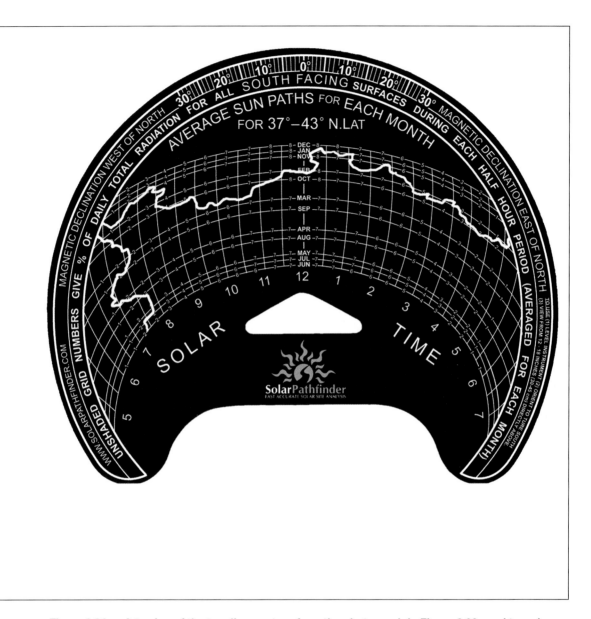

Figure 3.21 — A tracing of the tree line contour from the photograph in Figure 3.20 used to make a sun path diagram. For more information, see www.solarpathfinder.com/PF. [Courtesy Solar Pathfinder]

shown in **Figure 3.20** and **3.21**. Just align the compass for your magnetic declination and stand over the device with a camera pointed down and the hemispherical plastic cover will reflect an image of your trees and horizon into your camera for later analysis. For example, the lower winter angles might appear to be shade free from about 8 AM to 3 PM, and from about March through September the shade limit might extend to about 5 PM. That would be an excellent solar location.

Although every solar estimator has one of these devices and will do your estimate for free, I wanted to double-check the numbers. The particular estimator I observed did not understand the difference between magnetic and true north and he did not appear to be as careful as I would have been to make the device perfectly level. He also only took a single photo from the center of the array location instead of both edges.

Without such a device, you can still make the calculations yourself by measuring your trees with a compass and protractor. Simply plot your trees

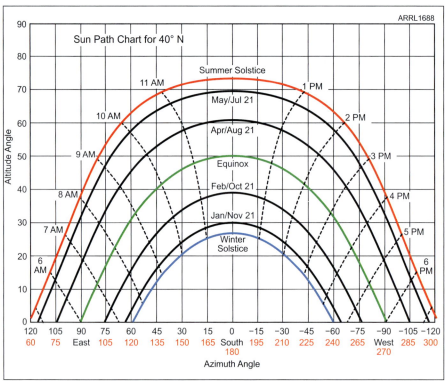

Figure 3.22 — The sun path across the sky in azimuth and elevation, as well as time of day, plotted on a rectangular grid.

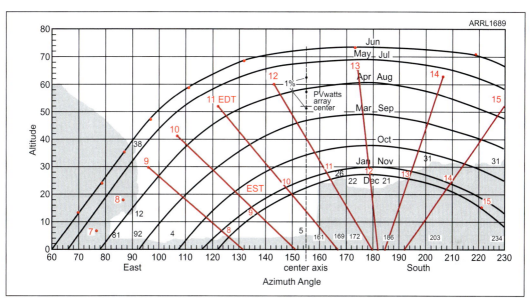

Figure 3.23 — The author's hand-plotted sun tracks taken from *InstantTrack* satellite tracking software with his shade angles plotted. He chose to point his array at that location to a 155 degree azimuth to maximize the total sun exposure, rather than just pointing south, because of western shade in that direction.

on any online plot of the sun path (**Figure 3.22**) for your latitude and do this prediction yourself as I have done in **Figure 3.23**. It is also important to consider where you are standing when you make your angle measurements. The western shade angles should be taken from the western edge of where the array is going to go, and the eastern shade should be measured from the eastern edge of the array. Just taking a single set of measurements from the center location can misjudge the effect of the shade by an hour or so.

Remember that the power production for any angle away from the pointing angle is reduced by the cosine of the angle. So at the far east and west angles the power is down as well. For ±45 degrees, the cosine is down by 0.707, but by ±60 degrees the power is down by half. With Earth spinning at 15 degrees per hour, this theoretically might suggest six and eight hours of sun above 0.707 and half power during the day. But that does not take into account the three-dimensional effects. Looking at Figure 3.21, this rule of thumb only applies at low angles near south. At higher summer angles, the sun is actually moving as fast as 45 degrees of longitude per hour! So in only four hours from 10 AM to 2 PM, the sun has actually traversed more than 135 degrees in azimuth.

Once you have the plot of your shade, you can follow the trace of the sun across the sky for each month, comparing the total hours from horizon to horizon minus those that are shaded. Then divide the unshaded hours by the total number of sun hours in the day and you have the efficiency of your array due to shading below what PVwatts predicts for clear sky. Be sure to discount the lower angles because the power production is much lower at low angles and more atmosphere, and also lower for greater angles away from the array direction. Generally, for properly tilted arrays, about 75% of total power production occurs within ±3 hours of the center-facing azimuth of your array.

Point to Maximum Sky

Once you have the shade plot, you can also then choose the optimum direction for your array. Don't just point it south. Point it to the center of the broadest patch of sky that is visible from this location over the course of the year. And don't count on the loss of leaves in the winter. Even trees without leaves still lose significant power. Earlier we noted that the exact azimuth only makes a few percent difference, but this is only in clear skies. The amount of shade, however, has the biggest effect of all the variables. So pointing to the center of your available sky is the most important. As you can see in my plot, I pointed this array at 155 degrees azimuth, which was my eyeball of the most sky.

After summing up all the sun hours that are shaded in my array over the year, I calculate I will get about 73% efficiency compared to an ideal south-facing and totally unshaded array. As noted elsewhere in this book, the optimization for solar on this southeast-facing array and shading starting after 3 PM allowed me to put up another array facing southwest on the other side of those trees and to connect that array in parallel with this one so that the same inverter was getting solar power all the way to sunset, but with no added cost in inverters.

4 Choosing Your Home Solar System

The previous section covered the general aspects of solar power and solar panel orientation. This chapter will deal with the hardware you will need to interface your solar panel to the grid via a grid-tie inverter system.

Grid-Tie (GT) Inverters

Since the output of a typical 3.3 × 5.4 foot solar panel in 2017 is about 270 W, this equates to about 30 V dc at 9 A (my first panels in 2012 were 220 W at 7.5 A). It is important to understand how grid-tie inverters work to convert this dc to grid power. They are not like a common 60 Hz dc/ac inverter that we use to generate power in the field from a battery. Don't think of a GT inverter as a 60 Hz generator at all. It is simply a current source that is designed to push current against an existing voltage waveform. This way it is constantly pushing into the grid. By Ohms law, $V = I \times R$, and that means that if the resistance increases (load decreases) then the voltage will go up. If the load goes away completely, then R becomes infinite, and so like all current sources, the voltage will soar to infinity too. This is why GT inverters have very narrow feedback sensors that have an upper limit on voltage and will shut down if the waveform ever goes away.

When you think about it, the grid is a nearly infinite load. Think about 100 million other homes, all in parallel, drawing their average 1 kW load. At 120 V, that is 15 Ω each. Combined in parallel then, theoretically the US grid represents about 0.00000015 Ω just for homes.

But of course, the wires have resistance and the grid is designed to keep distribution losses to less than about 5%. So, instead of working backward from the grid to our house, let's look at it working from our 5 kW array feeding forward into the grid. We can assume that about 4.8 kW will be absorbed by all the nearby homes in our neighborhood and that 5%, or 200 W, is lost in the lines. Now we have a better idea of what the grid looks like from our house by taking the 4.8 kW which is 20 A at 240 V. That is about 12 Ω at that operating point. But here is where this simple analogy breaks down. Do the same thing for a 10 kW system, and you end up with a 6 Ω grid. Do it for a 100 kW system and you see a 0.6 Ω grid.

The point here is that the grid will simply absorb all the power you push into it, no matter what the quantity, assuming your wires are suitable for that power and there will be no change in grid voltage other than the 5% loss from the resistance in the wires. So this is how a current source like a GT inverter is protected from pushing to infinite voltage. It will shut down if it detects the voltage rising by about 5% or less, otherwise it would go to infinity.

Spoofing a GT inverter (Not)

The purpose of all of this discussion is to show why you cannot spoof a GT inverter by running a 60 Hz generator or other 60 Hz source to make it think it is connected to the grid. What you don't have is an infinite grid load connected to infinitely absorb the GT inverter's current under all conditions.

Example: The grid is down. Your house presents the average American 1 kW load. Your 5 kW GT inverter has shut down, so you connect up your 60 Hz generator to make the GT inverter think the grid is back up. Let's say your inverter has none of the anti-spoofing protections built in. When this theoretical GT inverter sees the 240 V ac at 60 Hz, it will begin pushing 5 kW into your 1 kW load. Do the math, and the voltage will then shoot up from 240 V ac to over 550 V. You will fry your generator and everything in your house. That is why the over-voltage setting on the GT inverter is there — to keep the output from soaring on loss of load.

For safety, most UL-approved GT inverters have a second protection feature to keep fools away. They also watch the 60 Hz line frequency and will not operate if the waveform is not between about 59.95 and 60.05 Hz. Note that I have seen the inexpensive, smaller plug-in GT inverters designed for one or two panel operation have a much wider frequency tolerance. But they at least have the overvoltage shutoff.

Choosing the GT Inverter System

There are three general ways to tie solar panels as a system to the 120/240 V ac grid in your house. They are: a single string inverter for the whole array, or microinverters or optimizers on the back of every solar panel.

Usually, a given installer might have a preferred approach, but one size does not fit all cases, and it is useful to understand the differences.

String Inverters

The original method is to simply connect the solar panels in strings of 10 to 14 panels in series and then connect the 300 to 420 V dc to a single *string inverter* that converts the dc to 240 V ac to feed your house and the grid as shown in **Figure 4.1**. The string inverter is usually mounted in the basement or along the side of the house for easy access.

The advantages of a string inverter are simplicity, protection, and ease of maintenance (if any) because the inverter is in a sheltered, easy-to-reach location. There is also the significant advantage of lower copper wire costs. The amount of copper wire needed to bring solar power to your power distribution box is proportional to the square of current. If 10 panels were all connected in parallel, you would need wire capable of 10 times the current of a single panel, which means 100 times the amount of copper to safely carry the current from all 10 panels. Note that the voltage would still be the same as a single panel — 30 V.

But if the same 10 panels are connected in series, then the voltage goes up to 300 V, but the current remains the same as a single panel — 9 A. With series wiring, the whole array is only operating at 9 A, and so the array can be connected with inexpensive, common #14 or #12 AWG house wire. When

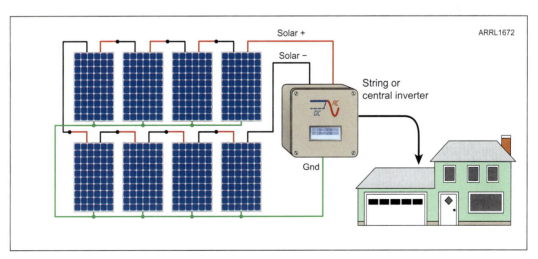

Figure 4.1 — In a string inverter system, all solar panels are connected in series and tie into a central inverter, which is connected to the electrical grid through the home electrical panel and a net meter.

the array is a long distance away from the distribution panel, for example on a roof or ground mounted far from the house, this can be a significant consideration in wire costs. The only disadvantage of series string arrays is that all of the 10 to 14 panels must be mounted in a single direction so that they all produce the same current under the same solar illumination.

Another consideration is that when you opt for string inverters and have more than 10 to 14 panels, you have the choice of using one big string inverter for the multiple strings (in groupings of 10 to 14 modules for each string), or using multiple string inverters connected in parallel. I went with multiple smaller string inverters because my arrays grew over time and because I like having three identical separate inverters for my three strings. That gives me redundancy rather than having all arrays going through a single possible point of failure. Of course it probably cost me about $300 more to go with separate inverters, but it was worth it to me for the redundancy. If one fails, the other two continue to produce while waiting for repair.

Peak Voltage Rating

I use a limit of 14 panels to stay within the maximum 600 V rating of most standard electrical hardware that is generally available. Although the nominal output of a solar panel is about 30 V while delivering maximum current in full sun, this is at about room temperature (25 °C, or 77 °F). As temperatures go up, output goes down. But as temperatures go down, the output and voltage go up. In addition, when the panel is not fully loaded, then the open circuit voltage can rise to 40 V or so.

By doing a calculation with the lowest possible outdoor temperature and the open circuit voltage, it is easy to see that when the outside temperature is –15 °F, the output of 14 panels can approach the 600 V maximum. This is a calculation you will have to make for your system as part of your documentation package to submit to the local utility with your GT application.

Microinverters

Microinverters (**Figure 4.2**) are small boxes attached to the back of every individual solar panel (**Figure 4.3**) so that the power produced for each panel is directly fed to a cable carrying 240 V ac down to the home's distribution panel. Microinverters are touted as an advantage in installation, and with electronics on each panel, each panel can report over an internet connection to give daily and hourly performance.

Microinverters are also considered to have an advantage compared to a

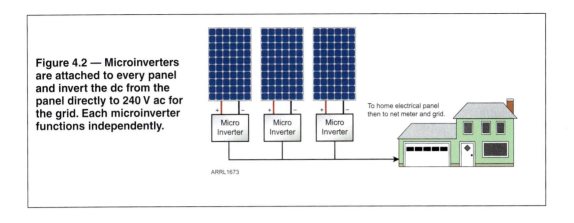

Figure 4.2 — Microinverters are attached to every panel and invert the dc from the panel directly to 240 V ac for the grid. Each microinverter functions independently.

Figure 4.3 — Microinverters mount outdoors, behind or under each solar panel, and are subjected to the elements and wide temperature variations throughout the year.

string array when there is partial shading or if there are mounting differences between individual panels. The claim is that each panel will still produce full power independent of other panels, which is claimed to not be the case with a series string. But this claim is simply not true in most cases and is a significant distortion of reality. As discussed in Chapter 3 and shown in Figure 3.18, each of the three sections of every panel has an inherent bypass diode built in to the back of the panel. If a section of a solar panel is shaded in a string array, then that section simply becomes bypassed so that all the other panels and sections in the string array can still produce full power with the system current bypassing the shaded subsection. This loss of a section still occurs for each of the three subsections, even when a microinverter is connected to each panel.

The only case where microinverters can actually produce more power than a string array is when the majority of the panels in a string array are shaded. In the string array case, when more than half of the panels are shaded, leaving fewer than seven panels in good sun, then the voltage is insufficient for the string inverter to operate efficiently and it simply drops out. But in a good installation, half-shading of the entire array should only occur at low sun angles in the morning and afternoon, well outside of prime production hours. In the same situation, the microinverter panels will still produce output from each sunny panel until the last one is shaded.

For a nominal sited array, significant shading only occurs in the first or last 30 minutes of daylight, when the sun is at such a non-perpendicular angle on the panels that they are only producing maybe 10% power anyway. Thus the microinverter advantage of squeezing out every last bit of power in waning light conditions is usually insignificant.

Microinverters made sense back in 2008 when a single solar panel cost $1200 and the microinverter cost only $250. But now that a solar panel costs about $120, and the microinverter costs about $150, it makes little practical sense when you compare the sum of say 12 microinverters at $2400 to the $1600 for a single string inverter for the same 12-panel array.

The main condition where microinverters are an advantage is on disjointed roofs where it is not possible to congregate at least 10 or more panels into one-direction string arrays. With microinverters, each panel can point at a different tilt and direction and still contribute full power when it is illuminated, independent of what adjacent panels produce.

In addition to cost, the other disadvantage of microinverters is that they are mounted on the roof under the solar panels where they see the full −10 °F to +140 °F temperature range. This is usually not a good idea for electronics. And finally, although the microinverter can identify a failure to a single panel module, having the electronics on the roof makes repair and replacement labor intensive compared to repairing a single string inverter on a wall.

I recently talked to someone who has had a microinverter array since 2010, and he says that over that time, all of his microinverters have had to be replaced, and many of them twice! And all that work is up on the roof, requiring the removal of panels to get to the failed inverters. In contrast, my large string inverters in my basement have been running for five years with no problems at all.

Whole House Transient Suppressors

At this point it should be mentioned that adding a whole house transient suppressor (**Figure 4.4**) right at your utility distribution panel is definitely a good idea. Most hams have probably already done this, but the power lines are notorious carriers of transients, not only from lightning but also from any other large transient event in the area. These transient suppressors are good insurance for all the electronics in your house. Of course each inverter, no matter what type, probably already has some input suppressors, but they are not as big as the ones for the whole house which bypass the incoming transients right where they enter the house and are a good first line of defense. That might be another reason that I have had no inverter failures.

Optimizers

Because of the declining economics for microinverters, the modern equivalent is an optimizer (**Figure 4.5**). Just like microinverters, these are small electronic boxes (though less expensive) mounted on the back of every panel so that the module can report on the condition of each panel and can adjust the output under a variety of lighting conditions. However, the bulk of

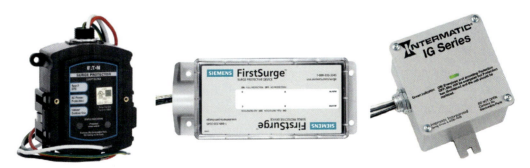

Figure 4.4 — A surge suppressor at the main electrical panel can protect the solar inverters and all the electronics in the house against transients.

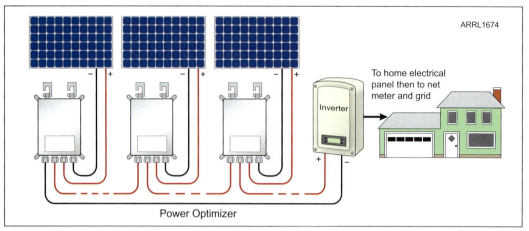

Figure 4.5 — In an optimizer system, there is a dc switching device at each panel that adjusts the voltage of that panel's incoming solar power so that they can be wired in series with identical currents to a single central grid-tie inverter.

the critical grid-interface electronics is closer to the ground or indoors on a wall somewhere, similar to a string inverter. Some claim that this approach has the combined benefits of microinverters and string inverters, but others, myself included, see that this is adding all the vulnerability of roof-mounted electronics to a wall unit and therefore is no net advantage over a simple string inverter.

A minor side note is that it has been observed that the optimizers generate significantly more radio interference. Having these electronic switching devices all over the roof generates electronic noise, and connecting the devices to wires that act like antennas can create interference to anyone listening on a nearby AM radio. For a ham radio operator such as myself, this is a deal killer from the get-go.

The solution to this interference problem requires removing all the panels and placing filters on every one of the modules, both their inputs and outputs. On the other hand, if noise is generated in a single string inverter, that is easily solved in the basement with a few $10 clamp-on filters over the four wires involved, at the one easy-to-reach location. Chapter 6 includes more information on RF interference from optimizer systems.

Maintenance

All three types of inverters require virtually no maintenance. With a leased array, the solar company is responsible for the array for the next 20 years and is only a phone call away. To some, this is an advantage. That is, unless the 20 year finance package has been sold by the solar company to a finance company. On the other hand, many direct-purchase solar systems these days are installed under 20-year warranties too. If the installation shows any problems during the warranty period, the installer is happy to come troubleshoot and make repairs.

Once early installation problems are corrected, solar systems are very reliable since there is nothing to wear out or replace. There are no moving parts, and the only risks are heavy hail (bigger than golf balls), direct lightning strikes (which should be covered by your homeowner insurance), and/or inverter failure.

Like microinverters, modern string inverters have the option of a WiFi module to report array performance on an hourly and daily and annual basis to your PC or smart phone. It just does not break down reporting to the panel level. If one panel out of an array of 10 panels fails, for example, the internal bypass diode will simply bypass the panel. This is observable in the reports because the overall array output will then be 10% less than for a similar day with all panels operating. A simple test with a voltmeter can locate a bad panel, though troubleshooting is more difficult if the array is on the roof.

Lease or Buy?

Choosing how to pay for the array is an important consideration for most people. And like any other investment, you get the maximum benefit when you invest your own money and do not pay finance charges to use someone else's money. But if you cannot make that upfront investment, then a lease deal is a good way to convert to clean renewable solar energy with zero initial investment.

With a lease, the solar company is investing in the solar production on your house. Instead of paying the power company for electricity as in the past, you will pay the solar company a monthly repayment on their investment on your roof. Usually, the solar lease company will guarantee that your monthly payments to them will be something like 10% or so less than what you used to pay for the same electricity from the utility.

Of course, with a solar installation you are grid-tied and so you still have a utility bill, but its amount is reduced by the amount of energy the array produces. There is always a minimum account fee just to have the utility account (which you need for storage during the day, and in the summer for use at night, and in the winter). In Maryland, that minimum fee is about $8 per month as of 2018, and is a bargain compared to having to have $10,000 worth of batteries in the basement to store the energy. (The minimum fee varies in different states.)

Lease

Be sure to look at the lease calculation numbers carefully. To make sure that your solar lease payment is less than what you used to pay for the same energy, the solar company makes some assumptions. The biggest assumption is that the annual cost of electricity from the utility will rise. A common figure is maybe 3% annually, and so they include that increase in your payment schedule, too. Of course this shows the rising value of your solar-produced power, but it also means that what you pay to the leasing company will also increase by that same percentage over the 20 year life of the lease.

Originally that was a good assumption. Back in 2008 at the beginning of the solar revolution, the utilities and analysts were in agreement that electric rates would have to rise and rise and rise due to rising demand and increased need to build more and more coal and gas-fired power plants to meet demand. But it did not work out that way. In fact, for many utilities, the death of coal, the low cost of solar, and higher efficiency appliances and lighting of the last decade have actually kept electric rates almost flat — and in some cases they have gone down somewhat. In that case, the 3% escalation in assumed utility costs built into contracts did not happen, and homeowners with solar leases from that era were actually paying slightly more than if they had stayed entirely on utility-generated power. But still they were happily living on emissions-free and fossil-fuel-free electricity, and they should have no regrets since that is the whole point. But do consider the escalation assumption that the solar leasing company is using in their long-term analysis.

Tax Incentives

One of the key elements of investing in solar is the ability to take a 30% federal tax credit (as of 2018), plus any state, county, and/or city credits. This only applies to those who purchase their array outright, and only to people who pay taxes.

For our nonprofit church, for example, none of these tax credits would apply if we purchased the array directly. But by leasing, the leasing company was able to take all of these investment credits up front and pass those along to the church in a lower overall lease rate. Although our church chose to lease due to these advantages, we did not want to pay 20 years of finance leasing charges to the solar company, so we took the fully-pre-paid option. We made a single up-front payment for the entire 20 year lease, and it turns out that payment was about half of what a full purchase would have cost. This is because the solar company folded back all the tax credits into the cost, which reduced up-front single payment.

End-of-Lease Negotiations

What happens at the end of the lease is still open for negotiation since none of the 20 year leases initiated during the rise of solar starting around 2010 have run their course as of this writing in 2018. For our church's 9 kW system lease, which cost us a single up-front, one-time lease payment of about $20,000, the solar company also offered a complete end-of-lease buyout for about $6000. They included a declining buy-out price table that decreased to about $4000 after 20 years. Given that the system would still be producing more than 80% of its initial power rating at that 20 year life point, this is still a bargain.

However, we are holding off. At the recent rate of price decline, our old panels would have practically no resale value for the leasing company at that time, compared to 20 years of advancement of solar panels over the same period. We think the value of the array to the solar company at the end of the lease will be less than the cost of labor to remove it. So we are waiting to negotiate at that later time and offer them the choice to leave it in place at no cost to either of us, and thus they avoid their cost of removal.

Purchase

For the homeowner who has been saving for retirement and their future life in a home where they expect to stay forever, outright purchase of the array is the best investment. By eliminating most of the monthly electric bill, generally the homeowner will see at least a 10% annual rate of return on the investment over the life of the array, and the real value of that return actually rises over time when compared to future rises in the cost of electricity. For example if the cost of electricity doubles over 20 years, then that rate of return is actually 20% per year at that time. These percentages of return on investment can easily beat the banks, or stocks or bonds and with a much greater sense of security. Other investments are just numbers on a piece of paper, but your investment in solar is actual hardware on the roof of your own house. You own it, and it won't decline in value through mismanagement or corruption.

The Certainty of Death, Taxes, and Utilities

Of all the sections in this book, this section and **Figure 4.6** make the most compelling argument for the value of solar to the homeowner. We've all heard the old saying, "nothing is certain but death and taxes." But this simplistic vision overlooks *utilities*, which are also inescapably a constant drain on our lives. We all need energy to live. So another way to look at the solar investment decision is to compare what you will have after, say, 11 years with

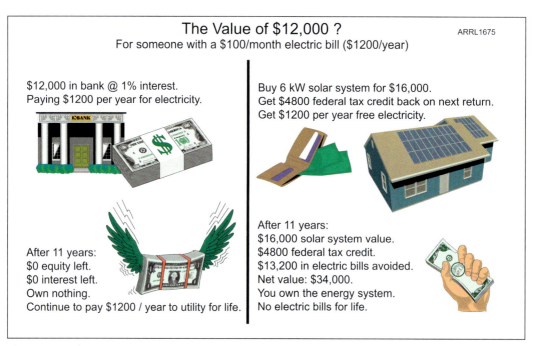

Figure 4.6 — Comparison over an 11-year period between leaving $12,000 in the bank at 1% interest and using that to pay a $100 per month electric bill, versus investing $16,000 in a 6 kW solar system, receiving the 30% federal tax credit, and avoiding $100 per month electric bills during that 11 year period. See text for more information.

$12,000 of savings in a bank earning 1% interest, versus the same $12,000 invested in a rooftop solar array.

See Figure 4.6. Assume that the cost of electricity is $100 per month ($1200 per year), and you use that $12,000 in the bank earning 1% interest to pay your electric bill. At the end of about 11 years, that entire $12,000 of initial savings has all gone to the utility. You have used all of it, plus any interest earned, to pay electric bills over 11 years — and you still face the burden of paying $100 a month for electricity for the rest of your life.

In the second scenario, let's turn that $12,000 from savings into a solar power investment. You will need to add an additional $4000 initially, to end up with a good sized $16,000 solar system for the roof of your house. That will buy about a 6 kW solar system. First, as of 2018 you get a 30% federal solar tax credit, so you get back $4800 (that additional initial investment and more) directly as a credit when you file your next federal tax return. That reduces your net investment to $11,200 out-of-pocket. Already, you have made an $800 profit compared to leaving the $12,000 in the bank. Plus, you have secured energy for life and eliminated some of your dependence on fossil fuels. You now own a physical energy supply system worth $16,000 of equity and have eliminated $100 per month utility costs for life.

After 11 years, instead of using *any* of the $12,000 in the bank to pay your monthly electric bill, you have simply exchanged it for $16,000 of equity in your own solar system, have received a $4800 tax credit, have avoided $13,200 in utility bills, and have energy for life with no utility costs for the rest of your years.

Some might argue that the original $16,000 solar investment depreciates over time and will be worth probably half that amount at the 11-year point. I would argue that if it still produces 90% of all your energy needs at the 10-year point, and more than 80% at the 25-year point, then it still retains its original value of providing your power to the last day of your life. Even losing 20% of the array production over 25 years (the standard aging rate of solar cell technology) is nothing to be concerned about, since in the same 25 years, it's likely that your appliances will have improved efficiency, so your array will still produce all you need for the rest of your life.

Bottom line for retirement: After 11 years of maintaining the status quo, you will have spent $12,000 and have nothing left to show for it. Or, if you choose to invest it in your own solar generation facility on your roof, you will have free power for life and still own the original equity.

Note: These are simple numbers given for a general example. You should consult your financial advisor for your own situation and for a much more refined approach to the analysis. As of this writing in late 2018, the federal solar tax credit is scheduled to remain 30% for 2019, then drop to 26% in 2020 and 20% in 2021, and then 10% for commercial and 0% for residential installations. In addition, some states offer Solar Renewable Energy Credits (SRECs) as well. Of course that may change.

Peak Power Value versus Distribution Costs

There is pushback from some utilities and the fossil fuel lobby, and some have initiated campaigns to convince non-solar customers that, because solar customers are reducing their bills substantially, it must somehow be costing the non-solar customers more. This is not true. The cost of generating electricity varies minute by minute throughout the day to meet the demand, as shown in **Figure 4.7**. Although the consumer is only billed the average, say 10 cents per kWh, the actual prices paid by the utilities for the power from the generators varies from 3 cents or less at night and up to 18 cents during the peak loads of the day. The nominal cost of electricity is

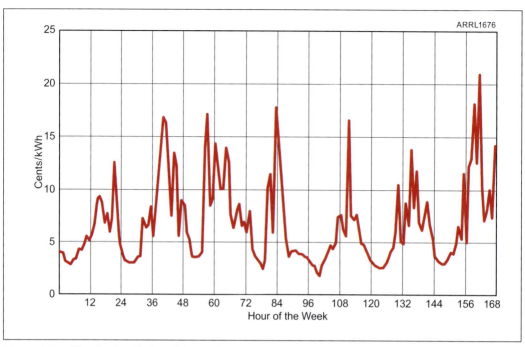

Figure 4.7 — Hourly electricity pricing varies over a 5-to-1 range throughout the day, yet consumers pay only a single fixed rate. (From energysystems.princeton.edu.)

established as the long term average of these drastic daily fluctuations.

At the high-price times during the day, the home solar net-meter producer is still only getting the same one-to-one 10 cent credit for his power, even though the home system is producing electricity when the utility needs it most, and when the utility is paying other sources much more than the 10 cent rate. At night, the solar array is not producing, and customer is still paying 10 cents per kWh consumed, but at a time when it only costs the utility a few pennies. This net peak value of solar more than offsets the modest costs to maintain the distribution hardware of the grid for solar customers.

So, it is not the other utility customers who are losing to solar customers. It is utility-owned fossil-fuel peaking plants that are fired up during the daily peak when they can sell electricity at 10 to 20 times the average rate. It is these fossil-fuel plants that are losing their monopoly on high-priced power. Yes, the utilities that own these plants are losing profit but, unfortunately, that is the goal of a cleaner energy future. We need to phase out the dirtiest and most expensive fossil-fuel peaking plants because solar systems can minimize the need for them. It is what must happen if we are to clean up the grid and our air.

Don't Wait, Do It Now!

The nature of home solar energy, electric vehicles, and the grid will still be evolving rapidly during the time you are reading this book. Solar is growing rapidly and has plenty of room to grow in most states, even though in 2017 two states (Hawaii and California) are beginning to worry about the *duck's back curve* (see Chapter 11) and the over-production of solar. In those states, the grid is getting less interested in encouraging more solar to be added to the grid without adding some form of storage. When solar overproduces in those states during midday, and the actual cost of power to the utility goes negative, then it is obvious that the present incentives to go solar in the future will be less.

By now, 46 of the 50 states are mostly on board with supporting solar net metering to customers. This is up from only 17 or so back in 2012. Some provide much better deals than others. Anyone who installed solar during this time frame easily recouped their investment quickly, and will continue to benefit for the rest of their lives. Even in California and Hawaii, although the value of solar (without storage) is going down as more oversupply is coming on line, it is still a good deal. In the other 44 states that support net metering, the economic value of solar is still rising. So, like anything else, the early bird gets the worm… but eventually everyone rises on the same tide of clean renewable energy from solar (and wind). But already we are seeing some states pushing back to reduce the incentives.

Any oversupply of low-cost solar power will only be temporary as low-cost solar power during the day will always find a willing customer and incentivize other uses of cheap electricity. A good example will be the trend toward increased daytime loads such as charging-at-work for EVs, plus battery storage for profit, plus industries that are power intensive such as aluminum or hydrogen production.

If you are ready to consider significantly reducing your monthly contribution to your local utility, check out the current net-metering deal from your utility and figure out what an investment in your own solar energy generation system would require. Other considerations might be how long your net-metering contract will last, and what the tea leaves are saying with respect to the future in your area. In one state, there are rumors that the utilities are facing so much change that they are only committing to

10 year or shorter net-metering contracts with customers so that they can make changes in the future.

On the other hand, for those without good solar properties, there is a growth in community solar that allows anyone to invest in community solar farms via their local utility. They subscribe to solar power from those farms for a fixed contract for a term. As this is written in 2018, in Maryland there are two such community power projects. One offers a long-term contract for 25 years that guarantees a cost of 5% less than the standard utility rate. The other offers the same 5% guaranteed savings, but for only three years. This is a better option for people who might move soon, while the longer term contract might be better to lock in lower-cost power for the rest of your life.

In the big picture, of course, solar will always be a great investment for everyone. Who can argue that a source of power that is now cheaper than even coal and completely carbon-free is not a good investment? The only question is who gets the benefit? You, the solar financing company, the utility, the fossil fuel lobby, or the politicians? Even if you can't go solar yourself due to your current situation, or shade on your property, consider advocating for future growth of clean renewable energy.

5 Solar DIY at Home and in the Field

Although the solar focus of this book is on accommodating solar into the home and ham radio station because that is where the economics of solar are revolutionizing our energy systems, it does not mean that solar is not economical where there is no access to the grid. If you have no grid, then solar is practical at any cost because it gives you continuing access to independent energy anywhere.

An excellent example was mentioned in the "Second Century" column in the August 2017 issue of *QST*, where the author mentions that batteries for our forward-deployed Marines and all of their associated electronics are more expensive than munitions. Other sources have placed the cost of gas for generators in these units to be as high as $800 a gallon when you consider the complete logistics train all the way back to the refinery, including heavily armed convoys just to deliver the gas to each camp. The military is rapidly adjusting to this reality, and solar panels are rapidly being integrated into these units.

Power Lines Not Available

Another example where off-grid solar can be economical is when the building is far from the existing power lines. Utility companies usually install a new service for free if it a typical installation. If the customer is in a remote spot, then the customer usually bears the cost of new poles, wire, labor, and other expenses of establishing service, and that can run thousands of dollars.

For example, the power company might want $20,000 to run a power line to a remote cabin that you only use a few weekends a year. Then a $1000 investment in a 1 kW battery-based solar system is clearly more cost-effective. The fact that the $1000 is only producing about $2 per week of electricity is insignificant to the joy of being there. Generally, the largest investment in this type of system over the long term is the maintenance of batteries. But that will become less of an issue as more and more electric vehicles are produced and used batteries become available.

Connecting an off-grid system is simple. Just connect the solar panels to a battery charge controller that is connected to a battery, and then run all your stuff on the battery. This is fine for Field Day when all your needs are met at 12 V dc and are right at your station. When you consider that wire

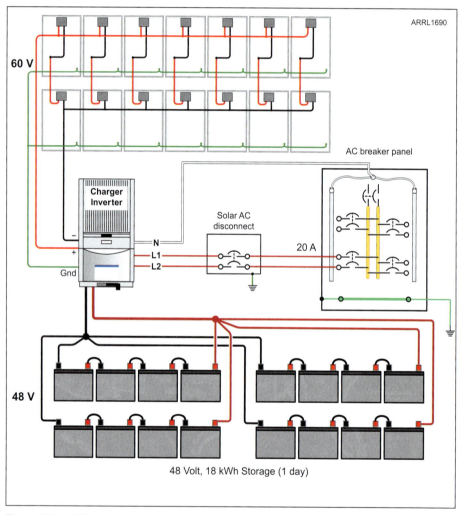

Figure 5.1 — Off-grid systems marry solar panels in parallel with heavy wires for use either directly at dc or via an inverter for ac distribution.

loss is proportional to I-squared times the wire resistance (I²R), however, it is easy to see that distributing power at 12 V requires 100 times the copper conductor size compared to distributing at 120 V for the same line loss.

When you want to distribute power throughout a cabin or over hundreds of feet between Field Day stations, then low-voltage dc becomes impractical. At that point, it becomes practical to simply invert the battery voltage to 120 V ac for distribution using standard distribution wiring as shown in **Figure 5.1** Another advantage of distribution at 120 V ac is the ability to use any off-the-shelf electronics, appliances, and lighting with no dependence on specialty (and rare) dc items. Modern inverters operate at over 90% efficiency and more than make up for the inefficiencies of wire loss at low-voltage dc. Additional coverage of this topic of distribution at even higher voltages is discussed in Chapter 10, High Voltage DC Emergency and Backup Power.

Designing the System

To choose the solar panel size needed, and the battery size, you need to know the energy demand. This is not simply adding up the power requirements of all the devices, lights, and appliances in the house. They are never all on at the same time. You have to include the duration of time that they are drawing power. Multiplying the device power required, times the duration that each is on, will yield the needed energy in watt-hours (Wh).

Minimum Case Example

Say your cabin has 10 LED light bulbs at 6 W each, and half of them are on for about five hours a night — that's 30 Wh. Your ham radio is on for 12 hours a day drawing 12 W (1 A during receive), needing 144 Wh. And it transmits 10% of the time, drawing 120 W (another 12 W average), for another 144 Wh. For this system, your energy needs for lights and ham operation are about 320 Wh per day.

In Maryland, the average daily solar energy available on a fixed-orientation solar panel is about four hours a day. So with the average four hours of good sun a day, a single 250 W solar panel costing about $150 will provide over 1000 Wh a day on average. This gives a good a factor-of-three safety margin to cover for days that are less than "average" solar days.

Choosing the Battery

Battery capacity also depends on watt-hours. If you only need a battery to store the average daily energy, then in the above example you need 1000 Wh of capacity, which at 12 V is about 80 amp-hours (Ah). But you usually want to double that to be sure you preserve the life of the battery by rarely discharging below 50%. Further, this assumes every solar day is an average solar day. You might want to increase this half again so that you can carry over some capacity from a good solar day to a bad solar day. Now you are up to a good-sized 240 Ah battery. That requirement can be met quite well with a pair of 6 V golf cart deep-discharge batteries giving 240 Ah capacity for about $350. Notice that these days, the cost of these batteries will be about twice what you paid for the solar panel.

In the old days, when the solar panel was the biggest cost, you could also trade off the size of the solar panels and the size of the batteries in applications that were not full-time. For example, a cabin used only on weekends can have a smaller solar array but a bigger battery to accumulate solar energy over seven days, but that energy is used only during the two-day weekends. A benefit of this approach is that the larger battery gives you a surge capacity on the weekend. However, this approach runs a greater risk of running out of power if you try to use the battery for more than two days a week, when the solar panel cannot replenish power quickly enough to meet a longer demand. On the other hand, you can get by with a much smaller battery if you use most of your energy-intensive loads during the day when you have plenty of solar power, and minimize loads at night when it all has to run off batteries.

Just remember that there is a significant difference in energy availability between summer and winter for off-grid systems. Not only is the solar day only half as long in the winter as in the summer, the nights are almost twice as long. When the only lighting available for night was incandescent, this lighting load was huge. Now, with LED lighting operating 10 times more efficiently, the lighting load can be much less than the ham radio load.

Field Day Solar Power and Air Conditioning

A great example of how far solar has come is the ability to run a small air conditioner from just three common solar panels in the field. This is handy when my communications shelter trailer (**Figure 5.2**) is sitting in the sun all day. Three panels provide 750 to 900 W when pointed at the sun, and a typical small 5000 BTU window air-conditioning unit draws only about 650 W (measured) once it is running. There are three things working in your favor. First, the air conditioning is the most desirable when it is hot, and it is the hottest when the sun is shining the most, and when the sun is shining the most, you get the most power. Second, modern Energy Star rated air conditioning units delay the compressor starting current until after the fan is running to minimize the starting surge. And third, modern modified sine wave inverters often have a peak rating twice as high as the average rating.

Figure 5.2 — My solar plug-in hybrid electric vehicle also gave plenty of power in the field.

My test involved running a small air conditioning unit from my 1500 W modified sine wave inverter in the back of my car. This inverter has a bar-graph LED display showing power level. With the air conditioning unit plugged in, the inverter had no problem starting the compressor and then settling down to a steady-state load of approximately 650 W, providing plenty of cool air to a station operating tent.

This type of operation would be entirely sustainable on a sunny day from three solar panels. In 2018, typical state-of-the art panels were up to 300 W each, providing 900 W continuous power for your comfort all day long if you move the panels to follow the sun.

DIY Solar While Grid Tied

The big conundrum about writing this book is that there is hardly anything simpler than connecting up solar, and nothing is more cost effective for energy than solar. But on the other hand, there is no economical cost effective way to use that power in the home and ham radio station without being grid-tied. And there is no way to grid-tie without having a net meter, and there is no way to get a net meter without all of the applications, licensing, permits, certifications, inspections, and approvals needed for the utility to give you one. The problem for this book, then, is that radio amateurs often fall into the do-it-yourself (DIY) class and may want to use their fundamental skills to do their own solar installation, where possible.

Because of all the requirements imposed by the utility, doing it myself, it took about three years from the time of my solar awakening in 2010 until I was finally grid-tied in 2013. That is why I can give such great advice as to how not to do it (and the final workaround). A lot of that delay was caused by two things: my limited hobby time, and my unique situation of being the first person in Maryland to face outdated environmental rules near the Chesapeake Bay. Another delay was that as soon as I got my first batch of solar panels in the fall of 2011, I couldn't wait to use them somehow — even without net metering.

Bulk Heating Project

While waiting to find an electrician, I hooked up my 8 kW of solar arrays to a 10 kW resistance heater to make full use of the free power until I could complete the grid-tie process. I had found a 10 kW coil heater designed to fit inside a large HVAC duct tossed in a dumpster during a commercial building renovation. I now had a use for it!

Shown in **Figure 5.3**, this unit consisted of multiple coils designed for operation at 440 V. I added a few jumpers to be able to series/parallel the coils and the arrays to maximize the heat delivered. Remember, you have to match the load to the incident solar power under all sun conditions in order to get maximum power.

I placed these coils in a box in the center room of the house, and it was pleasant to see the orange-hot coils during the day delivering about 8 kW

Figure 5.3 — These 10 kW resistance coils provided a quick and dirty use of solar arrays in the winter for home heating.

of heat in the winter. Although this was about 1/3 the efficiency of running a heat pump, it was easy to do and it allowed me to drag my feet in getting around to finding an electrician to make my arrays grid-tie-legal.

Finding an Electrician

Every electrician I contacted explained that he was so busy making thousands of dollars a week installing solar, that he had no interest in spending a day doing nothing but paperwork for my system where he did not get to make any money in labor, hardware, and profit markups. Finally I found a hungry licensed electrician via his handmade sign beside the road leading away from a home center. It said in effect, "Master Electrician Needs work." Since I had done all of the preparations, the engineering, the drawings, and had collected all the UL certifications, all he had to do was file the paperwork and be there for the county inspection. His standard rate for this service — "drawing a permit" — was $500.

Radiator-Based Hot Water Heating

The problem with the 10 kW resistance wire heating was that all the heat went into just the central part of the house. So another distraction in my DIY progression was due to the imminent failure (leaking) of my oil-burning radiator boiler. This delayed the project another winter as I cobbled together a cheap way to inject all my 8 kW of solar power into my radiator hot-water system to spread the heat throughout the house, instead of heating just the central room. The solar powered system would also serve as backup to the failing oil burner.

The result is shown in **Figure 5.4**. I took two standard $10 water heater elements and screwed them into a "plumber's special" made from off-the-shelf 2-inch galvanized pipe and two T fittings from a home center. Since each element is about 4800 W, this matched my 8 kW of solar arrays just fine. These heating elements are about 12 Ω and yield 4800 W at 240 V. My solar arrays put out 400 to 500 V, so I wired the elements in series to give full power at 480 V dc from the solar panels. I also added some jumpers so that I can wire directly to the grid (240 V) to get emergency backup power when the boiler fails.

Do Not Do This At Home

It worked well, but with one very important safety caution. Although I mounted this heating pipe vertically to take advantage of convection circulation, that was not enough. At modest solar illumination, all was going well without powering up the water circulation pump. But then the sun came

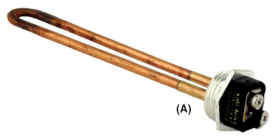

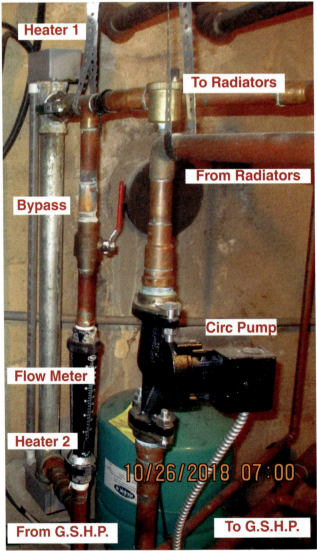

Figure 5.4 — Two 4800 W water heater elements (A), screwed into the ends of a 3-foot piece of galvanized pipe, are used for backup resistance heat in my house radiator system (B).

5.8   Chapter 5

out full-strength and I heard very loud *bangs* throughout the house as the solar power going into the two heater coils was flashing the water to steam, which then bubbled to the colder water above it, where it condensed with a *bang*. This would have destroyed the structure, and so I learned that I always had to have a circulating pump running, and it must be failure-free.

Since the pump was running from the ac mains and the solar was heating the elements, I was vulnerable to overheating from loss of power to the pump during a power outage if I ran the system unattended. The only safe way around this was to install thermal cutouts that would disconnect the solar whenever the pipe got too hot. And these had to be fail-safe at switching 480 V dc. This is not trivial. (See the sidebar, "High-Voltage DC is Now Everywhere" in Chapter 1 for cautions on switching high-voltage dc.)

By this time, I realized that playing around with inefficient resistance heating (1/3 the efficiency of a heat pump) was a waste of time when I had plenty of free solar electricity. I decided to solve the failing oil boiler problem by simply replacing it with a heat pump. So I disconnected the homemade heating element plumbing device and keep it in reserve only for attended-backup solar power if the grid goes down. So far I have never had to use it, nor develop all the fail-safe hardware needed to allow it to safely run unattended.

High Voltage Disconnects

You will notice throughout this book that I have a number of circuits that I need to reconfigure manually that operate at high voltages and currents, and which will produce a blinding arc-flash on disconnect. Such high-voltage dc switches are very expensive, so I have found an easy solution. I use a simple air conditioner outdoor pull-out disconnect box. These are designed for up to 60 A and are rated at 600 V ac.

Of course, they are not rated for dc because there is no common use for such dc. I choose the ones that have a pair of contacts on a large plastic-handle (**Figure 5.5**). The handle simply pulls the contacts out of the

Figure 5.5 — Air conditioner pull-out disconnects (less than $10 from home centers) make good cheap DIY high voltage, high current switches for manual operation. The pull-out contacts leave no gap for a dc arc.

socket, instead of using an actual disconnect switch. When you pull out the contacts, you still get a white-hot plasma arc-flash, but with the pull-out there is no gap remaining for the arc. Just remember to not look at the contact as it comes out. The amazing thing is that you get not only a high-voltage, high current disconnect switch, but it comes in a weather proof outdoor enclosure — all for less than $10 at your local hardware store.

Other DIY, Non-Grid Ideas

Still searching for ways to use these very cheap (50 cents per watt) solar panels at home without grid-tie, another idea was to heat hot water. The idea was to connect a few solar panels to the lower heating element in an electric water heater to provide day-long warming of the incoming water via solar energy. See **Figure 5.6**.

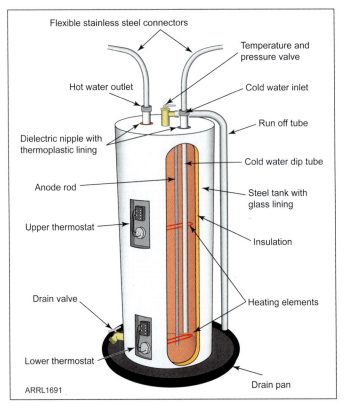

Figure 5.6 — The conventional water heater has both upper and lower elements and thermostats.

I would not need 4800 W of solar to drive the heating coil since the idea was not to heat incoming hot water fast (within an hour or so at 4800 W) but to heat it more slowly over the solar day. Four solar panels (240 W each) for five hours would provide the same water heating as 4800 W for one hour. It takes 1 BTU to raise one pound of water one degree Fahrenheit. And with 3.4 BTU per watt-hour, that would be 40 gallons raised 50 degrees, heating just about a full water tank to 110 °F while letting the thermostatically controlled top coil running on grid power bring it up to 120 °F and also fill in on cloudy days.

Do Not Do This At Home

Anyone who has seen a water heater explode several hundred feet into the air through the roof of a house (examples can be seen on the Myth Busters TV show or YouTube) will realize that you need to have a fail-safe mechanism to stop the solar heating when you don't use all the water every day.

The first level of protection is the relief valve that is standard equipment on every water heater. The relief valve should dump any excess pressure, and it must be in working order.

Second, you cannot just wire dc solar power to the lower element with its existing thermostat and be done. Since dc arcing will destroy any unprotected contacts when they try to open, it is imperative that these contacts can only be used if they are protected with an RC snubber circuit or by using a high-voltage, dc-rated contactor. The safety of your house depends on this circuit. Even one test without a snubber circuit will ruin the thermostat contacts permanently when they open the first time. More than likely, the failure will be shorted contacts that will cause an overheating condition, so the water heater is protected only by the pressure relief valve.

Solar Thermal Water Heating is Dead

While on the topic of hot water... Prior to about 2005, the high cost of solar photovoltaic (solar PV) panels made solar thermal hot water heating one of the best choices for direct conversion of sunlight to useful energy. But still, it was only about 75% efficient and was a high maintenance system with pumps, motors, anti-freeze, valves, and so on. This was when solar PV panels still cost over $8 per watt and was only about 15% efficient, as shown in **Figure 5.7**.

But over the next decade, several things happened. First, the price of solar PV dropped by a factor of five or more. Second, new heat pump-based electric water heaters came on the market that could heat water about two to

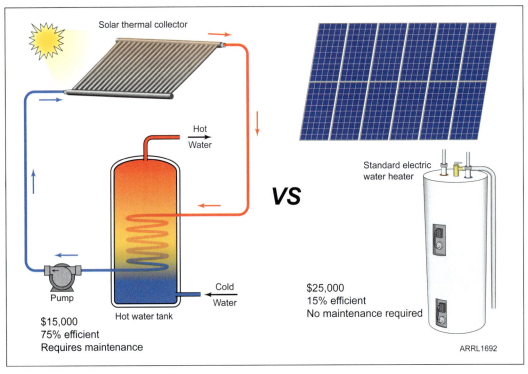

Figure 5.7 — Prior to about 2005, solar hot water heating was the most cost-effective form of using solar energy to heat water.

three times more efficiently than with resistance heat. And third, PV panel efficiency went up from about 15% to more than 20% for home panels. These three things drastically changed the dynamic on water heating as shown in **Figure 5.8**, and by 2012, thermal hot water heating for the home was considered dead (see **www.greenbuildingadvisor.com/article/solar-thermal-is-dead**).

But there is an even more important thing going on for domestic hot water in the home that might not be so obvious. In order to reach the efficiency claimed for thermal water heating, the system must be producing hot water all day, every day. But to do this under the variety of weather conditions, the solar thermal water system has to be oversized to cover for overcast or less-than-optimum sunshine. This means that on a good day, or when fewer people are using the water, the hot water tank might be fully hot by noon and all the rest of that day, the solar investment on the roof of the house is producing nothing. That's a wasted investment.

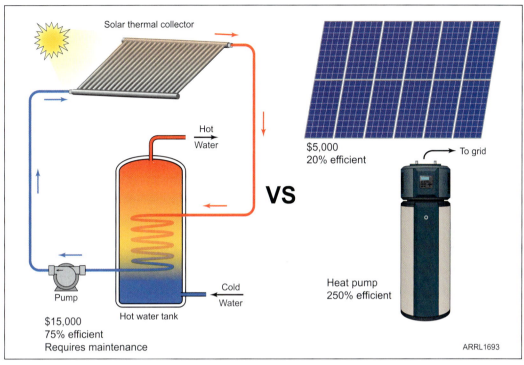

Figure 5.8 — Drastic reductions in the cost of PV solar panels and introduction of affordable, efficient heat pumps for water heating, spelled the end of thermal solar hot water.

On the other hand, for solar PV-based hot water heating via a heat pump, once the tank is hot, the PV panels continue to produce electricity all day long. This excess is stored in the grid at full retail rates via the net meter and can be used later for hot water on poor solar days, as well as for any other electrical purpose in the home any time for the rest of the year. Under these conditions, by 2014 thermal water heating was really, really dead (see **www.greenbuildingadvisor.com/article/solar-thermal-is-really-really-dead**).

Master Electrician Required

To connect to the grid, you have to have both building and electrical permits, full detail and signed engineering drawings of the complete system, and certifications of UL-approved equipment. Then (in most states) you have to have a master electrician file for the permits and sign for an inspection. Once you pass the required local government inspection, you can turn on the system temporarily to check it out. Then you have to submit an additional formal filing with the electrical utility, get approval, and pass another on-site inspection, this time by the utility, which may or may not consider your solar generation as a threat to their income model. When you pass that, then you will be scheduled to receive a net meter. Once they install the net meter, then you can turn on your system and begin generating free power for the rest of your life.

Remember, not until you get the net meter will your grid-tied power actually count your kilowatts backward. This was not entirely clear to me, because during the test phase, I did watch the eddy disk in the utility meter actually run backward whenever the array was producing more than I used. So, after the first inspection, but before I got the net meter, I figured I could just leave the system connected until the utility came back with the net meter and get a two-week head start.

Two weeks later the meter was installed, and I was good to go. Watching the meter spin backward, I couldn't wait to get my first electric bill and see how much I had produced. You can imagine my chagrin when I received the next bill and found that my normal $200 per month electric bill had *doubled* to more than $400. Turns out, to prevent fraud, all electric meters for at least the last 40 years either have differential gearing, or a ratchet pawl, or if they have an electric counter will only count kWh one way, and that is *up* no matter which way the disk spins. So what I had done was paid $200 for all the solar kWh I pushed into the grid, *and* I paid another $200 for the kWh I drew back out at night. I could only chalk it up to another lesson learned, because I could not complain about getting overcharged while being connected without permission.

And that is the reason why economical solar (which demands grid-tie for storage) simply cannot be done without a net meter, and you cannot get a net meter without all the permits, inspections and approvals.

A Single Panel Without Net Metering for Your Minimum Loads

Although this limit of never overproducing what your house can use in real time without a net meter installed applied to my 8 kW array producing about $200 a month, it even applies with something as small as a single solar panel and a single $100 grid-tie inverter plugged into an outlet to help offset power used in your house. Any time you are producing more than you use, you will pay double for it.

It used to be that the phantom loads of all the inefficient home appliances, along with low-voltage wall transformers, incandescent bulbs and other things in the house, probably added up to a few hundred watts and would consume whatever you generated with a single solar panel. So you could plug in a 250 W solar panel and inexpensive grid-tie inverter as

Figure 5.9 — Inexpensive grid-tie microinverters simply plug in to any 120 V ac outlet. The one on the right accepts full-size 30 – 45 V solar panels up to 600 W, and the one on the left is only for 12 V panels up to 300 W.

shown in **Figure 5.9** and be okay. This panel and inverter are temporary and/or portable and only interface to your house grid when you plug them into a wall outlet, so the usual electrical permit is not required.

The energy produced would never leave your house because the phantom loads would absorb all the power, and the electric meter would never go backward. But in recent years, with Energy Star appliances that minimize inefficient standby losses, it is likely that a house might at times actually drop below the power production of even a single solar panel, and you will end up pushing the meter backward when this happens. Without a net meter, the kWh will count upward and you will pay for the power going into the grid, and later pay again for it coming back out — double for that excess solar power you produced.

Even a refrigerator cycles on and off. Say it draws 250 W while running, absorbing all 250 W from your single solar panel during that time. When it kicks off, if there is no other load in your house running at that time, the 250 W from the panel will go into the grid, and without a net meter you will pay for that. Then you pay again when you draw 250 W back out. So your simple single-panel grid-tie inverter can actually cost you more money to operate than it will save.

So the rule is, if you want to back feed the loads in your house with grid-tie solar, you have to measure the minimum load of the house under all conditions to find the absolute minimum power the house draws. Then that is the only grid-tie power you can produce without paying extra for the privilege if you don't have a net meter. And in many cases, this is just not enough power to bother with. Or, once you identify these minor remaining loads, it is almost as easy to replace them with modern, efficient Energy Star loads to simply reduce your wasted always-on power in the first place.

Two Panels for the Limit of One

Let's say you find that the absolute minimum loads in your house total 250 W. So it would appear that you can only add a single solar panel and a 250 W micro-grid-tie inverter without being charged for excess power. But it turns out that you can actually double that amount in total energy produced by spreading that power out over a longer period of time. That is, you connect two 250 W solar panels in parallel, but point one of them east, and the other one west. Now you are still only producing a maximum of 250 W at a time, but you are doing it for twice the number of hours per day without exceeding the minimum 250 W load of your house.

I have the 600 W inverter shown in Figure 5.9 wired to four 250 W panels in parallel — two pointing east-ish and two pointing west-ish. It is plugged into an outdoor outlet in my backyard normally used only for lawn mowing. Since I have a net meter, I don't have to worry about overproducing, and the added $200 per year of free electricity for a kilowatt of handy panels was worth the hour or two to prop up the panels on a quick wood frame. Another advantage is that you still only need the single 600 W grid-tie inverter because it now just operates twice as long. This demonstrates the value of just moving forward with installing a legal net meter and being able to go with far more panels

Using a Window or Portable Heat Pump as a Minimum Solar Load

Here is an idea for an efficient DIY load you can use to absorb the excess free DIY solar power from a system not connected to a net meter. I wanted

Figure 5.10 — My daughter was able to put a single solar panel and small grid-tie inverter to use at a rental house.

to give some solar panels to my daughter (**Figure 5.10**). She lived in a rental house, and I just could not figure out any way to make sure the solar system did not overproduce her minimum loads when she was not home during the day. Nor could I figure out a way to always be measuring the house load and only connect the solar panels and grid-tie inverter when the load exceeded the solar capacity. Every scheme I came up with just seemed too complicated.

I finally came up with the brilliant idea to connect the solar panel and grid-tie inverter to a window or portable air conditioner/heat pump unit, connected on the load side of the thermostat and not the line side. This way the grid-tie inverter would only be connected to the grid when the thermostat called for the compressor to be running. I could connect four 250 W panels, to generate the 1000 W used by the air conditioner/heat pump whenever it was on, but not feed any power to the grid when it was off.

At first I thought this might be only half the time, as the unit cycled on and off during the day. A 50% duty cycle on the air conditioner/heat pump would effectively only give me 50% of my solar value. But then I realized that rather than use the thermostat to control the air conditioner/heat pump, I could simply use an appliance timer. I could set the air conditioner/heat pump thermostat to maximum cold in the summer or maximum hot in the winter.

Then, when the timer came on at midday when the panels could produce maximum power, the compressor would always be running and the solar panels would always be producing maximum power.

Since the portable or window air conditioner/heat pump unit was only on part of the time and supplementing the existing house system (oil heat), then it would not likely overheat or overcool the house. The house would be cooled with free solar energy during the day while she was at work, or in the winter, the heat pump would warm the house while she was gone. The heat added to the house from the heat pump would keep the oil heat thermostat satisfied, and she would be using less fossil fuel and getting heat during the day for free.

I forgot two things. Spring and fall. During those seasons, she didn't need to heat or cool the house, so I was back to square one. If we could only use the solar panels to produce maximum power half the year for only heating and cooling, then we were only going to use 50% of the possible solar power from the investment. But since you can do solar DIY at 1/4 the cost of a contractor-installed net-metered system, then getting power only half the year at 1/4 the cost is still a good deal. Another only saving grace was that my son-in-law worked at home a lot of the time. With his PC and several other devices always on, we might be assured that the house load never dropped below the possible solar output.

That was a lot of "ifs," so we ended up with just the single solar panel and a single 250 W grid-tie inverter, so at least they could use some renewable power. We could double the total energy gained by hooking two orthogonal solar panels to the same inverter and still stay within the minimum power limit, but for twice as long during the day as described in the previous section.

That has always been the solar power DIY conundrum. You either have to use all of it while you are producing it in the middle of the day, or you have to store it. Storing it in batteries triples the cost, and you cannot store the longer summer day's excess for use later in the winter when you need it more. And it cannot possibly compete with the cost of grid storage (free), and storing it in the grid can *only* work if you have a net meter.

Solar DIY Car Charging

Another stand-alone DIY possibility for absorbing several kW of solar power without back-feeding a net meter is illustrated later, with a solar car port for an electric vehicle described in Chapter 13. As long as the car is charging at either 1.5 kW (6 panels) or 3 kW (12 panels), then a grid-tie inverter's power will all get absorbed into the car battery.

But the problem is, how do you know that the car needs a charge? One way is to simply schedule your car to always charge from 10 AM to 2 PM, when the sun is maximum on your south-facing panels. But then this also means you have to be retired, work at home, or work the night shift so that your car is at home during the day. But if you are retired or working from home, then you are not commuting 40 miles a day, and so the car does not need a charge!

In other words, back to square one. You need to be grid-tied with a net meter to be able to absorb the solar-generated power whenever the sun is shining and to be able to charge whenever the car is parked there.

Grid-Tie, Still the Best Solution

After learning these lessons during my decade of solar experimentation, I've concluded that there is still one and only one way to easily add DIY solar to your house and get the true economics of modern grid-tie solar. And that is, to simply bite the bullet and hire a contractor to properly install a permitted, certified, engineered, approved, inspected, licensed, and activated grid-tie system with a net meter.

If you like to DIY and want to do some yourself, you could simply contract for the smallest grid-tie system the contractor will consider. At 2018 prices of about $2.50 per watt, this would cost around $5000 for a 2 kW system, but you would get back $1500 via the tax credit for a net cost of about $3500. Then after it is fully approved and installed, you will have your net meter. Now you will get full credit for any watts you produce.

Now, if the contractor-installed 2 kW system was installed on your roof pointing east, for example, you can add another 2 kW of DIY solar panels pointing the opposite direction and theoretically connect this second array in parallel to the first (following all the National Electrical Code requirements and practices). Many inverters have dual-terminal or three-terminal blocks that are diode-isolated for combining multiple arrays anyway, or you should use 10 A isolating diodes from each array when connecting in parallel. With solar panels costing as low as 25 cents a watt at bargain prices, you can double your power production for only another $500. Of course, in most states anything that connects to the grid must also meet all NEC codes and must be permitted and approved, so you are still going to have to pay a licensed electrician to legally hook it up. Or, you might consider it a temporary system and simply plug it into an existing outlet.

Plug-in Solar Around the House

Once you have a grid-tie system and net meter, there are many other opportunities around the house for the DIY individual to optimize a solar investment. For example a recreational vehicle (RV), boat, or special Field Day trailer might have solar panels for use away from the power grid or out in the field. But the other 99% of the time, these panels just sit in the sun with their free solar power going nowhere once their batteries are fully charged. But you can still get full retail value for all that solar energy all year long if you simply add a cheap plug-in micro-grid-tie inverter (such as shown in Figure 5.9) and plug them into the house while not in use.

One example is the 1 kW of solar panels on the roof of my rarely used van as shown in **Figure 5.11**. This old van is only used occasionally for hauling and for Field Day. The other 99% of the time, its 1 kW of solar panels feed retail power worth about $140 a year into an outdoor outlet on my garage via the inexpensive grid-tie inverter shown in the figure. The 1 kW at 120 V is only injecting 8 A into the outlet and is well within the NEC limits for continuous use in a standard 15 A outlet. I even report the vehicle as being in storage to my insurance company, and the insurance drops to only about $40 a year (liability coverage only), while the car remains registered with tags and can be reactivated with 24 hours' notice. The fourth panel (slightly visible) is usually on a hinge that flips over the windshield while parked to give the full 1 kW.

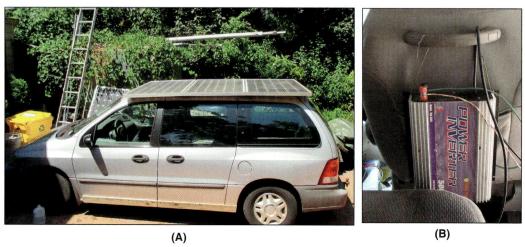

(A) (B)

Figure 5.11 — The 1 kW of solar panels on the roof of my van (A) are useful at Field Day, but they also feed retail power into an outlet via an inexpensive grid-tie inverter sitting in the backseat (B) the other 99.6% of the time.

Another good example is an old boat I found with a non-running gas engine shown in **Figure 5.12**. I sold the old 40 horsepower Evinrude to a fossil fuel enthusiast and got back half the cost of the old boat. Then I put on a pair of electric trolling motors and added some deep-cycle batteries and 500 W of solar panels to keep it going all day long. When it is not in use (99% of the time), it is also back-feeding my home grid with about $70 a year of electricity.

But this boat project back in 2008 was not big enough (go figure). So the ultimate plan when I retire is to finish out supplying my total annual home electric load with my final 3600 W of solar installed on a floating deck. I can take it out for an afternoon on the creek, but for the other 99% of the time it is plugged into "shore power" backfeeding my grid-tie system as shown in **Figure 5.13**. With 3.6 kW of dc power at 28 V, there is plenty of power for several trolling motors — even on overcast days. But while plugged into shore power, it will generate about $600 worth of power that will be deducted from my electric bill every year.

Figure 5.12 — With 500 W of solar panels and an electric trolling motor, my DIY electric boat can toodle around the creek all day. The panels feed retail power into an outlet the other 99% of the time.

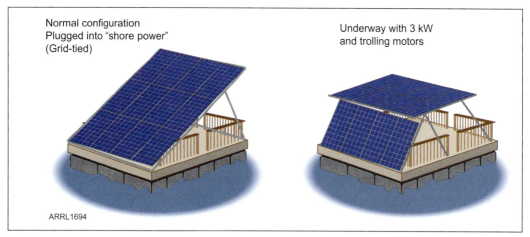

Figure 5.13 — My first retirement project will be this floating deck (solar boat) that has 3.6 kW for its electric trolling motors but also can backfeed my grid when plugged into shore power. The floating dock needs only 4 inches of foam underneath to support the structure and people using it.

I checked with the state. As long as this floating deck has a battery and trolling motors, it must be registered in the state as a boat. And, as a boat (with the required lights and personal flotation devices, first aid kit, and fire extinguisher), it needs no building permit or electrical permit to plug into my previously installed (permitted) outlet on the pier (shown in Figure 1.14 in Chapter 1). The floating deck (boat) will be 16 feet square, since any boat 16 feet or under in Maryland has no excise tax. Not shown is the central picnic table in the center and some seating around the rails for guests. The array has a hinge for a flat overhead while in use and an angled shape pointing south while moored.

Tracking the Sun

I have even considered tracking the sun with this floating deck because it would be so easy. The idea is to only tie it to the pier at one corner (with some kind of hinge pin) and then use a clockwork motor and cable of some kind to pivot the deck about that corner to follow the sun across the sky. This single-axis tracking would pick up another 20% of power every day.

Solar Power for the Ham Shack

A common ham radio project is to install a solar panel at home to charge a battery in the ham shack for backup and emergency power. But when you think about it, the panel is only producing full power for one day (to charge the battery) and then the next 364 days, while the battery is fully charged waiting for the rare power outage, the solar panel is producing nothing. While it is nice to have this Armageddon solar power source, it is not needed 99.9% of the time and so is really only about 0.1% efficient (the once a year you use it).

On the other hand, you could decide to run your ham shack on the battery every day to take advantage of the free power, But it will wear out the battery in a year or so (typical lead-acid batteries are only rated for about 500 discharge cycles). And buying replacement batteries every year or so to take advantage of the free $35 worth of solar makes no sense.

It is far better to add a cheap grid-tie inverter to the panel so that once the battery is fully charged (and not used but in emergencies), then all the other days while the grid is up, you are not wearing out the battery but are getting the full $35 per year retail value for the solar panel electricity fed into your house as shown in **Figure 5.14**. But again, only as long as you have a grid-tie net meter, or your panel does not overfeed your house and push a standard (non-net) meter backward.

The only remaining consideration is that inexpensive grid-tie plug-in inverters mostly come from China and are probably not UL listed. There are all kinds of things we plug into outlets that are not UL listed, and there is no requirement on the homeowner to only plug in UL listed items. But the onus is on you to be sure that anything you plug into an outlet is safe.

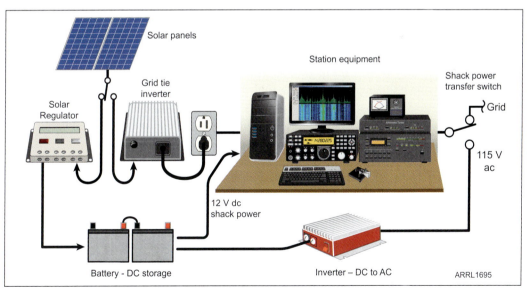

Figure 5.14 — If you use a solar panel and battery to provide emergency backup power for your ham station, you can also use the panel and an inexpensive inverter to supply full-retail-value grid power the other 99% of the time, after the battery is full charged from a power-out event.

Commercial DIY

It turns out that there are many suppliers of DIY solar kits. There is nothing magic about these kits because they will not be of any practical use until you get a legitimate grid-tie contract with your utility, along with a net meter. As discussed previously, you can hire a licensed electrician to inspect the system and sign off on the application paperwork, but recognize that an electrician may have little interest in doing just paperwork when he can make far more down the street doing a full system install.

On the other hand, several companies sell DIY grid-tie kits that include everything you need, as well as materials guiding you through the licensing process. Prices seem to be around $2/watt and appear to include everything (panels, microinverters, connectors, mounts, and so on). This is about 25% less than the contractor installed prices in Maryland as this is written in 2018. To help you get licensed these kits may also include additional options to buy their engineering and drawing kit if you want to handle all the paperwork yourself, and they will direct you to a local electrician/installer.

One kit offers this engineering and application kit for about $350, but you still have to submit the application. (In my state, only a licensed master electrician can even file the application, and the minimum price for that was about $500.) But at this point, the DIY kit plus all the extras ended up being not much different in price from an equivalent turn-key system installed by a contractor.

It also might boil down to the attitudes of the local utility and local inspectors in your area. If they are progressive and encouraging solar power, they may be helpful in guiding you through the process. But if they see solar by the homeowner as a threat to their monopoly, then it might be quite hard to get through the licensing process on your own.

When I asked one of these DIY solar companies about the licensing process, I received a relatively comprehensive response:

From (Company Owner)
Date: Thu, Jun 21, 2018 at 4:58 PM
Subject: Re: Licensing of DIY Kits

I appreciate your interest in our company. We recently shipped our 500th kit so we're pretty happy with our progress.
When someone orders from us, they can then call us for any technical assistance they need. We do have a permit option for

$350 and about half our customers buy that option. We work with an engineering firm and they prepare technical documents and drawings for permits. We work with the customer to get the correct information so the documents are acceptable for permits. Our documents have always been accepted although occasionally a municipality requires an engineer stamp and the customer needs to get that from an engineer registered in their state.

We also provide the technical resources on our web site so a competent person can prepare their own drawings and that works for the half of the customers who don't buy the permit option. We generally tell people to try it themselves to save the $350.

Applying for net metering is simply a matter of talking to your utility and then they let you know if they support net metering and take the customer through the process. In most cases the utility will replace the customer meter for free with a meter capable of doing net metering once all the paperwork requirements are met.

It's not always easy but it's part of the DIY approach and most people get through it fine.

Our kits are all tailored for DIY so they use simple mounting, micro-inverters and standard, tier 1 components. Our panels and micro-inverters all carry 25yr manufacturer warranties.

Unfortunately, in my state, Maryland you can do all the paperwork you want, but only a licensed electrician can apply for the needed permits. For those states that do not have that requirement, then DIY should be something anyone can do if they are willing to meet all the requirements.

Living Off-Grid

Historically, solar has always been very practical for remote, isolated applications with no access to the grid. Generators can provide short-term peak power needs, but the cost of that power is at least seven times the cost of grid power and is unsustainable in the long run.

There simply is no long-term option in a remote area other than solar, and in that case, cost is not an issue. A few panels, some batteries, an inverter, and you have power. As the cost of solar in my lifetime has gone down by 100 to 1, and the cost of battery technology has gone down about 25 to 1, many DIY experimenters think that simply combining the two is a great project even if they have access to the grid. Some seem to relish the idea of disconnecting from the power company and "going-off-grid," even though it makes no economic sense and the costs would be three times higher.

Although the cost of solar panels and batteries is orders of magnitude less expensive than 50 years ago, the batteries are still 2/3 of the lifetime cost of an off-grid system. This means for the same investment, not only can grid-tie generate three times the total annual power compared to an off-grid system, but it can provide it consistently throughout the year, any day, any night, any season, and for half the cost of power generated by the utility.

This is in drastic contrast to a battery-based solar system that not only costs three times more over its lifetime (because of the batteries), but also can only provide *half* the lifestyle power in the winter. Compounding that minimal lifestyle in the winter is that typically you will generate nearly twice the average lifestyle power you will need in the summer.

This annual cycle in energy availability demands significant lifestyle adjustments. For off-grid living with batteries, you cannot carry over excess power for more than a few days. On every good solar day, when the batteries are fully charged by noon, then the rest of the power produced by your arrays just goes nowhere, and during that period your net power production from your solar investment is practically zero.

In addition, solar arrays and batteries in an off-grid system have to be sized big enough to provide lifestyle power on cloudy days. In Maryland, only half the days produce full power, and there can be strings of four to seven days of cloudy weather. This means you have to at least double, and perhaps triple, your investment in solar and batteries to get your average power. And it is impossible to store the summertime double energy production for six months to use later in the winter.

Repeating the mantra, solar power is economical power when it is grid-tied and requires no restrictions on lifestyle. Whereas living off-grid is much more expensive and requires significant changes in annual lifestyle to match the 2-to-1 seasonal variability of sunshine and the many-to-1 seasonal variability need for heating and cooling.

Solar Panel Cleaning

After seven years of service in Maryland, my solar panels have never needed cleaning. But when I went to dig out some spare panels that had fallen over into my swampy lower lot and hook them up to an extra 600 W inverter, they were covered in a glaze of grime. I attempted to clean the panels with a sponge and water, but they dried exactly the same — dirty.

It turned out that the haze and some algae and some other crud really needed scrubbing with an abrasive cleanser to clean the stuff off. Then I remembered why. In **Figure 5.15**, you can see that solar panels have a non-reflective surface, meaning the surface has some microscopic texture to it. A simple wipe-off will not do. You need some abrasion to get the dirt out of the pores.

Figure 5.15 — In the inset photo, I am holding a solar panel and a window pane so that the sun reflects onto the wall of a building. In the main photo, you really cannot even see the reflection from the solar panel (it would be in the rectangle on the left side in the main photo). The reflection from the window is in the rectangle on the right. (Unfortunately, the window I used was 90 years old and not perfectly flat, so you do not see the rectangular edges of it either, but the reflection is obvious.)

6 New Energy Sources of Radio Frequency Interference (RFI)

The one downside to the energy revolution is the potential for radio frequency interference (RFI) to the ham operator. Throughout this book I discuss the movement to high-voltage dc, not only in solar systems, but also in new appliances, power supplies, solar, and the coming wave of electric cars. To do useful work, all of this dc has to be chopped into square waves to be able to control it or transform it to other voltages. When you put a 10 W LED lamp chopping dc at tens of kHz in your station next to your radio, you will likely hear some RFI somewhere. Or, when a 50,000 W generator in a hybrid vehicle is operating with square waves at up to 20 kHz or higher, this is like sitting inside a local AM radio station transmitter. It takes excellent engineering design and built-in RFI mitigation in every aspect of the vehicle or electronics system to minimize this problem. This not only applies to high-voltage dc systems, but also to any modern electronic device — including those as simple as LED bulbs and phone chargers.

In reviewing the topic of RFI, it is interesting to note the top 10 exemptions to certification testing of FCC Part 15 limits normally required for electronic systems (see **emcfastpass.com/could-your-product-be-exempt-from-emc-testing-altogether/**). Not only do EVs and hybrids and any other car electronics get an exemption (#1) but also it is noteworthy that #4 includes electronics inside an appliance, which can include microwaves, washers, dryers, air conditioners, and so on, and also #7, computer mice. Although *all* devices must still meet the limits, the ones that did not have to submit to FCC certification testing might make a good shopping list as to where to start first in any RFI snooping search:

1) Electronics in vehicles and aircraft.
2) Utility electronics located within utility buildings.
3) Industrial, commercial, and medical test equipment.

4) Electronics inside an appliance.
5) Specialized medical digital devices.
6) Devices operating at powers below 0.006 microwatts.
7) Joysticks and mice that only have analog or A/D chips.
8) Battery powered digital devices operating below 1.705 MHz.
9) Anything with clock speed below 9 kHz.
10) Home built devices (no more than quantity 5).

Just because the best devices meet FCC RFI limits, that does not necessarily result in a clean RF environment. The FCC limits keep RFI from a single device to *reasonable* levels to a receiver at some distance, but this does not protect us when we are surrounded every few feet by some electronic device, or light bulb, and every one of them is emitting their "fair share" which all accumulates at our antenna.

Mobile Operation

The success of RFI suppression is probably not of much concern to the average consumer with ear buds listening to digital music, but it is of extreme importance to the radio amateur or anyone who has a receiver in the RF spectrum. For hybrids and EVs, some consumers might notice the higher noise level down on the AM broadcast band at every harmonic of the car's pulse-width modulated (PWM) motor drive system. In fact, BMW even eliminated the AM band in their first production EV, the model i3, several years ago and now Honda has dropped AM from their Acura NSX hybrid sports car and Tesla has dropped AM From all current models. (See **www.warc.com/newsandopinion/news/video_didnt_kill_the_radio_star_but_electric_cars_might/41298**.)

Their goal was to avoid the problem entirely and not have customers complain that the AM band radio was significantly impacted from all the noise. Though it might curtail your ability to operate HF mobile inside an EV or hybrid, at least the RFI from an electric car only affects you in the car, and you can turn it off and get away from it.

In my heavily modified salvage Prius with several of my own wiring connections invading various high-voltage boxes in the system, I noticed that my reception range while traveling was about half of what would be expected on VHF. People could hear me fine, but I could not hear the repeaters well. That was when I noticed that the squelch would open and close at various speeds during acceleration and deceleration (regenerative breaking). Testing with the squelch revealed very high levels of noise on the S-meter, but only when the squelch was open. I have to drive with the squelch at its highest setting as a matter of routine so that I don't hear the squelch opening on noise generated by the vehicle. I do not feel comfortable blaming this entirely on the Prius itself because of all my hacks that took no care in RFI shielding and attenuation on penetrations into the high-voltage boxes, and some of the boxes are missing their covers. But even with the engine off and the gear in park, the multi-kW dc/dc converter is still running and the noise does not go off until either accessory mode is selected or the hybrid system is completely off.

Other Perspectives on Hybrid Car RFI

Here are some other comments from hams on hybrid car RFI:

The Prius with my mobile HF screwdriver definitely had broadband noise when running. One of the problems is that the electrical systems on modern vehicles may be bundle-shielded, making every wire an antenna.

I bought a 10-acre site in rural California, some miles away from a paved road or wired electrical power. Unfortunately this does not make it RF-quiet (except at night when solar is not active), and I will have to work with the neighbor farmer and perhaps some others. The neighbor is friendly, but by the look of some of the other locals, maybe not so much. — *Bruce Perens, K6BP*

I have a 2006 Honda Civic Hybrid and the hybrid engine's RFI into my FT-857D transceiver is more than S-9. The RFI is so strong that when I am driving, I can't hear any signals less that S-9 + 10 dB.

I have written to Honda asking for help, but they have not written back that they can help me solve my hybrid RFI problem. A Honda customer service rep did telephone me and told me that since my ham installation is an aftermarket device, I am responsible for solving the problem. — *Ken Witkin, W3XAF*

LED Lighting RFI Problems

The recent explosive shift from incandescent lighting to LED lighting and the five-fold savings in energy solves one problem, but it can produce another. Every LED bulb has a dc/dc voltage converter to prepare the dc for the LEDs (**Figure 6.1**). This has the potential to produce RFI if the bulbs were not manufactured with RFI suppression as a primary requirement. A prime example of this problem with LEDs is the US Coast Guard warnings about using LED bulbs on boats. Here is their Safety Alert 13-18 issued on 15 Aug 2018:

> The U.S. Coast Guard has received reports from crews, ship owners, inspectors and other mariners regarding poor reception on VHF frequencies used for radiotelephone, digital selective calling (DSC) and automatic identification systems (AIS) when in the vicinity of light emitting diode (LED) lighting on-board ships (e.g., navigation lights, searchlights and floodlights, interior and exterior lights, adornment). Radio frequency interference caused by these LED lamps were found to create potential safety hazards. [*snip*] Strong radio interference from LED sources may not be immediately evident to maritime radio users. Nonetheless, it may be possible to test for the presence of LED interference by using the following procedures:
> 1. Turn off LED light(s).

Figure 6.1 — Every LED bulb has a dc/dc voltage converter to prepare the dc for the LEDs.

2. Tune the VHF radio to a quiet channel (e.g. Ch. 13).

3. Adjust the VHF radio's squelch control until the radio outputs audio noise.

4. Re-adjust the radio's squelch control until the audio noise is quiet, only slightly above the noise threshold.

5. Turn on the LED light(s).

If the radio now outputs audio noise, then the LED lights have raised the noise floor. [*snip*] In order to determine the full impact of this interference, the Coast Guard requests those experiencing this problem to report their experiences to Coast Guard Navigation

(From **www.dco.uscg.mil/Portals/9/DCO%20 Documents/5p/CG-5PC/INV/Alerts/1318. pdf?ver=2018-08-16-091109-630**.)

Recommended RFI Test on FM Radios

There is one problem with the Coast Guard's recommended test described above, and that is that it does not work for many FM radios. It is easy to overlook RFI on an FM radio, not only because that is the advantage of FM over AM — it eliminates AM noise in the limiter — but also because RFI is noise power, and it is noise power that keeps a squelch circuit *closed*. So the opening and closing of an FM squelch as suggested by the Coast Guard is not a solid test for the presence of RFI.

What does work most times is to manually open the squelch and see the background noise level. That will include RFI that will show on the S-meter but otherwise would not open the squelch. On my typical ham radios, when the squelch is closed, the S-meter is inactive and shows 0 signal, again, giving a false sense of immunity. So, any such recommended test for RFI with FM radios should include additional testing with the squelch open.

Although RFI in the home is as old as ham radio, there are many new sources invading our spectrum.

Other Perspectives on LED Lighting RFI

Here are some other comments from hams on RFI from LED lighting:

I have many LED bulbs on my boat. Most are fine, but one wipes out everything well into the VHF spectrum. The USCG has been all over this, it makes AIS targets vanish. — *Joe Della Barba, N3HGB*

Had problems with LED RFI. See my article several pages in on our newsletter: **www.skyviewradio.net/2018_10_Q5er.pdf** .— *Dan Walter, NM3A*

RFI from LED lights has been a well-known problem in the VHF/UHF EME (moonbounce) weak signal community for years. The first generation of LED lights were very strong RFI generators. The most recent generation of LED lights are much better but can still cause problems. LED lighting RFI tends to be broadband noise and not visible birdies.

The best way to see LED lighting broadband noise is with an SDR and waterfall display. The SDR or radio AGC must be turned off. It's easy to find offending LED lights in your own home. It gets trickier finding RFI lighting and devices in neighbor's homes. Turn off all the lights in your house and start turning them on one at a time. Watch your noise floor. RFI will be obvious.

The good news is that typical amateur satellite communications are not really weak signal and low-level RFI is not usually a problem. However, if you are trying to work satellite passes on the horizon, LED noise can be an issue for high gain directional Yagis with mast mount preamps.

I have at least 100 RFI generating LED lights in a box in my basement that I removed from my home and my neighbors. I have exchanged bad LED lights for good LED lights. My house is 100% incandescent and fluorescent. No LEDs as long as I'm operating EME on 144 and 432 MHz. LED noise does not reach up into 1296 MHz.

Good luck with your LED RFI issues. They can be solved but it's a bit of a "wack a mole" effort. — *Paul Andrews W2HRO*

We had some LEDs installed in the kitchen, and our adjacent garage door opener ceased to work. Turned out it was 300 MHz noise from Chinese cheap cans (recessed lights).

I used a handheld VHF scanner, and qualitatively can tell you the difference between good and bad was readily apparent, especially as you approached the base of the bulb with a stubby duck. At the garage door antenna, which was our problem, quantitatively there was about 20 dB noise above ambient with the bad lights, and the replacements showed 0 dB additional, using an attenuator to measure the difference.

If you have or can get your hands on a portable spectrum analyzer for a while, it's worth the effort to just cruise the premises. After getting one, I discovered noise from my wife's router on the FO29 downlink that made about a 3-4 dB improvement once I reoriented her antenna. And don't even ask about her landscaping lights. Good luck. — *Scott McDonald KA9P*

I ran into an LED situation last year when we rebuilt the kitchen. We installed low-voltage LED strings over the counters under the cabinets. The contractor had two different brands, and he asked me to choose. I took the power supplies and lamp strings out to my truck, where I have an IC-706, and checked them across 160 meters to 70 cm in CW receive mode (no squelch).

One set emitted serious RF noise clear across the spectrum, and the other was as quiet as a mouse. The good one had the FCC Part 15 compliance notice, and the other one did not. — *Gordon Davids, WJ3K*

I have investigated VHF RFI and before retiring, managed a lab that was responsible for product validation (performance to specs), RFI measurements, EMC (electromagnetic compatibility) and UL approval.

I have an 18 W desk lamp that produces more HF RFI when it is off than on — yes, *off*. It has a lighted-touch-button on-off and needs a switched mode power supply to light the button and run the button detect.

The issue with LED bulbs is not whether a bulb meets Part 15, but that there will be [are] hundreds of them in your neighborhoods and all that noise adds up. Ten bulbs means the noise can be 10 dB above the legal limit! It's not that simple, but bad nonetheless.

Part 15 has a limit to the amount of interference each can emit. It is not zero. Also, that is for *one* bulb in some fixture. If you're close enough to one, it can still cause problems.

With many of them in random fixtures, who knows. This has been a gloom-and-doom bad omen since CFLs came out, since they also used electronic switching to generate the high start and run voltages. — *Steve Noskowicz, K9DCI*

The ARRL Lab and LED Lighting

Here are some thoughts on the topic of LED lighting from ARRL Lab Manager Ed Hare, W1RFI:

> The ARRL Lab has the ability to make quantified measurements of field strength and conducted emissions from all types of devices. We use calibrated antennas and spectrum analyzers with CISPR detectors to make accurate measurements in microvolts/meter. Our in-situ measurements can give a very good indication of how these devices would perform if measured under the laboratory conditions used by manufacturers and regulators to authorize devices.
>
> There are probably literally thousands of LED bulbs made today, so we can't act on a simple report that "LED bulbs need to be measured." When they first started coming out, the ARRL Lab bought a large number of them and measured them, finding that the ones being sold by the big box stores at the time complied with the emissions limits. (Interference is still possible.) That could change, though, so what we need are model numbers and where they are being sold. The Lab can then buy a couple of the suspect devices, test them, and if there is an apparent emissions-limit violation, ARRL can turn this over to the FCC as a formal complaint.
>
> Unfortunately, most of the reports we receive do not provide enough information to act. They can range from "LED bulbs are noisy" to "my neighbor had noisy bulbs so we threw them away and replaced them with quiet ones."
>
> Send specific RFI reports, including model numbers of bulbs if possible to: **RFI@arrl.org**.

Home Solar System Noise

If your solar array or your neighbor's array produces RFI whenever the sun is up, or even worse, if your neighbor's array wipes out most of the HF spectrum on all bands, it can really have an effect on your operations. As described in Chapter 4, there are three types of grid-tie inverter systems — high voltage dc string inverters, microinverters, and optimizers. So far we do not have enough data to be able to conclusively say to which systems are better or worse, but the consensus of reports I have seen so far suggest that the dc string inverters and high quality microinverters are relatively quiet, but installations with optimizers (**Figure 6.2**) are very noisy and require extraordinary effort on the roof to tame.

My inverters shown in Chapter 3 in Figure 3.5 are high-voltage dc string inverters, and all the wiring to the panels on the roof of a dc string array carries only dc. With all my full-sized dipoles up in the air, I listened with the arrays on and off. I have inverter noise about 12 dB above the noise floor every 38 kHz on 80 meters, but couldn't really find anything on 20 meters. I did not do a thorough search, but enough to finally say, "yes, there is some noise..." For my rare HF operating, the solar ac disconnect switch is about three feet from the kitchen door. It's easy enough to pull if I want HF silence. I could also install a 40 A disconnect relay from a switch in the shack.

Although I can hear moderate RFI on the lower HF bands, I know I can suppress that with simple RF chokes on the dc lines where they enter the central inverter. If needed, I can also add chokes on the Line 1, Line 2, Neutral and Ground wires leaving the inverter. But with my occasional operating style, I'll probably do nothing till I retire. Of course it is perfectly quiet at night for operating.

Figure 6.2 -- Reports from a number of hams indicate that solar systems with optimizers can be very noisy and difficult to tame. Tony Brock-Fisher, K1KP, added chokes to each of the optimizers in his rooftop system, and took other measures as described later in this chapter. Note that this photo does not show the additional chokes needed on each solar panel dc leads as shown later, in Figure 6.7. [Tony Brock-Fisher, K1KP, photo]

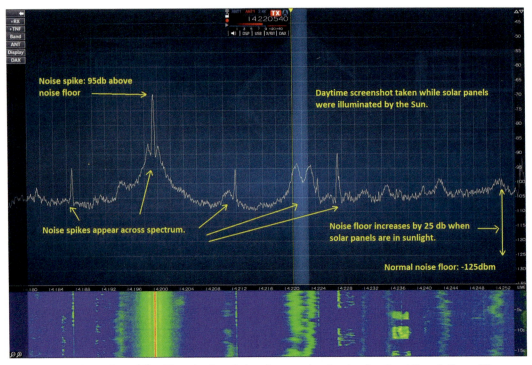

Figure 6.3 — A portion of the 20 meter band showing received noise levels at the station of Tony Bombardiere, K2MO, while his neighbor's solar panels and inverters are active during the day. [Courtesy Tony Bombardiere, K2MO]

Other Perspectives on Home Solar RFI

Here are some other comments from hams on RFI from home solar installations:

Tony Bombardiere, K2MO, has an ongoing solar panel RFI case in Kings Park, New York. **Figures 6.3** *and* **6.4** *show a portion of the 20-meter band with the solar panels active during the day and inactive at night.*

Some of you may recall that I've been dealing with RFI generated by a neighbor's solar panel installation since the day it was installed in August of 2016. I promptly notified the manufacturer about the noise and they acknowledged (eventually) that their components were the cause of the RFI.

Now, last week, on June 21, 2018, they sent a contractor to install RFI suppression to eliminate the RFI. The engineers from the

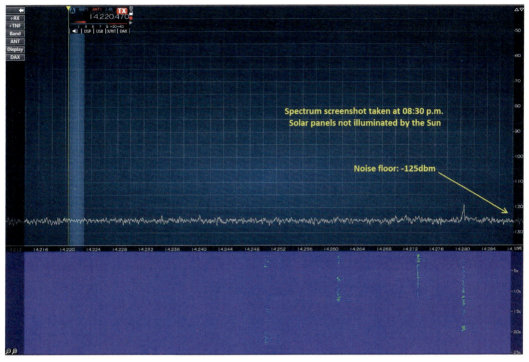

Figure 6.4 — The same spectrum as in Figure 6.3 after dark with the solar panels inactive. [Courtesy Tony Bombardiere, K2MO]

manufacturer told me that they guaranteed it would work and that they've installed this type of RFI suppression many times before.

Unfortunately, it had little to no effect. They used small clamp-on ferrite cores at the optimizers (noise generators) with one turn of cable around each core. The reason they gave for not using a large ferrite with multiple turns was that multiple turns could damage the cables — go figure.

They apologized for not solving the problem and are now flying their engineers in from the west coast to New York to inspect the work done by the installer. Once again, they assured me that problem will be solved.

In my case, my neighbor's installation is 150 feet from my antennas yet the RFI is strong at that distance. It's heard on 30 through 10 meters so HF is essentially unusable during the day while the system is active.

My advice to fellow hams is this: take a good look around your neighborhood and notice the number of solar panel systems popping up everywhere. Imagine trying to figure out which system among them is causing RFI and the task of knocking on doors to find out who manufactured the system or who the responsible party is.

Solar panel systems are not going away so the potential for RFI issues are likely to become widespread. In fact, California plans on making solar panels mandatory on new homes beginning in 2020.

I think most would agree that it's time for us to organize with our other ham radio advocates to make a serious effort to let the FCC know how serious a problem this is. Signed petitions by the 160,000 members of the ARRL sent to local congressmen might be a good place to start. Or, we can sit on our hands and say goodbye to HF. — *Tony Bombardiere, K2MO*

I have an end fed wire feeding two SDR-IQ remote server receivers about 30 feet over my home/repeater shed's back up diesel genny. A small (50 W) panel sits atop the genny housing and keeps the starting battery charged. The charge controller was a PWM type, and essentially wiped out several HF bands. Swapped out the expensive controller for a cheaper one and problem solved. — *Kriss Kliegle, KA1GJU*

Another one of the reasons I left my old QTH was all the homes around me had solar with many different styles and HF RFI during the day was awful, but I had no switch to shut them up. — *Kevin Schuchmann, WA7FWF*

I enjoyed your comments about "Solar Can Be Simple and Quiet" in Technical Correspondence in September 2016 *QST*. We have an Enphase solar panel system that features ac microinverters behind each panel and I do not have any HF radio noise. I do have good station grounding with copper tubing around the house foundation.

Our power company solar year ends with our mid-March bill. We were pleased to have a surplus of 3,500 kWh at that time and got a $100 credit against future electric bills. So for this last solar power year we paid no electric power bill, except the $19/month grid connection fee. Power to the People! — *Tom Brooks, KE1R*

I had no idea how bad the solar panel QRM was by me until we had a hurricane knock out the local power grid for a day or so. I was delighting in the absolute quiet the blackout brought until dawn, and then the noise started. It's really bad by me on Long Island, NY and the #1 source of cold callers are solar suppliers taking advantage of people who don't care what goes up on their roof. The biggest topic at the clubs by me and the SDR groups I follow is noise mitigation, and how we're looking for different ways to handle ever increasing levels of QRM. It certainly is a big deal for those of us seeking to get on 630 meters and lower. — *Jim Minor, W2DSX*

Here's a letter from Jim Wallace, N3ADF, to the FCC:

I am a member of the Prince George's (Co., MD) Amateur Radio Service; PGARES.org. I live in Bowie, MD 20720. My neighbor just had Solar City install 72 solar panels and two inverters. The inverter panels are causing severe RFI on all Amateur Bands but especially 20 m. The inverter panels are 135 ft. from my 20 m antenna. During the day when the panels are generating, the noise levels on 20 m are 20-30 dB over S9. I have physically turned off the inverter panels and the noise levels dropped to S3 to S5.

The inverters seem to be generating RFI very near every 100 kHz as shown below.

80 m — During the day I can hear the RFI around S4-5 but turned off the noise is S2-3.

40 m — During the day I can hear the RFI around S5-6 but turned off the noise is S2-3.

The RFI seems to be concentrated in the 20 m band. The below signal levels were recorded with my Icom IC-7410 in SSB mode on a 20 m dipole on my roof at 45 feet above ground, oriented almost broadside to the neighbor's house. Day and nights signal strengths are indicated.

Frequency (MHz)	Day - May 8, '17 1245Z (Full sunshine) Signal strength	Night – May 14, '17 0245Z (Dark) Signal strength
13.980	S7	S3
13.990	S9	S3
13.999	S9+20	S2-3
14.010	S7	S2
14.090	S9	S4-5
14.099	S9	S3
14.190	S9	S4-5
14.099	S9	S3
14.199	S9+20	S3-4
14.210	S7	S4

I called Solar City and talked with a supervisor in their Customer Department and he didn't understand the problem. He also said that it is the actual homeowner that must make a complaint, not a neighbor. Well, the neighbor doesn't have the problem. He just rents space on his roof to Solar City. — *Jim Wallace, N3ADF*

Bob, I read with interest your comments on the implications of NEC 2017. You said "I hope I am not being alarmist." I don't think you are — however you are tackling the issue on the wrong front.

The issue that you need to raise concerns the "standards" that govern the interfaces between solar panels and optimizers — and any other ancillary equipment. There are IEC and IEEE standards that state the permissible levels of emission from the ports of this equipment, and the frequencies they use in the standards are for the most part derived from standard agreed by CISPR.

As a contributor to CISPR through my work at British Standards Institute, and CENELEC in Brussels, I am aware of many licenced radio amateurs from the USA who are involved in this work. In fact the lead representative for the USA on the subject of harvesting of solar energy is an active licensee. He is also involved with all aspect of near field charging of vehicles — another topic which should cause radio amateurs great concern.

I would recommend two things. Firstly that you encourage ARRL to increase its support for this important and valuable work. [*snip*] Secondly, find a way, if this does not already exist, to become involved in NEC affairs — it should be possible to have ARRL representation involved in their work. The objective is to ensure that "best practice" is used on all solar harvesting schemes and every installation.

To summarize, the steps should ensure that the items of equipment (apparatus) are compliant with international standards that are designed to protect radio services, and then ensure that the equipment is installed in such a way that it does not negate compliance with the standard. For example, if the equipment is connected with twisted pairs in order the meet the compliance test, the installer must follow the same practice — and so NEC 2017 (or later versions), must make that clear.

I acknowledge that best practice is followed when safety issues are concerned, but are rarely understood when EMC matters are important. That is what you have to get across with NEC and we have to get across here in Europe, where we face exactly the same challenge.

All of this is an international effort, because for the most part solar harvesting equipment is manufactured around the world. Here in Europe the systems come from China or Germany. Which means that it may be compliant with CENELEC requirements to carry the ubiquitous CE mark. Note that little word "may".

CISPR — Special International Committee for Radio Interference, affiliated with International Electro-Technical Commission (IEC)

CENELEC — European Committee for Electrical Standards

I hope this helps. Do let me know if I can provide any additional background. — *John Pink, G8MM, F5VKU*

And just imagine what RFI might be like in southeast Asia as reported here:

I don't want to be a pessimist, but I think HF (and lower) is history anyway. If it's not this new breed of solar arrays, then it will be something else. Residential noise levels are up so high in many places already that HF is unworkable anyway. Even VHF is starting to suffer from increased noise levels. The only hope is that when any commercial or government service using that particular part of the spectrum is affected, then the solutions are available before you know it. Sad but true. — *Hans, BX2ABT*

I've had solar panels with optimizers for 4 months and they definitely cause RFI on both HF and VHF. I think they are Solar Edge panels. By the way, I specifically asked the installer about RFI and he told me that he never heard any complaints about it. Selective listening?

To follow up, I purchased ferrite toroids from Palomar Engineers, specifically recommended for solar PV system RFI, and the electrician that installed the panels was able to come back and retrofit the toroids onto the wiring following Palomar's published instructions.

It seems like the RFI has been reduced at VHF frequencies. However, I did not perceive a reduction in RFI at HF frequencies where I like to operate QRP CW. I finally bought a TimeWave Antenna Noise Canceller which actually does reduce the noise enough that I can work on 40 m now. Without the noise canceller I cannot hear anything but loud static on 40 m during the day. — *Steve Hamre, AI9N*

I have a 25 kW array using SMA inverters right under my antenna and have not noticed any RFI at all. However, I notice a bunch of RFI from Ethernet connected devices that may be masking anything from them. For microinverters, I have generally not heard any significant complaints. — *Rob Frohne, KL7NA*

RFI Mitigation

Fortunately, we do have a well-documented case in the April 2016 issue of *QST* written by Tony Brock-Fisher, K1KP. In the article "Can Home Solar Power and Ham Radio Coexist?," Tony describes the drastic measures needed to get the noise from his optimizers down to a reasonable level. As you can see in **Figure 6.5**, he has a premium HF installation and went to significant measures to suppress RFI as much as possible.

Step 1 was to plan for paralleling the positive high-voltage dc line and the negative return into a twisted pair transmission line as shown in **Figure 6.6** instead of a big loop as normally done by installers.

Step 2 was to put five bifilar-turns of these wires between every optimizer and panel though large RF chokes as shown in Figure 6.5.

Step 3 was to install another three turns of bifilar wound wire onto solar panel pigtails and put those between each panel and its optimizer as shown in **Figure 6.7**.

Figure 6.5 — A view of the solar panel installation at the home of Tony Brock-Fisher, K1KP, taken from his antenna tower. [Tony Brock-Fisher, K1KP, photo]

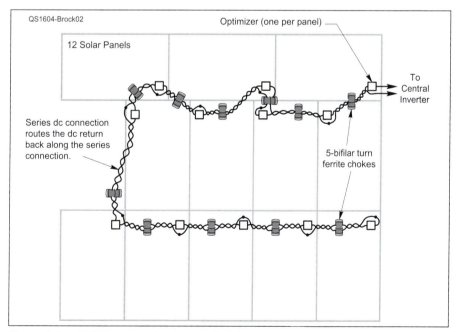

Figure 6.6 — K1KP arranged solar panel wiring as a twisted pair transmission line with large ferrite beads to suppress common mode RF currents.

Figure 6.7 — Three bifilar turns of #10 PV wire on Fair-Rite 2631626202 core with MC4 connectors installed. [Tony Brock-Fisher, K1KP, photo]

Step 4 was to enclose the high-voltage dc wires from the roof into metal conduit instead of PVC (metallic conduit is required by the NEC for high-voltage dc inside a building anyway).

Step 5 was to pass the wires as they entered the central inverter through three more chokes.

And finally, he passed the ground, neutral and 240 V ac outputs of the central inverter all through another long string of 30 RF chokes.

This experience demonstrates the significant challenge of dealing with RFI from solar optimizers or other solar installations that were not designed with the radio amateur and FCC emission limits in mind.

If you operate HF or plan to during the rest of your life, you might consider being proactive and contact all of your neighbors within say 1000 feet to ask that they work with you when they consider solar, to make sure to get a system that complies with FCC emission requirements. Even that will not guarantee an absence of noise, but it is a start.

I have no idea what approach would work best, but you don't want to find out after the fact that a neighbor has just spent $16,000 on a solar system installed in just a couple days that will be the end of HF in your neighborhood for the next 25 years. Solar is inevitable on every roof without shade. Every ham who hopes to operate HF should consider getting out ahead of it.

7 Electrification of Transportation

The largest single source of energy use in the US is oil for transportation as shown in Figure 3.1 in Chapter 3, and about 78% of that energy is just thrown away as waste heat and toxic emissions. We have been doing this now for a century, and it is simply not sustainable. Fortunately, the electrification of transportation is actually easy to do, and it can beat oil hands down in more than 95% of our transportation needs.

Electric Vehicles (EVs)

Total EV sales in the US exceeded 1 million by the end of 2018, and insiders were predicting that 2018 will represent the peak of fossil fuel car production. Gas car sales were already starting to decline at the end of 2018, and in January 2019 it was not only reported that 22 of the major auto manufacturers doing business in the US were on record to invest hundreds of billions of dollars into at least 550 models of EV plug-in vehicles worldwide over just the next six years (by 2025), but also Ford announced an EV version of their top-selling F-150 pickup truck. For details, see the Reuters report available on line at **graphics.reuters.com/AUTOS-INVESTMENT-ELECTRIC/010081ZB3HD/index.html**.

Electric Vehicles were invented in about 1834, and by the 1890s were outselling gasoline powered cars 10-to-1 (see the EV History page on the Electric Auto Association website, **www.electricauto.org**). Henry Ford even bought one for his wife because it always worked, and she just flipped a switch instead of using the heavy crank to start his Model T. But, when the electric starter for the gas car debuted in 1912, it was the end of EVs for a century. Now, a hundred years later, batteries have improved 25-to-1 over those early electric cars and EVs are making a striking comeback that is revolutionizing our transportation sector.

Since the electrification of transportation is the largest disruptive change to transportation and fossil fuels since the automobile replaced the horse a century ago, it is important to fully understand the nuances of this revolution at hand and not be misled by misinformation about EVs. (I have written quite a bit on this topic on my website, at **aprs.org/EV-misinformation.html**).

It's important to understand that an EV is not a replacement for every vehicle, but it is an excellent replacement for the 95% of our transportation needs that are local and daily. The average daily mileage of American drivers is about 40 miles (15,000 miles a year), and 98% of all daily trips begin and end at home. This kind of travel is the ideal application for EVs. Not only do they leave the home in the morning every day with a fully charged battery providing maximum range, but they also return home every night for a very convenient overnight charge. This costs about $2 a day or less while giving us the convenience of never having to stop at a gas station.

A Battery is Not a Tank

Early models of electric cars up to about 2012 had daily ranges of about 100 miles, which is more than 2½ times the average American daily travel. By 2017, several manufacturers were producing 200 mile EVs. With a range almost five times more than the average American daily miles driven, these EVs can fulfill almost all local travel plus contingencies.

Although most people think they are going to want the largest range available, the smart EV purchaser should consider, or may prefer to buy, no more daily range than they need to avoid paying a large premium for a large capacity battery that they almost never use. As shown in **Figure 7.1**, a battery is not a tank. It is not something you fill up once a week inconveniently somewhere away from home, then ignore it until it gets close to empty,

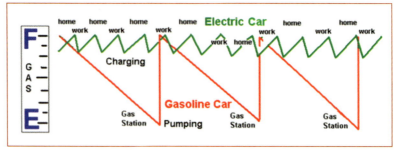

Figure 7.1 — A battery is not a tank. But it is ideal for using every day after an overnight charge.

and then look for another public place to fill up. EVs bring an entirely new refueling paradigm because they charge conveniently at home whenever the car is parked and not in use.

An excellent example of this tradeoff was the expensive and popular Tesla Model S luxury sedan introduced in 2012 at more than $107,000. While this car has more than 260 mile range, Tesla also sold the exact same car with a half-size battery option for $50,000 less. Choosing this lower cost model gave the same luxury, prestige, performance, and acceleration, and all the other advantages of driving electric, while also giving more than three times the average American daily range — all at a huge savings of $50,000. Yet, this model was eventually dropped from the lineup, because customers with that kind of money to spend on a luxury car were not interested in the savings, only in getting the best car with the longest range available whether they needed it or not. (For more on Tesla's performance in 2012, see **www.motortrend.com/news/2012-tesla-model-s-test-and-range-verification/**.)

However, to the purchaser who saved $50,000 by buying the smaller battery, there was hardly any daily impact because it was fully charged overnight and began each day with its full daily range of 140 miles. That's already more than three times the national average. The only time the difference would be apparent was when the driver would have to charge twice (40 minutes total) to get from Washington, DC, to New York City instead of once (20 minutes) using a fast dc charging station. Note that the $50,000 saved on the smaller battery could pay for a gas car rental every weekend for 10 years in order to make any long trips needed.

Public Perception about EV Charging Costs

A problem with EV charging anywhere is that most homeowners still do not understand how inexpensive electricity is for charging an EV. Although it is only 20 cents an hour, or about $2 for an overnight 10-hour charge to provide about 40 miles daily range, the uninformed public sees something quite different. Since they pay maybe $30 for a fill up for their small gas car, they are very leery of someone asking to plug in for an overnight charge, thinking that their electric bill will go up the same $30 (**Figure 7.2**). It is beyond their experience to believe that it only costs about $2 a day to help out their neighbor with an EV.

This huge disparity shows why we need everyone to become EV-aware so that the true low cost of charging an EV is understood by everyone. That is, that an EV can charge anywhere, anytime, from any standard 120 V outlet for 20 cents an hour, and never have to go stand in long gas lines to refuel. It's even better if they can plug into their own unlimited home solar every day.

Figure 7.2 — Only pennies an hour to charge an EV and only a dollar or two a day depending on mileage.

Grid Load of EV Charging

It is frustrating to see the media focus on the need for widespread EV charging infrastructure before EVs will be a common commodity. This is simply the carryover of gas-tank/gas-station legacy thinking without understanding the complete paradigm shift from refueling gas cars inconveniently at public gas stations to conveniently charging an EV while parked at home or work. With more than 200 million people living in single family detached homes (with outlets), that is almost 2000 times more charging opportunities than there are gas stations in the whole country.

A second major misunderstanding of the media and public is the common claim that the grid cannot handle the load if all the cars in America become EVs. This simply is not true. Recent estimates suggest EV charging by 2030 — with 40% of new car sales being EVs — will only add 1% load to the grid. By 2050, when 95% of all sales are EVs, the added load will only be 4%. (See **www.mckinsey.com/industries/automotive-and-assembly/our-insights/the-potential-impact-of-electric-vehicles-on-global-energy-systems**.)

That does not take into account the exponential growth of solar and wind rapidly rising to be the majority of all new power plants being built. And when you consider that an EV owner can put up his own 12 solar panels to fully charge an EV every day forever for the national average 40 miles a day, it is clear that the load of EVs on the grid is inconsequential.

EVs typically spend more than 22 hours a day parked and available for charging, so there is great flexibility as to when to charge. If charging is postponed to off-peak times, then the load of EVs on the grid has no impact at all because they are using power that is otherwise considered a surplus. In recent years, in some areas, there is so much wind and solar on some days that the wholesale price of grid electricity actually goes negative, and the utilities actually have to pay customers to use it. This is why the marriage of EV batteries and charging at work with the variability of renewable energy is a match made in heaven.

EVs Best for Local Travel

Generally, an EV is not designed to be a long-distance traveling car. And a battery is not a tank to be filled up once a week during an inconvenient 5 minute stop at a public gas station. A battery EV is simply plugged in every night and begins each day with full range in the morning, and the total impact on the owners is about 10 seconds a day. Five seconds to unplug in the morning, and five seconds to plug in at night. The paradigm changing value-promise of the EV is in local daily travel, where it does the job better,

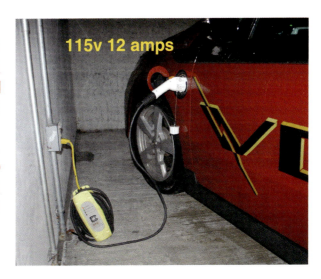

Figure 7.3 — Plugging in any EV to a standard 120 V ac outlet adds no more load to the grid than another coffeepot. Businesses often pay for coffee at work, and should consider allowing employees to plug in their EVs for a modest fee.

cheaper, and more conveniently than gas and never has to go anywhere but home to charge. Even then, if needed, it can charge anywhere there is a standard electric outlet. Yes, simply plugging into a standard 120 V outlet (just like your cell phone at night) can maintain 40 miles a day and puts no more load on your house grid than another coffeepot, as shown in **Figure 7.3**. Also, plugging in while parked at work can double that range to 80 miles a day from standard outlets.

EV Commuting

As shown in **Figure 7.4**, about 68% of all American commuting is 15 miles or less one-way, and 92% of commuters are less than 35 miles a day. This is the reason that the Chevy Volt, one of the first modern EVs to come out in 2011, targeted a basic EV range of 40 miles. Adding in the 20-mile commuters, then 78% of all commuters could drive the Volt to and from work on electric power without burning any gas and charge only at home overnight.

For the longer distance commutes with the typically shorter EV range of a plug-in hybrid, employees need to plug in at work if they also want to drive home on pure electric. Figure 7.4 also shows how many hours at work an EV must be plugged into a standard 120 V outlet to restore batteries to full charge. Notice that the 68% of commuters with 15 miles or less can be fully charged by noon, while those who drove up to 35 miles to get to work would be fully charged in eight hours for the trip home.

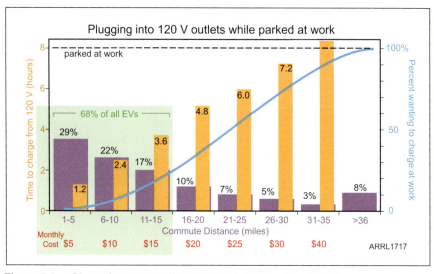

Figure 7.4 — Plots of commute distances and time and cost to charge.

Superimposed on this plot is an estimate of how many of those commuters would want to actually plug in at work. Those with the shortest commutes and those with the biggest batteries see little need to plug in. But for those with plug-in hybrids, which all have relatively small EV batteries, almost all with commutes that are longer than half of their EV range would want to plug in.

I first used this chart back in 2012 to justify a request for lots of Level 1 (120 V) charging outlets at my employer's garage. But now, a decade later, we are actually up to 40 employees driving EVs, but only three of them express a real need to charge at work. Another handful said they would only want to plug in on some days when they knew they had many errands to run and might exceed their range.

Federal Employee Charging-at-Work

As mentioned in Chapter 1, after more than a decade of letter writing, presentation, and general activism, I feel instrumental in getting the Department of Energy (DOE) to push Congress to include in the 2016 Congressional FAST Act the provision that federal agencies may permit federal employees to plug in to existing outlets for a payment of about $6 per bi-weekly pay period. Doing the math, that about equals the cost of daily charging at the national average 10 cent electric rate for the average government employee commute of 15 miles. A simple placard on the window would show that the employee has pre-paid for daily charging (**Figure 7.5**).

EV Buyers Also Favor Clean Energy

A 2014 survey in California by the California Clean Vehicle Rebate Project revealed that about 48% of all EV purchasers used (or will use) 100% clean solar or wind power for charging their EV. A survey by Ford in 2015 showed that 83% of their EV purchasers either used solar from their own solar system, or bought clean solar or wind electricity from the local utility, or would do so as soon as the utility offered it (see **www.greencarreports.com/news/1099531_electric-car-drivers-tell-ford-well-never-go-back-to-gasoline**.)

It can be shown that even with a grid running on 50% coal, the average of EVs charged in that area still only generate about 8% of the emissions compared to a gas car. Since 50%

Figure 7.5 — Charging outlet signs and payment placards are one way to allow employees to charge EVs at work for an appropriate fee.

of EV owners use only clean energy, then only 50% use the coal-generated electricity. Since an EV only uses about 33% of the energy consumed in a gas car, then, the combined effective average "emissions" of an EV is 50% of 50% of 33% which is about 8% compared to a gas car emissions.

EV Cost

Although the EVs introduced in 2008 to 2010 were more expensive than gas cars, in just five years, by 2015, the average cost was about equal to gas cars. By 2018, the cost of 70% of all battery EVs (BEVs) with incentives cost less than the average gas car as shown in **Figure 7.6**. And the typical cost of several three year old used models coming off-lease was less than $10,000. Similarly, the plug-in hybrids, which are really two cars in one — an EV and a backup gas engine — showed that about 40% with incentives cost less than the average gas car.

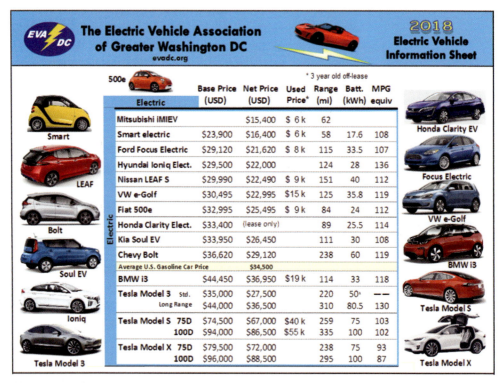

Figure 7.6 — In 2018, about 70% of all battery EVs cost less than the average new gas car, and some three-year-old used ones coming off lease go for well under $10,000. (Based on the 2018 Electric Vehicle Information Sheet from the Electric Vehicle Association of Greater Washington, DC — evadc.org.)

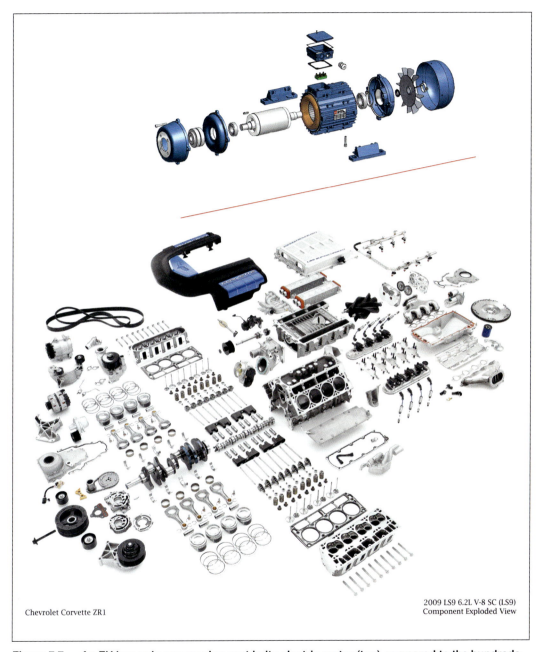

Figure 7.7 — An EV has only one moving part in its electric motor (top) compared to the hundreds in a gas engine. (Electric motor image courtesy wonderfulengineering.com and LS9 V8 image courtesy General Motors.)

Not only do most EVs now cost less than fossil fuel powered cars to buy and operate, they are also much simpler, and cheaper to own, operate, and maintain. With 1/3 the energy cost and without oil changes, mufflers, exhaust systems, radiators, friction brakes, automatic transmissions, catalytic converters, and emissions control systems, they are far simpler and less expensive to maintain. The engine in an EV has only one moving part compared to the hundreds in a gas engine as shown in **Figure 7.7**. Some estimates suggest that the maintenance costs of an electric car are only 10% of the maintenance costs for a gas car. This is a real threat to the dealership model which makes much of their profit on expensive service of gas cars. (See section on the dealership bottleneck later in this chapter.)

Another very dramatic cost savings with EVs is evident to anyone who has had to disassemble their dashboard to install a ham radio transceiver in their car. Compared to the several dozen buttons and switches and levers and associated complex wiring harnesses in a typical car, almost all of the functions in the Tesla Model 3 are simply on the very convenient and powerful central touch screen shown in **Figure 7.8**.

(A)

(B)

Figure 7.8 — The Tesla Model 3 dashboard (A) is a lot simpler and easier to manufacture than the dashboard in a typical conventional car (B). (Images courtesy Tesla and Ford Motor Company.)

The rate of adoption of EVs will be even faster than the revolution in the industry brought on with hybrid technology. Hybrids were introduced by Toyota with the Prius in 2001, and in 13 years were generally accepted as the best way to achieve the low emissions and high MPG goals being set by governments around the world. The adoption rate of EVs is the next step in the reduction of transportation emissions and has achieved the same rate of growth in half the time.

Once the full understanding of the value promise of EVs for local daily travel sinks in for the general population, the tipping point will have been

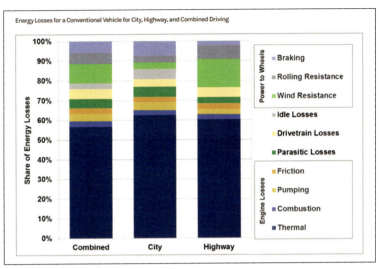

Figure 7.9 — About 70% of all energy in a gas/diesel car is waste heat and toxic emissions. (From www.energy.gov/eere/vehicles/fact-880-july-6-2015-conventional-vehicle-energy-use-where-does-energy-go.)

reached and predictions are that the adoption of EVs will be as dramatic as the replacement of the horse by the automobile at the turn of the last century. Just looking at the Department of Energy's assessment of energy loss in an internal combustion car is shown in **Figure 7.9** should convince anyone that the 70% or so waste energy to heat is just not sustainable.

Gasoline Hybrids

It is important to understand that although hybrids such as the Prius have both an electric motor and a battery, they still run 100% on the burning of gasoline. What the hybrid electric motor and battery do is fill in when more power is needed and then absorb electricity from the regenerative brakes when there is excess at every stop. This reduction in wasted energy and heat results in an improvement to over 50 MPG and does reduce emissions by half compared to older gas cars. However, hybrids are still fossil-fuel powered with the resulting toxic and carbon emissions.

Plug-in Hybrids

To simplify the distinction between hybrids and all the various electric vehicle types such as battery EV (BEV), hybrid EV (HEV), plug-in hybrid EV (PHEV), and extended-range EV (EREV), it is important to understand that the only thing that matters for driving on clean renewable energy is whether the car has a *plug*. If it has a plug, then it can run on external sources of electricity generated from hydro, solar, wind, or any other form of 100% clean renewable electricity, and is called a "*plug-in*."

Although the optimum application of EVs is for local travel and commuting, the plug-in hybrids (PHEVs) now offer electric car solutions

Figure 7.10 — For the plug-in hybrids, about 40% of all models in 2018 cost less than the average new gas car, and some three-year-old used ones coming off lease go for under $15,000. (Based on the 2018 Electric Vehicle Information Sheet from the Electric Vehicle Association of Greater Washington, DC — evadc.org.)

for everyone (**Figure 7.10**). The lower-cost, all-electric models commonly referred to as BEVs (battery electric vehicles), such as the top-selling Nissan Leaf, are ideal for daily commuting and local travel and for families that have more than one car and can dedicate the all-electric car for local use. But for the individual with access to only one car, or for the daily road warrior who may be called on any day for trips of several hundred miles, then the plug-in hybrid fully meets that need. The plug-in hybrid not only includes sufficient all-electric daily miles with home overnight charging, but also has a backup gas engine for long trips at any time, and anywhere.

The top sellers over the last eight years in the plug-in hybrid category are the Plug-in Prius and the Chevy Volt. Although the original 2012 Plug-in Prius (called the PIP) only had 12 miles of usable EV range, this was sufficient for many people with short commutes. The car also offered 500 mile range on gas. It was finally replaced in 2016 with the Prius Prime, with almost 30 miles EV range and more than 600 miles range on gas while remaining a very cost-effective car.

The other most popular plug-in is the Chevy Volt (shown back in Chapter 1 in Figure 1.8) which has the greatest daily EV range of all PHEVs — around 50 miles, backed up with more than 300 miles range on gas. This maximum EV range and seamless gas backup made the Volt the best transition experience for single car owners who are switching from gas to electric.

Second to commuting and local travel, the pickup work truck is another excellent EV application. Tesla, Via Motors, Ford, and Workhorse (**Figure 7.11**) are all working on EV models of the popular pickup. This is not a truck you would use to haul an RV trailer across the country, but it is perfect for the local contractor who needs a dependable work truck on the job site.

Figure 7.11 — The Workhorse W-15 electric pickup truck. (Courtesy Workhorse.)

These EVs pickups would offer maximum torque for pulling and hauling, yet get to and from the jobsite on efficient and emissions-free electric drive. In addition, they typically can generate plenty of power at 120/240 V ac at the job site and can provide that power silently and even indoors if needed. Typical projected ranges for these pickups are currently about 100 miles, but at worksites with utility power, the truck can be plugged in to keep the battery topped off for material runs and errands too.

EV Range

To the EV buyer who purchased an EV with battery range that matches his daily commute and local travel needs, the popularly misconstrued topic of *range anxiety* vanishes as an issue. After all, every morning when he gets in the car, he begins with full range for the day from charging overnight at home. But to the media and general public who do not yet understand the concept of charging-while-parked every day when the car is not in use, or beginning each day on full, there remains the concern over range.

To give a better understanding of this topic, I have prepared a summary of the ranges of the 45 EVs currently on the market in 2018 in **Figure 7.12**. Note that about 50% of all EVs and PHEVs have ranges greater than 350 miles, and about 78% have ranges greater than 200 miles. For the long-range traveler, 20% have ranges over 500 miles, with the low-cost plug-in Prius Prime topping 640 miles. That's 10 hours of driving without stopping (and far beyond most travelers' needs).

The only time that range is of any concern in an EV is when one is driven on a long trip and needs to run for hours at a time between refueling and pit stops. That is why more than half the EVs on the market are PHEVs, so that they have the backup gas engine for such occasional needs. These PHEVs give the local daily miles on battery alone, but magically and seamlessly transition to gas whenever needed.

MPGe

Miles Per Gallon Equivalent, or MPGe, is a concept that makes it easy to compare the efficiency of EVs to fossil fuel cars. To get MPGe, the energy content of electricity is converted to the same energy units of gasoline so they can be compared "apples to apples." The 100 to 120 MPGe rating of modern EVs is equivalent to getting 100 to 120 miles per gallon on gas. This is more than double even the best gasoline hybrids (Prius), with the added value of elimination of emissions and the ability to charge at home.

Electric Car Ranges 100 to 600 Miles!

The daily miles for the average American car is about 40 miles. The smart EV shopper buys the minimum range battery that meets their specific daily routine everyday use. Plugin overnight and have full range every morning.

A battery EV (BEV) is an ideal second car for all local travel and daily use. A plugin hybrid (PHEV) is ideal for a car that must do both routine local travel but also long trips. These cars have smaller EV batteries because they have the gas engine for seamless backup and for long drives.

More than half of all 46 EV's now on the market are PHEVs in 2018. Of all EVs,

| 78% have total ranges over 200 miles. |
| 50% have total ranges over 350 miles. |
| 20% have total ranges over 500 miles. |

Further, 50% cost LESS with incentives than the average $36k gas car!

```
Rng  EV Cost  Plugin EV/Hybrid model
----  --  -----  -----------------------------
666   29  $30k   Kia Optima Plug-In
650   27  $30k   Hyundai Sonata PHEV
640   25  $23k   Toyota Prius Prime
630   29  $20k   Hyundai Ioniq PHEV
610   21  $27k   Ford Fusion Energi
580   33  $33k   Chrysler Pacifica hyb.
580   26  $23k   Kia Niro PHEV
560   24  $93k   Porsche Panamera
540   13  $59k   BMW X5 xDrive40e
480   14  $75k   Porsche Cayenne
460   20  $23k   Ford C-Max Energi
460    8  $62k   Mercedes GLE550e
450   12  $92k   Mercedes S550e
450   18  $48k   Volvo XC60 T8
440   30  $68k   Cadillac CT6 Plug-In
410    8  $44k   Mercedes C350e
410   21  $59k   Volvo S90 T8
380   53  $26k   Chevy Volt
380   16  $35k   Audi A3 e-tron
372   16  $48k   BMW 530e
350   22  $42k   BMW 330e
350   19  $60k   Volvo XC90 T8
340   47  $26k   Honda Clarity PHEV
340   14  $86k   BMW 740e xDrive
335   EV  $87k   Tesla 100D
330   14  $143k  BMW i8
310   EV  $37k   Tesla 3 extended range
310   22  $29k   Mitsubishi Outlander
295   EV  $89k   Tesla X 100D
259   EV  $67k   Tesla S 75D
270   12  $33k   MINI Cooper S E Countr
240   37  $123k  Karma Revero
238   EV  $72k   Tesla X 75D
238   EV  $29k   Chevy Bolt
220   EV  $28k   Tesla 3 std
180   97  $41k   BMW i3 Range Extender
151   EV  $22k   Nissan Leaf
125   EV  $23k   VW e-golf
124   EV  $22k   Hyundai Ioniq Electric
115   EV  $22k   Ford Focus Electric
114   EV  $27k   BMW i3
111   EV  $26k   Kia Soul Electric
 89   EV  $26k   Honda Clarity Electric
 84   EV  $26k   Fiat 500e
 58   EV  $16k   Smart
```

Rng column is the total combined range and **EV** Column is the EV only range. Some standouts are highlighted in red. **Cost** is net after federal incentives.

evadc.org

Figure 7.12 — Range comparison for 45 EVs of all types on the market in 2018.

Hydrogen Fuel Cell Vehicles

A lot has been made of the future of the hydrogen economy since the byproduct of combustion or from a fuel cell is simply water. What could be cleaner? Well, there is a reason that some engineers refer to the hydrogen fuel-cell EV (FCEV) as a *fool*-cell car. This is because there is no source of natural hydrogen on Earth. It is always combined with something else, such as water or natural gas for example, and there is virtually no distribution system.

Although we can drill for more natural gas (more hydraulic fracking and its host of issues), this is not economical nor clean. To separate the hydrogen from natural gas, some of the gas has to first be burned to generate steam from water which then reforms into a mixture of hydrogen, carbon monoxide, and some carbon dioxide. What's wrong with this picture? 1) Significant contamination of ground water through hydraulic fracking to get the gas, then 2) the consumption of more water to form the steam, then 3) burning of some of the gas to get the heat to make the steam and the result is the hydrogen you want and 4) all the carbon and carbon monoxide into the air that we are trying to avoid in the first place.

Hydrogen from Water Hydrolysis

Similarly, getting hydrogen from water takes much more energy from some other energy source to separate the hydrogen from the oxygen. Instead of first wasting energy in the conversion to hydrogen, more energy compressing the hydrogen, distributing the hydrogen through a distribution system (that does not exist) to a car tank, where the hydrogen is then inefficiently converted to electricity in a fuel cell back to electricity to drive a motor, we could, much more efficiently, simply drive an EV motor directly from electricity in the first place.

Hydrogen fuel cell cars made sense to the "tank dependent" way of thinking of energy storage for vehicles maybe a decade ago, before modern batteries made electric vehicles practical. With the cost and weight of batteries having dropped 25-to-1 and the cost of 100% clean solar electricity having dropped 100-to-1, there is little economic business model for the hydrogen FCEV with its lack of a hydrogen source and complete lack of a distribution system. That's especially true compared to electricity already being distributed to more than 200 million of us.

Hydrogen in the Far Future

Despite the prior paragraphs enumerating the lack of a business model for the FCEV, hydrogen may eventually have a niche market in the long run. In the future, when there is excess renewable wind or solar production and there is low demand, the excess clean power might simply be dumped into water tanks to generate free hydrogen. Then, rather than face the insurmountable problem of how to distribute this hydrogen to 200 million cars through a distribution system that does not exist, the answer instead, is to keep the hydrogen in tanks where it was generated and then burn the hydrogen in turbines to feed that stored energy back to the grid when needed. Another small niche might be in long-haul hydrogen trucking and railroad transportation hubs where distribution can be done more easily in bulk just to the hubs.

Tipping the Scales

One last factor that keeps FCEV cars in the news is the California Air Resources Board (CARB) regulations that, decades ago, assumed hydrogen cars might make sense someday. So the CARB rules not only gave hydrogen car makers a degree of bonus points for low emissions just like EV makers get, but in addition, the rules gave an additional five times multiplier to the bonus points to any system that can refuel in the same five minutes as a gas car.

These bonus points are what allows car manufacturers to *still* sell large numbers of gas cars in California and, because of the point system, they can sell five times more gas cars for every single hydrogen car they sell compared to every EV they sell. This is why the manufacturers only make exactly the minimum requirement of FCEVs to sell in California and no more. They only wanted the bonus points so they could sell more gas cars.

A decade or so ago, no one foresaw how rapidly the EV would overtake the FCEV concept and beat it in every measure of efficiency, practicality and cost. But now with at least three major car companies having invested in this technology, the CARB will never be able to pull back those rules even though there is no near-term future in the FCEV.

Battery Swap Technology

Just as the fantasy of hydrogen cars won't die, neither does the idea of using battery-swapping stations for EVs. Just like the fast-fueling bonus points for hydrogen, EVs were also given a significant multiplier bonus points for five-minute fast charging. This is why Tesla made their Model S cars able to swap the entire battery pack in the magic five-minute requirement and demonstrated it with great fanfare. After the demo, they collected the millions of dollars' worth of bonus points, and we have not seen a single battery swap since, nor will we. If the battery represents nearly half of the $120,000 investment in a Tesla, it is no wonder that an owner is not going to give up their known $50,000 battery for an unknown battery at some roadside swapping station. The battery swap concept is simply a continuation of the obsolete gas-tank/gas-station legacy thinking.

A classic and spectacular failure of the battery swap idea was the bankruptcy of A Better Place in 2012. They spent a billion dollars, mostly in Israel, on the concept of battery swap stations and automobile usage not as an ownership model, but as a service across the country. But they overlooked the fact that in a country that is only 40 miles wide, typical 80-mile EVs have battery ranges sufficient to go almost anywhere in the country before coming a border. There was little reason to swap the battery for a range-extending quick refueling. The founder's business model was that people wanted cars for transportation only, and they would pay for the battery and charging service in the same way they pay for cell phone services (ie, he could almost give away the car for free, and they would pay a service charge). Turns out, people like to buy their car, and just like with cell phones, they tend to hate their service providers. (For more information, see **www.fastcompany.com/3028159/a-broken-place-better-place**.)

Long Distance Travel

The electric vehicle has always been considered the ideal match to the 95% of our transportation needs, which largely consist of local travel and commuting. But for the other 5% of the time when we do have a need to travel long distance (interstate travel), there are many options:

1) Public transportation by bus, rail or air.
2) Rent the most appropriate car for the trip.
3) A second family hybrid gasoline car for distant travel when needed.
4) A plug-in hybrid that runs on clean electricity locally but can still run on gas for long distance travel.
5) A long-range EV (240 mile battery) that not only meets 100% of local needs, but can also travel for four hours or so between highway fast charges.

Making a choice of these options is a very individual consideration. It is uniquely based on your amount of daily commute and local usage, compared to how often you need to go on longer trips, and the distance of those trips. Also important is your access to another car in the family for times when you need more range, or how much you are willing to pay to have a huge 250-mile battery that is usually used less than 50 miles a day. The rest of the time that 240-mile battery is being hauled around doing nothing, and the initial cost was about five times more than a battery sufficient for your daily routine.

EV Charging Types

There are three types of EV charging options. The first is called Level 1 or L1 and comes with every plug-in car. Level 1 is suitable for overnight charging from any convenient 120 V ac outlet to provide about 50 miles a day. It consists of a standard 15 A, 120 V plug and an interface box that contains a ground fault circuit interrupter (GFCI), some simple signaling circuitry, a contactor, and then the special J1772 plug that connects safely to the car as shown in **Figure 7.13**. The combination of all these components is called an EV Supply Equipment, or EVSE. Every EV in the world has standardized on that J1772 connector for ac charging.

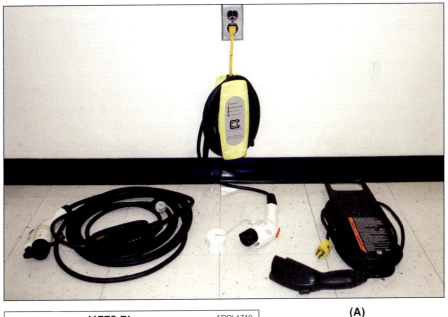

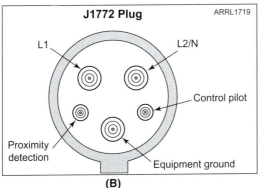

Figure 7.13 — Several different Level 1 EVSE chargers that plug into any standard 120 V ac outlet and charge at 12 A up to 50 miles overnight (A). At (B), the larger pins in a J1772 connector are for Line 1, Line 2, and Ground, while the two smaller pins are for safety and control circuitry.

The EVSE signaling circuit simply puts out a 1 kHz pulse train with a set duty cycle to tell the car how much current is available. For all stock L1 EVSE devices in the US, the default pulse duty cycle signals 12 A since that is the maximum sustained current that should be drawn from a standard 15 A ac outlet. Some plug-in hybrids, such as the Prius and Volt, default to only 8 A. Even at that current, the car will be fully charged overnight, and at 8 A there is less concern about overloading some unknown outlet or an outlet shared with other devices in the house. Similarly, some EVSE chargers can be set for 16 A if they are plugged into a 20 A circuit. At 8, 12 or 16 A, the typical L1 EVSE can deliver 1, 1.5, or 2 kW charge rates.

EVSE Level 2

Level 2, or L2, connects to 240 V ac and is usually wired to 20, 30, or 50 A ac circuits (or more). On these circuits, the EVSE will draw either 16, 24, or 40 A which is the 80% derating for long-duration current on those circuits. L2 can deliver 3, 6 or 10 kW of power.

The EVSE hardware for L2 looks the same as for L1, but has a higher rated cord and contactor. The internal signaling matches the capacity of the current available from the outlet it is connected to, and it is assumed to be operating at 240 V ac. These L2 EVSE chargers can be had now for about $250 each, and for convenience many come with simple 240 V, 20, 30, or 50 A ac plugs.

Just remember that the internal circuit tells the car how much it can draw. So it is okay to make an adapter to plug in a 20 or 30 A EVSE into a 50 A outlet, but it would be a huge error to make an adapter for a 50 A EVSE to plug into a 30 A or 20 A outlet without doing the internal modifications to tell it that it is operating on a lower rated circuit. Most public chargers are also L2 that are hardwired and contain some kind of billing equipment to pay for the electricity.

Charging Speed

Rather than trying to remember all the diffcrent L1 and L2 specifications for charging amps and charging times and the two voltage levels, it is easy to convert these to charging miles per hour or MPH. The simple rule of thumb is that an L1 EVSE charges at about 4 MPH, a 240 V L2 running the minimum 16 A charges at about 11 MPH, and 30/50 A chargers charge at about 22/28 MPH.

Although all cars can charge L2 on a 20 A circuit at 11 MPH, many cars only provide faster charging as a purchase option. Looking at the specs on most cars, the difference between charging on a 30 or 50 A circuit is often

Figure 7.14 — Since Tesla EVs were the first with big batteries and can travel longer distances, Tesla built out a "Supercharger" network of Level 3 chargers across the country that can charge in about 20 minutes. [Map as of late 2018, courtesy Tesla.]

only the difference between the 22 and 25 MPH range because few cars include the expense of a 10 kW charger on board every car. But the 50 A connector is common for plugging into campground or dryer outlets.

High Voltage DC — Level 3

These fast Level 3 (L3) dc chargers are completely different from the ac EVSEs, which are really not chargers but are simply signaling and safety circuits between the car and the grid. But for Level 3, the battery charger is actually outside of the car in the charging station and has to have critical communication with the car to properly charge the battery. The capacity of these chargers is huge, since the goal is fast charging, and the operating voltage is usually 480 V or higher.

The original cross-county Tesla network of high voltage chargers (**Figure 7.14**), the Superchargers, are typically rated at 120 kW. When a car plugs in (for only 30 minutes), the power drawn is equivalent to a full neighborhood of 120 homes, and the charging rate is more than 100 MPH for comparison to the examples in the previous section.

These high voltages and currents require a special connector, and unfortunately there are three separate standards. One is the Tesla since it was the first EV on the market. This was followed by CHADEMO developed in Japan and supplied as an option in all Nissan Leafs and subsequently other models. Then the SAE (Society of Automotive Engineers) got involved and came up with the Combo Charging System (CCS), which combined the J1772 and high voltage dc connecting pins in the same handle.

There are three distinctions of dc charging levels. Level 1 dc charges at 240 to 480 V up to 36 kW; dc Level 2 charges 240 to 480 V up to 90 kW; and dc Level 3 charges at 200 to 600 V at up to 240 kW. To meet these growing charging speeds, new installations of roadside high-voltage dc charging stations are being built with up to 350 kW capacity from the grid (**Figure 7.15**).

A small side note about these high-voltage dc connectors on the EVs

Figure 7.15 — EVgo Level 3 public chargers (A) and Tesla Superchargers (B) are now widely available (these are located at a rest area on the New Jersey Turnpike). Level 3 dc chargers are much, much faster than plugging the vehicle in at home, but also demand more than 100 times more power than the average home. The neighborhood-size power substation is behind the fence.

(A)

(B)

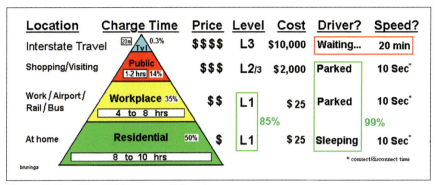

Figure 7.16 — The EV Charging Triangle.

is that they give external access to the EV's internal battery. So any future applications that intend to use the EV battery for external purposes such as vehicle-to-grid or home backup power will be using this connector. Of course, significant digital handshaking between the vehicle and application are required for safe use. We'll cover these topics in later chapters.

The Charging Triangle

The charging triangle shown in **Figure 7.16** represents the wide range of charging options available. The base of the triangle indicates that the vast majority of EV charging is at home. Since the car is usually parked there overnight, at least 8 to 10 are hours available for charging. In that time, even a standard 120 V Level 1 (L1) charge cord can be adequate. The time to charge is inconsequential because the owner is spending that time sleeping and charging is the ultimate in convenience. The actual impact is the time to plug in when you get home and unplug when you leave.

The next most practical time for EV charging on a daily basis is while at work. Here too, for most people, the car is parked several hours a day. If simply plugged into a standard 120 V outlet (L1 charging), 20 to 40 miles a day of range can be replenished. Combined with charging at home, it's easy to maintain more than 80 miles of daily range from just standard outlets, while charging during times that you are not normally using the car.

The next level of the charging pyramid is for daily travel that might be beyond the American average of 40 miles a day plus lots of errands. In this case, one might look to plug in while parked for shopping or while visiting other locations. This is the focus of most public charging for a fee, and it can be as much as 14% of the charging pyramid.

In these locations, speed of charging begins to be an issue, and so these chargers must be Level 2 and they typically cost much more than a simple L1 charger. And since each car can fill up by quite different amounts, a metering system to count the charge and a billing system has to be included so the customer can pay for the energy received, all of which drive up the costs of this kind of charging station to well over $10,000 each. Fortunately, this kind of charging is still occurring while the car is parked, so the impact on the driver remains only the typical 10 seconds total to plug in and unplug.

Highway Charging

The tiny tip of the triangle, which studies have shown will represent less than 0.3% of the total charging pyramid, is the charging option that gets all the press. Fast charging along the interstate on long trips is the only process that even comes close to mimicking the gas-tank/gas-station legacy thinking, and so people focus on it entirely even though it is the most rarely used.

In this sense, it is the ultimate in *inconvenience*. Charging while parked and not normally using the car — the other 99% of the charging pyramid — is a brief inconvenience to plug the charger in when you get home, and then unplug it when you leave. In comparison, the fast interstate charging on the road is actually the slowest and most inconvenient. This is because it is being done while you wait, just like at the gas pump. But unlike the five minutes to fill a gas car, even the fastest fast charging takes 20 minutes or more while you wait to resume your trip — four times longer than a typical gas fill-up.

Yet to those who do not yet understand the true value promise of the EV — charging at home or at work while parked — this fast charging along the interstate is the focal point, even though it represents less than 1% of the EV charging need. This aspect alone is why the number one thing we need to move forward on the electrification of transportation is simply the education of the consumer. EVs are for local and daily travel, and charging while parked. There are many other alternatives for distant travel.

Charging by the Week

An often-quoted concern for gas drivers considering a 240-mile EV and using a simple L2 charge cord is the statement "but it will take 20 hours to a full charge." They say this with grave concern, while ignoring the fact that the car will sit parked for typically 22 hours a day with plenty of time for that full charge anyway!

I like to make the comparison about charging on a weekly basis. For example, say you have a 240-mile EV, a 20 mile daily commute, and the ability to, overnight, charge the EV enough for 40 miles from a standard 120 V outlet. You are not only meeting all your commuting requirements, but are also accumulating charge for 20 additional miles a day (140 miles a week) for longer weekend trips. If you can also plug in at work, you can accumulate another 40 miles a day and have 240 miles every weekend for travel… and all from simple 120 V ac outlet charging when you are not normally using the car.

With a simple $250 L2 charge cord that operates from a 240 V ac outlet, then overnight charging can gain 110 miles a day, for a weekly budget of 770 miles, which is more than double what the average American gas car is driven. You would never have to go for public charging except for long trips over 240 miles in each stretch. With a higher-capacity 7 kW L2 charge cord, overnight you can pick up 240 miles and be fully charged every morning no matter how far you drive.

The Dealership Bottleneck

When most EV purchasers are asked what is holding back the widespread adoption of electric vehicles, the topic of dealerships invariably comes up. There are many ways that this impacts the sales and growth of EV adoption:

1) Most dealers steer customers away from EV to gas where they make more profit.
2) Most dealers are not fully trained on the true value promise of an EV, and most salesmen do not own, operate, drive, or understand one.
3) Most dealers make much of their income from gas car routine service, not sales.
4) The estimated 90% less maintenance for an EV is a threat to the dealership model.
5) Without the need for frequent maintenance, the dependency on the dealer disappears, especially when updates can be made directly to the car via the internet instead of a service call.

Over the last century our dependency on the automobile for transportation grew, so did the power and influence of car dealerships that sold and maintained them. This influence has led to laws providing dealerships a virtual monopoly on selling cars and has actually made it impossible for some new car manufacturers to enter the market. This grip of the dealership model is unrelenting.

As of January 2018, with 10 year history of selling EVs, Tesla is still only allowed to sell cars direct to customers without a dealership and with no restrictions in just 20 states. The legislature in Michigan even passed a special change in their dealership laws to block Tesla from selling in the state (see **www.mlive.com/news/grand-rapids/index.ssf/2018/03/anti-tesla_law_ michigan_auto_d.html**). On the other hand, about 26 states do allow Tesla to have galleries in malls where they can show the cars but not sell them. It seems overly protectionist and short sighted of these states to not only be blocking sales in their states, and at the same time pushing business and jobs to nearby states.

Rapid Change and Visibility

By now you can see why this book focuses so much on the EV as an immediate and personal transition to clean energy. When the EV is better, cleaner, faster, and cheaper to buy, cheaper to operate and cheaper to maintain than a gas car, when purchased by an informed and prepared individual, the transition is inevitable. But why is it not happening faster? Several reasons:

1) Human nature abhors change and clings to past held beliefs often in spite of clear and present new information.

2) It is hard to abandon the century old legacy of gas-tank/gas-station public refueling thinking, and it is hard to grasp the convenience of refueling at home and waking daily to full daily range.

3) Dealers are not advertising EVs or steering buyers toward EVs (they make more profit in selling SUVs and big gas cars).

4) Gas prices are cheap compared to nearly $4 per gallon a few years ago.

5) Many people just buy what's cheapest now instead of investing wisely in their future

8 Electric Vehicle DIY Projects

Although tinkering around inside the design of a modern EV is far beyond the scope of this book, there are a few DIY projects that are quite possible. These range from designing your own charge cords to doing a full EV conversion of your favorite old classic automobile for proudly tooling around locally on your own clean solar electricity.

Mild Hybrid Project

This is a solar EV project that can be added to many cars relatively simply. Not only does it give a nice source of solar power for a mobile radio while parked, it can also save about 15% or more on gas mileage. The idea is to replace the wasted mechanical losses from the typical fan belt with solar power. To test this idea, I removed the fan belt on my son's 1995 Geo Metro Tracker. Actually, I just slipped the belt off the motor pulley, but left it in place for the several day duration of the test. I just wired it out of the way for a while so I did not have to mechanically remove all the pulley powered stuff as shown in **Figure 8.1A**.

Disconnecting the fan belt eliminated several lossy mechanical loads. First is the alternator, but that energy is easily replaced with a solar panel (Figure 8.1B) and possibly a backup battery. The belt also powers the water pump and the very lossy radiator fan. Fortunately, very few cars made during for the past several decades actually waste power in a mechanical radiator fan, but instead use a thermostatically controlled electric fan that comes on only when needed.

In the Geo Metro, removing the belt disabled both the fan and the water pump. I found that by running the cabin heater on high (this was in the winter), I could go to and from work with relatively modest driving and not overheat the engine. A proper conversion would add a thermostatically controlled 12 V water circulator pump (perhaps $30 from the hardware store) and a modern thermostatically controlled electric fan to control engine heat.

Figure 8.1 — The fan belt removed in the 1995 Geo Metro Tracker (A). At (B), a solar panel on the hood helps keep the battery topped off with the alternator disconnected.

I ran the car without the alternator, water pump, and fan for a week on a full tank of gas, and at the end of the week I had achieved 33 MPG instead of my typical best of about 29 MPG for a 15% energy improvement.

Without the alternator, the bulk of the 12 V electrical load while driving was drawn from the battery. The solar panel on the hood was only about a 24 W panel, and its main job was to charge up the battery while parked at work for eight hours, not supply power for the car while driving. The battery was also charged from a trickle charger at night for a full charge by morning.

For a practical project for long-term use, a full size solar panel of more than 200 W would be needed to maintain all electrical systems while driving over long distances, and then only during the day. But still, it makes for great ham radio power in the mobile and might be practical in sunny climates.

Car Pre-Heating Hacks

The first hack I did when we began driving Priuses was to work on a way to preheat the car for the cold weather. In those early days, everyone was trying to *hypermile* and see how many miles per gallon above the EPA ratings on the window sticker were possible. When driving efficiently in a hybrid to work every morning, I used a stopwatch once to time how long the gasoline engine was actually running. Turns out the engine only ran for about 11 minutes out of a 30 minute commute. Otherwise it was coasting, regenerating during traffic slowdowns and running on battery at light loads.

The problem I experienced is that this type of operation really reduces the normal waste heat of a gas engine, and there is not enough waste heat to fully supply the passenger compartment heater. So, turning on the heater would cause the engine to actually keep running at traffic lights just to create waste heat used just to heat the passenger compartment. You can spot a hypermiler because he is all dressed for the cold and never turns on the heat in his hybrid. Also, preheating any car by remote-start (burning gasoline for nothing but heat) was a definite no-go for the energy conscious driver.

My solution was to add a standard 120 V plug and socket on the side of the car so I could plug in some heat before I left the house in the morning as shown in **Figure 8.2**. The plug went to several things. First, it powered a

Figure 8.2 — I added this 120 V extension cord port so that engine, cabin, and seat can be pre-heated in the winter.

400 W engine block heater under the hood. Second, it ran to a standard 120 V outlet below the dashboard where I could plug in a $20 heating pad for my driver's seat, and a small space heater on the passenger side floor that was set to half power (700 W). The 120 V connection box includes a female 120 V socket as well so that while the car is plugged into an extension cord, there is also an accessory outlet still available for power tools.

The cord from the car was plugged into a permanent extension cord from the house that was connected to a switch in the bedroom so that I could turn on the heat when I got up and get maybe 20 minutes before leaving. Actually it was a dual-box switch plate, and the switches were labeled *His* and *Hers* for both of our salvage Prius cars. This was great. When I unplugged the cord and got in the car, it was comfortably warm, the seat was warm and the engine was warm. And when I sat on the warm heating pad, the heat was trapped between the seat and my butt, and it stayed warm most of the half-hour drive to work.

The 400 W engine block heater was not so much for the cabin, but for greatly improving gas mileage as the engine would start warm. A Prius only gets maybe 30 MPG during the initial warm up period, so pre-warming the engine on renewable energy can save fossil fuel. That shows up well on the Prius MPG monitor display (**Figure 8.3**.) There were of course debates as

Figure 8.3 — All gas engines have poor MPG and much higher emissions until warmed up. This shows up well on the Prius MPG monitor display.

to how long to pre-warm the car. And there are three answers depending on whether you want the most heat, the least overall energy use, or the least overall emissions. I think the consensus was something like 30 minutes for best comfort, 20 minutes for least emissions, and 10 minutes for least overall energy use — or something like that.

Steering-Wheel Heater

In order to add steering wheel heat, I came up with the idea of a simple circuit on the wheel shown in **Figure 8.4A** consisting of a single AA NiMH cell and a heating element made of about a half ohm of wire (50 feet of #20 AWG magnet wire) wrapped around the bottom of the wheel where my hands usually were. Plugging in a single cell 2500 mAh NiMH battery would

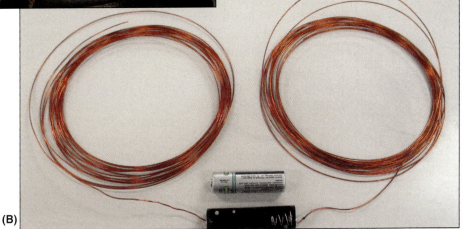

Figure 8.4 — My steering wheel heater, installed where I normally place my hands while driving. It's made from two coils of wire and a single AA-size NiMH rechargeable battery (B).

give about 3 W of power at 2.5 A for the full 30-minute drive. Every evening, I just removed the cell and brought it back in the house for charging overnight.

To simplify wrapping the wires I soldered half the wire to each side of the battery holder as shown in Figure 8.4B, and then folded each side of wire in half. Then I taped the two ends temporarily near the battery to be joined later. Then I folded those halves in half, so then I could make the windings four strands at a time working outward. Then I pulled the windings tight and made the center connection between the loose ends and covered it all with tape. All the while, I made sure that the battery and wires were nowhere near the air bag!

J1772 EVSE Operation

Although every EV comes with a 120 V charge cord, when the new EVs came out in 2011, a replacement or spare J1772 EVSE charger cost more than $900. There was a lot of incentive to reverse engineer the device, and a project called Open EVSE began online to make it easy to build a charger (see **www.openevse.com/index.html**). But that approach used a microcontroller and required the usual code, libraries, programming, and special skills to make it work, and the costs rose as it became more professional.

I took the approach of a simple 555 timer chip and a few other gates to do the same thing. The J1772 spec is relatively simple, and all communication is via just two pins as shown in **Figure 8.5**. When idle, the EVSE puts 12 V on the Pilot pin. When plugged into a car, there is a fixed 2.7 kΩ resistor to ground in the car, which pulls the 12 V signal to 9 V or less. This signals the EVSE to activate a +/− pulse train at 1 kHz. The duty cycle of this pulse train indicates the available current at the EVSE.

If the car needs a charge, at this point, it closes its contactor and adds another 1.3 kΩ resistor in parallel with the original 2.7 kΩ resistor, and this load pulls the positive cycles of the pulse train to 6 V or less. This signals the EVSE to close its contactor and begin the charge. If the car puts another 270 Ω resistor in parallel and pulls the positive voltage down to 3 V, then this means the vehicle also needs ventilation.

The reason this signaling uses a pulsed square wave instead of just dc is so the negative side of the pulses, to −12 V, is for detecting errors. If the J1772 plug is just sitting on the wet ground and happens to find a resistance that looks like the car resistor, it could signal a charging session and dangerously activate the handle with ac power in a puddle. But in this case, notice that there will be no diode in this phantom water puddle circuit. So the −12 V will see the same drop as the +12 V, and so if the positive side drops to +6 V, then the negative pulses would also drop to only −6 V, and the loss of the unloaded −12 V pulses indicates something is wrong.

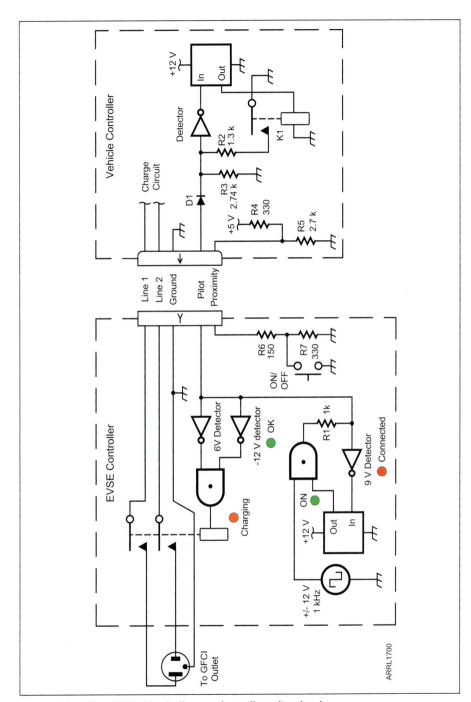

Figure 8.5 — The J1772 block diagram is really quite simple.

The other signal pin is the Proximity pin. This tells the car that a J1772 connector is inserted by the presence of a 150 Ω resistor to ground. If the handle button is pushed, this opens the contacts around a 330 Ω resistor, which is now in series with the 150 Ω resistor, and the rise in resistance signals the car to disconnect its contactors immediately.

An Example DIY J1772 Design

My approach also wanted to avoid the expensive J1772 handle, which cost more than $100 just for the plastic handle and 5 pins, plus $90 shipping from China. So I made a small disk PC board to hold my own scavenged pins plus a circuit board to fit inside a plumbing fixture. The biggest item is the 12 V dc power supply transformer shown in **Figure 8.6**. Note that I would not do it this way again, as the transformer limits the handle to operation at 120

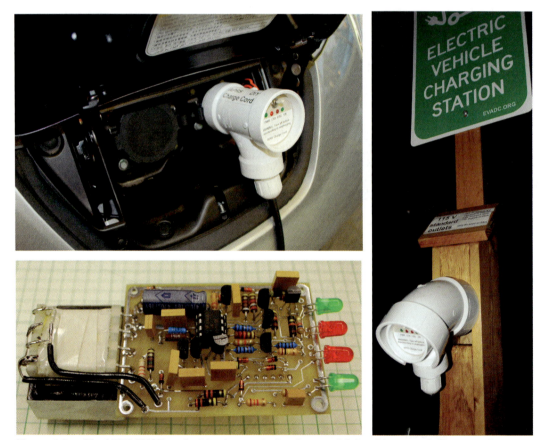

Figure 8.6 — My J1772 EVSE project to demonstrate a low-cost "plumbing special" approach.

V only. Since tiny universal switching supplies for cell phone and other small portable devices are now the size of a golf ball, I'd use one of those circuits so the handle could operate on either 120 or 240 V interchangeably. The charging post shown on the right might be misleading. It is simply showing the same plumbing charging handle, but held to the post out of the weather inside a much larger 4-inch PVC pipe elbow

But There Were Some Challenges

First, at the time, I did not own a real EV with a J1772 charge port. So I then had to build an EV simulator so that I would have something to plug it into. That EV simulator is shown in **Figure 8.7** and included 1200 W of light bulbs to simulate the load of the car's battery charging system. Second, my project did not include a GFCI circuit because I assumed that every outdoor outlet is now supposed to be GFCI-protected. So to give the same protection as the real J1772, it would have to be plugged into a GFCI outlet. Since I couldn't guarantee that a user would always do that, I began to get cold feet. Also I was hesitant to ask to plug into someone else's $30,000 car to test my circuit.

By the time I finally got a real EV with J1772 charge port, commercial EV cords were widely available for around $200, while the basic J1772 handles still cost an arm and a leg. Further, although the pins I had scavenged from the junk box were a perfect fit, I learned later that there is an added depth on the J1772 pins. This is because the pins on the car have a plastic tip to make sure the actual power pins do not connect until about 1/4 inch after the signaling pins connect. Without this added pocket depth in the female pins I had found, there was risk of a bad connection and arcing. Even today, the only way that I could find the correct special pins was to buy the whole J1772 handle, which still costs more than $100 and is not worth the trouble.

Figure 8.7 — My J1772 charge tester emulates the action of an EV when plugged into an EVSE.

Retractable L1 Charging

So next I turned the J1772 project into the design for a retractable cord. Since L1 charging from a standard outlet can provide more than 90% of all at-home and at-work charging, it has been frustrating that cars do not come with a simple retractable standard cord like a common vacuum cleaner does.

The response from the experts was to point at all the safety circuits involved in the EVSE design. But since I was still going to have all those features in the EVSE, and the EVSE was going to be attached to the car, then their claims were not an issue. Further, the house end of the EVSE cable has nothing more than the same three-pin, 120 V plug as a vacuum cleaner or any other standard appliance. When you plug that into the house, it is absolutely no different than plugging in anything else.

But there is one other unusual EVSE requirement — the length of the cord from the 120 V plug to the EVSE electronics cannot be more than about a foot. The idea is that this keeps anyone from plugging in the EVSE when it is sitting on the ground submersed in a puddle of water. It is this extreme requirement that seems to me to have actually caused more hazards than what it is trying to protect! So far, I'm not aware of reports of anyone foolishly plugging in a submerged EVSE, but there are hundreds of reports of damage to an L1 EVSE and the outlet it is plugged into because the 1-foot requirement means that the entire weight of the EVSE is hanging on the plug. Standard inexpensive 15 A home outlets were never designed to hold this weight. The unsupported weight causes the plug to loosen, the contact to get worse, and then possibly overheating and a fire. So I ignored this 1-foot requirement and assumed I would always plug into a GFCI outlet, and that I would always make sure the EVSE circuit was not in a puddle or under water (which it couldn't be because it is in the car!).

My approach was to simply build all of the EVSE safety circuitry into the car and then just connect that to a longer 120 V retractable cord coming out to the house. We even demonstrated this on a Nissan Leaf as shown in **Figure 8.8**. I was able to build all of the EVSE circuitry into a small box with its own pins coming out the back, so that it could plug into the J1772 connector and the whole thing still remain inside the car's charging port. My box is plugged into the J1772 port on the right and the unused Level 3 dc charge port is on the left. Below my box you can see the standard 120 V retractable plug ready to be pulled out up to 25 feet from the spool and connected to any available outlet. Since my box only plugs in to the J1772 socket, it could be unplugged at any time when using any other L1 or L2 charging option.

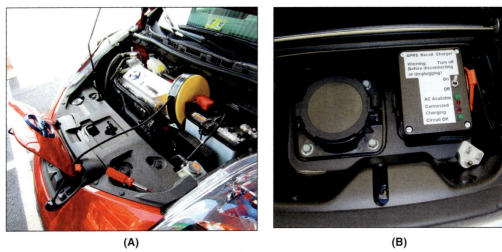

Figure 8.8 — A convenient hack puts a retractable cord in the car for easy plug-in charging anywhere (A). In this Nissan Leaf, the EVSE charging box plugs into the J1772 port on the right inside the charging port, with the unused Level 3 port on the left (B). It can be unplugged at any time if a different charging cord is used.

It should be noted that the retractable cords typically available from home centers are only rated for 10 A. If you apply the same NEC recommendation to derate any device to 80% when used for long periods, then you should use this cord at no more than 8 A. But after disassembling the retractable spool hardware and seeing the plastic slip rings and rivet-on-plastic connections, I decided the risk of having this inside the car even at only 8 A was just not worth it.

Spool Cautions

When using any kind of power cord on a spool, it is imperative to always unspool the entire length of cord even if only a few feet are needed. The current ratings of wire always assumes the wire is in free air so that any heat can be dissipated. I have seen one of those plastic spools for a 100 foot extension cord become a solid mass of melted rubber when a heavy duty load was drawn continuously through the cord wound on the spool. So if this retractable cord idea is implemented, it must always be used with the cord fully out of the spool.

EV Conversions — Build your own Electric Car!

Adding Instrumentation

Upon getting my first salvage Prius, the first thing I noticed was the complete lack of instrumentation on what was actually going on in the hybrid system. The display does show dotted lines showing the movement of power between the gas engine, battery, and two motor generators, but there is no indication of the magnitude. To be able to see what was actually going into and out of the battery, I added a voltmeter and ammeter to the high-voltage battery, along with some other useful gauges and indicators as shown in **Figure 8.9**.

In this photo, I have not yet changed the meter scales. The left-hand meter measures 200 – 260 V dc on the top scale, and 0 – 15 V on the bottom scale (switched by pushbuttons on the dash). The right-hand meter measures –100 to +200 A current. On the right is a conventional vacuum gauge so I can see when the gas engine is spinning (even if not providing power), and on the left is a conventional tachometer. Sometimes the Prius just spins the gas engine as a mechanical load when it has excess regenerative braking or battery power to keep the charge within bounds. A small 8-conductor Cat5 cable connects to the sensors in the back battery compartment.

Figure 8.9 — Added gauges and indicators on the Prius dashboard to better monitor the hybrid action and see the energy flow. The scales on the two meters in the center have not yet been changed in this photo. The meter on the left reads 200 - 260 and 0 - 15 V (using a pushbutton to switch), and the one on the right reads –100 to + 200 A current.

The Prius Hack (Then)

Back in 2007, when I began my recent renewed interest in electric cars, the easiest path to electrification was just to add batteries to a Prius hybrid as shown in **Figure 8.10**, to increase the electric miles available. Most people are surprised to learn that the all-electric range of a typical hybrid is only a mile or so. Although the battery is more than 200 V, it has only about the same capacity (1.5 kWh) as two golf cart batteries. In a hybrid, the battery is not intended to go any real distance in EV mode, but to provide propulsion power and torque in place of, or in addition to, the gas engine at times when the engine would not be efficient — crawling along at low speed or when nearly coasting at high speed, for example.

But since the Prius could run on its electric motors, a significant aftermarket developed for the DIYers, and numerous outfits sold conversion kits to add the batteries and to hack the CAN (Controller Area Network) bus for the multiple computers in the car to fool it into running mostly on battery power. Even with the modifications, the range in EV mode was about 50 miles or less, and you didn't have full power for maximum acceleration unless the engine was running. The complexity was in the software to hack and fool the Prius system, and fighting software

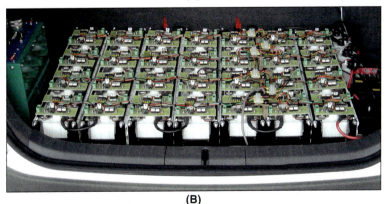

Figure 8.10 — The original 1.5-mile Prius battery (A). A typical 50-mile EV conversion for Prius back in the 2008 timeframe added batteries for more range (B). Quite a bit of information on plug-in hybrid conversions is available from the Electric Auto Association's web page at http://www.eaa-phev.org/wiki/Plug-In_Hybrids.

and computers in cars was not my cup of tea.

When the modern EVs came out starting in 2008, these additional battery kits declined in popularity, and the last surviving one used a simpler approach. It used the added batteries to simply provide a boost to the normal Prius operation. By adding batteries at lower voltage (48 V) and an inverter rated at several kW, the energy from the batteries could be paralleled into the Prius high-voltage electrical drive system so the Prius would find its battery well charged. It would operate normally but use more of the electricity than gas. This approach still required significant software hacks to convince the Prius to use this energy.

The Prius Hack (Now)

Used Priuses (Generation 2 starting in 2004) are more than 14 years old, and those that have traveled beyond 200,000 miles on the original battery can be had at nearly scrap prices. The idea of modifying one of these inexpensive cars for local battery travel could appeal to the DIY hacker again. The easiest modification for a DIYer who didn't want to hack the Prius computers was to simply add more batteries in parallel to the original and add a switch to disconnect the fuel injectors to the engine. Upon loss of gas flowing to the injectors, the Prius computers would panic and display all kinds of error codes, but they would still let you drive entirely on electric power (in emergency mode) without all the normal restrictions to protect the battery. In this mode, with the additional battery capacity the car could run at up to 50 MPH and keep going as long as your added battery arrangement lasted.

The problem with this hack was that when you stopped, the Prius computers were still convinced the car was dead and would not allow the car to restart with all the error codes. This was easy to clear by simply disconnecting the 12 V battery for a few seconds to reboot everything for the next drive. The only downside to disconnecting the battery is losing the radio preset channels and other user settings (if any). Two switches and lots of batteries could let you drive your Prius all electric if you were willing to put up with that hassle.

Today there are thousands of these cars out there for the asking, and there is also a much larger supply of salvage batteries available from the 10 years that EVs have been on the road. My three salvage Prius have been reliable and have never been to the dealer. As of 2018, they were 13 and 14 years old with 220, 180 and 100 thousand miles on them (though one had to have another battery at 180,000 miles at a cost of about $800 from salvage).

Convert Your Own EV Without Any Computers

Another way to have a nice low cost, RF-interference-quiet electric car is to build your own. Not only will it be quiet (while parked), but it will have thousands of watts of available power for your dream ARRL Field Day operation.

EV conversion kits are available for almost any old car. Conversion kits are in the range of $6000 plus battery, and they can use either an ac or dc motor. At the high end, Jaguar recently started offering EV conversions for their classic E-Type from the 1960s and 70s. If you don't already have an E-Type Jaguar for conversion, they also offer the Jaguar E-Type Zero shown in **Figure 8.11**.

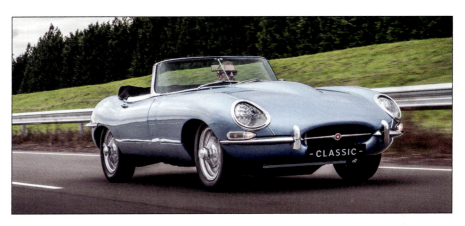

Figure 8.11 — The Jaguar E-Type Zero marries the beautiful lines of the classic Jaguar E-Type from the 1960s and 70s, fully restored with a modern plug-in electric drivetrain. You may have seen the photos of Prince Harry driving off to his honeymoon in his EV modified 1968 E-type Jaguar. (Photos courtesy Jaguar)

The only part unique to any model is the transmission adapter plate (see **Figure 8.12**). If they don't have a particular plate in stock for your favorite car, just trace around the transmission bell housing on a piece of paper with a pencil and they will manufacture one.

The dc motor with brushes has a simpler controller, and when all else fails, you can just clip a 12 V battery to the motor with jumper cables and crawl the car around your yard as the project develops. The only disadvantage to dc motors is the lack of regenerative braking. Of course the dc motor makes a perfect generator for this purpose but the load/lag of the physical angle setting of the brushes is important in a dc machine, and the angle for the best propulsion is not the optimum placement for generation. As a result, drawing power from the motor for regenerative braking causes significant destructive arcing of the brushes, which will quickly wear out the brushes and commutator. On the other hand, the ac controllers are more complex because they must generate the rotating field waveforms, but they do have the advantage of simple diode regenerative braking, which is important for overall EV efficiency.

What attracts me is the ultimate simplicity of such EV conversions. No computers, no downloads, no software, no drivers, no complexity at all. Just

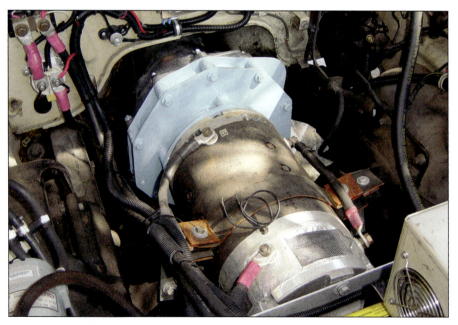

Figure 8.12 — Adding an electric motor to almost any car requires an appropriate transmission adapter plate. (Photo courtesy Leonard G. at English WikiPedia)

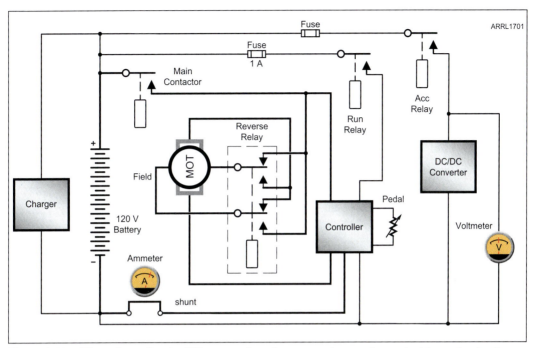

Figure 8.13 — The schematic of a DIY conversion of a gas engine car to an electric car is simple. The heavier lines indicate 100 A circuits.

a two-terminal battery, a two-terminal dc electric motor, and a three-terminal shoe-box sized controller connected by two hookup wires to an accelerator potentiometer. Add a heavy-duty contactor and relay or two as shown in the schematic in **Figure 8.13** and you have a working electric car. This is something that I can maintain for the rest of my life.

After my youthful MGB sports car died 35 years ago, there has not been a modern car that I feel I can troubleshoot and fix without taking it to the dealer. We are more and more dependent on proprietary test equipment, proprietary software, and special tools at the dealer. Even if we could fix it, the onboard computer still might not allow the car to run without some kind of secret computer reset using equipment available only to dealers. And this dealer dependency will only get worse as cars become more dependent on computers.

So I say, keep your eye open for that classic car you have always wanted. When you find it, buy it, add a $6,000 conversion kit and maybe $2,000 worth of batteries (which can even be lead-acid if you want to really keep it cheap). That will give you a reliable, short-range EV with a classic appearance that you can maintain yourself for the rest of your life.

My EV Conversions

What got me interested in this was finding an ideal, pristine 1968 MGB, garage-kept, fully repainted for only $800 without engine. I even found some running ones for less than $3,000. My goal was not to soup it up to a speedster or give it long range (nothing like a modern EV), but wanted just to be able to drive locally around town with the top down on nice days and tool back and forth on local errands with a big EV grin on my face. And I wanted to be able to fix it and maintain it for the rest of my life.

Also, prior to 2017, cars in my state that were more than 20 years old could get historic tags and be exempt from all modern safety and emissions inspections if they were used only for show and not routinely on the road. Unfortunately, too many people were doing this and then using the cars every day for commuting, so the state changed the law. Now, even historic vehicles have to meet all modern safety and emissions requirements. I got mine registered one week before the new law took effect so that I can continue to easily maintain the car without new inspections every two years. Check out applicable laws in your area.

But then I saw an already-converted-to-electric 1995 Honda Civic for sale with batteries for half the price of a conversion kit. I figured I would buy the Civic, drive it around for a while, get familiar with it, and when I had time, take the motor, controller and batteries out and just move them to the MGB with a new MGB adapter plate. But then entropy set in, and it was easier just to drive the Civic as-is and put off the big project of rebuilding it into the MGB.

Of course, the whole idea of the conversion was to have a unique, one-of-a-kind vehicle — or else, why do it? So my idea then evolved to convert the 1995 Honda Civic coupe to a woodie pickup for my weekly runs to the home center, as sketched in **Figure 8.14**. I'd remove the rear window and trunk and build in the wooden bed all the way to the back of the front seat where there would be a vertical window like a pickup truck.

The real reason for the pickup truck type bed was the ability to then make the bed tonneau cover from a standard 3.3 × 5.4-foot 300 W solar panel. That, plus some flexible panels on the hood and roof, would sum to over 500 W and give me about 10 miles of free solar mileage a day when parked in the sun. I have to retire first to be able to finish this project, my last EV. As noted, it will be my last because I can maintain it with a voltmeter for the rest of my life, and there are no computers in the car anywhere (other than the APRS radio)!

Figure 8.14 — To make the DIY EV more interesting, my retirement project will turn a Honda Civic into a *Truck-e* with full-size solar panel tonneau cover.

9 Conventional Backup and Emergency Power

In the Chapter 3 discussion on solar grid storage, we went to great lengths to convey that batteries have nothing to do with the recent rise in the highly economical use of solar for the home. With access to the grid, batteries for solar storage — and their significant cost and lifelong maintenance and periodic replacements — are simply not needed, nor are they economical.

When discussing solar with newcomers, the question always arises, "But what about when the grid goes down?" The answer is very simple. "Do whatever you do now." Adding grid-tied solar as a source of *economical, lower cost, emissions-free* power does not change anything with respect to what you do when the grid goes down at your house.

What you do when the grid goes down depends entirely on your unique and individual situation. Where I live in Maryland, our power company provides about 99.96% reliability, which means on average we lose power only about four hours a year. How much do I want to pay to replace this four hours a year, or less than $1 worth of power? Of course you may live in an area where power outages are more frequent or longer in duration, and may occur at times during the year when power is necessary to keep the house from freezing.

Whole House Emergency Battery Backup System

When you have no power at all, and need to keep warm, or keep the well pump running, or keep the freezer cold, then price might not be a concern. One solution is a whole house battery system. There was an excellent article on the subject in the May 2011 issue of *QST*. Jim Talens, N3JT, detailed his 12 kWh battery system and automatic switch-over inverter charged from a generator or two modest solar panels as shown in **Figure 9.1**

Figure 9.1 — Jim Talens, N3JT, stands by the solar panels that power his whole house battery backup system detailed in the May 2011 issue of *QST*.

He sized his batteries at 12 kWh to provide about 600 W for up to 20 hours to fully operate his ham radio equipment during major emergencies such as he experienced with Hurricane Isabel in 2003. When he built this system in 2011, solar panels cost about $5 per watt. So his modest 330 W of solar panels are small for long-term power outages, since they can only replenish about 1.2 kWh per day (about 10% of the capacity of his batteries). His system makes up for that with an auto-start 6500 W generator that can run the whole house and charge the batteries as long as gasoline is available, as shown in **Figure 9.2**

The overall cost for this system was on the order of $10,000, less some significant tax incentives at the time. Although solar panels are much less expensive today, Jim says the cost of the batteries is actually higher now. Of course, as we are approaching a million electric vehicles on the road, it will

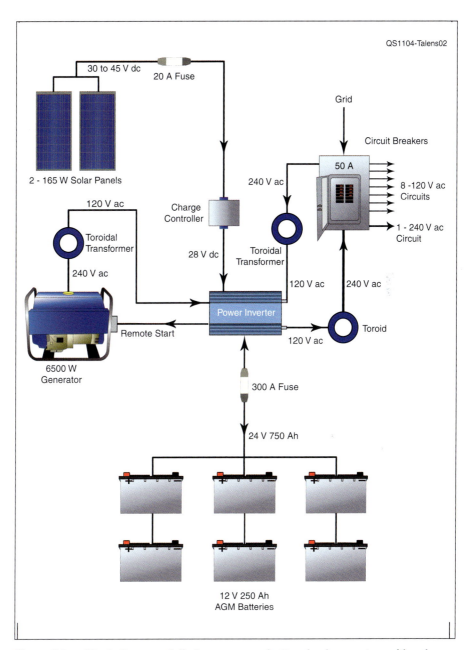

Figure 9.2 — Block diagram of Jim's emergency battery backup system with solar and gasoline generator charging and operation.

be easy to find very large batteries for surplus prices. Also, in 2018 solar panels cost only 10% of what they did back then, and so a much larger array could be built for long-term operation during emergencies. Jim's inverter and battery system is shown in **Figure 9.3**.

Economic Considerations

Assuming an initial cost of $10,000 and needing fresh batteries every five years or so, whole-house battery backup is an expensive proposition. I am

Figure 9.3 — The batteries and inverter for N3JT's emergency battery backup system.

reminded of a well-off family that retired to their dream home, added solar, and included such a whole-house battery backup system. They were in a rural area, and so power outages of a day or more were not uncommon every year. After about five years, when the big week-long power outage finally came along, they were happy with their whole house backup system and just continued living normally… for about eight hours. Then the batteries were dead. After a call to the installer, they discovered that the batteries are only good for about five years before they have to be replaced. So much for whole house economical backup power…

So, after investing several paragraphs in the earlier chapters of this book describing how batteries are not part of the economics of a modern grid-tied, net-metered home solar system, it turns out that there can be a small place for them as part of a minimal backup system for those rare emergency grid outages. If your area does not suffer frequent outages, and you can operate your house for a while on minimal needs, then there are other ways to meet your energy needs when the grid is down. This chapter discusses the various means to provide backup emergency power.

Sizing Your Emergency Power Needs

The first thing to consider when planning a backup system is how much emergency power you really need, to what level of comfort, and for how long? Even if you have someone on a respirator that makes it a life/death need for emergency power, it is far more economical and reliable to have a special backup just for the respirator and not for the whole house. So again, backup power is a very personal and individual consideration.

Lighting

With modern LED bulbs, candles and propane lanterns for emergency lighting are simply obsolete. A single candle consumes about 50 W of carbon energy just to put out a feeble light. A propane or gas lantern consumes about 5,000 W of carbon energy to put out about 100 W equivalent of light. That same need can now be met with a 10 W LED as shown in **Figure 9.4**. A propane lantern is dependent on a continuing supply of fuel. On the other hand, a simple LED lantern or flashlight can be charged every day with a small solar panel and used every night forever.

LED bulbs are not just for emergencies — they offer economy in the home the rest of the year. My home has about 50 light bulbs. If all of them were incandescent and the kids were home, we'd need about 5,000 W to light them, and this is spread over five or ten separate 15 A circuit breakers

Figure 9.4 — It takes 50 times more energy to run a gas/propane lantern (A) than a battery operated LED lantern (B). The LED lantern can be operated from alkaline cells or from rechargeable batteries and charged every day from a small solar planet.

in the house distribution panel. With LEDs, these same 50 bulbs can *all* be lit at the same time and need less than 500 W total. Every LED bulb in the whole house could be wired to a single 15 A breaker for convenience of lighting them with backup power, though it will get awfully dark throughout the whole house if the one circuit breaker trips. For sizing the load, if we only use about 1/5 of the lights during an outage, we need only about 100 W capacity for lighting. The problem is how to get backup power distributed to them all. There are three legal methods.

First, you could simply have enough extension cords to run from your backup power source to lamps in the main rooms where you want to have emergency lighting.

Second, you could have a whole-house generator transfer switch installed by a licensed electrician. A variation on this is a special circuit breaker panel for your house that includes a mechanical interlock to manually switch the panel between the power grid and backup power.

Third, you could have the electrician wire all your lights to perhaps two circuits, and wire these circuits to two standard 120 V plugs that can then be plugged into a single 15 A outlet by the panel. When the grid goes down, just unplug from the panel and plug one or both plugs into an extension cord to a generator or other backup power source to restore whole-house lighting.

There is a fourth method that is illegal, and that entails just throwing the main breaker to off to disconnect from the grid, and then back feeding your generator or other backup power source into any nearby outlet. This is strictly illegal and cannot be recommended. Forgetting to turn off the main breaker can injure or kill a power company lineman working on your power lines, or it can burn out your generator when grid power is restored.

Refrigerator/Freezer

Another very important consideration during any extended outage is, of course, the refrigerator and freezer. A typical refrigerator or freezer is usually rated at about 1 kW or less. The interesting thing is that the running power is usually 250 W or less, but the higher rating is needed for the defrost cycle. Most refrigerators run an 800 W or so strip heater coil to defrost the freezer coils periodically, and it is this power that drives the 1 kW or more specification on the nameplate.

Unfortunately, the manufacturers do not give us control over the defrost cycle, and there is no easy way to turn it off. Fortunately, if the appliance is Energy Star rated, then it will most likely reset the defrost cycle timer each time power is lost. This feature makes sure that when 500,000 refrigerators that were involved in a big power outage all come back on at once, they also do not all come on demanding the full defrost power too.

Let's assume that the refrigerator will run on about 250 W and that the compressor is really only running less than half the time, so the long-term average is on the order of about 125 W average per appliance. You still need a power source that can provide at least 1.5 kW surge, because the compressor draws at least 10 times the average current for a fraction of a second each time it starts.

For LED lighting (about 100 W) and the refrigerator (about 250 W plus surge power), all you need is about 1500 W of emergency power to survive long-term power outages. Of course you may need to also run a well pump, sump pump, furnace blower or circulating pump, or other device. In that case, you will need to figure in those power requirements. There are several methods to generate backup power, but you will need to decide what is appropriate for your individual needs.

Backup Generator

A gas powered portable generator is the most economical source of stand-alone temporary emergency power. An efficient generator can provide about 4 kWh per gallon of gas. (At $3 a gallon, that's about 75 cents per kWh — compared to 10 cents per kWh for power from the utility.) The cost for a 1500 W generator is probably less than $400, plus $15 for a can of gas (5 gallons). Just have plenty of extension cords to get power into the house where needed. This is clearly not a bad solution as long as you can get gasoline and can tolerate the noise and emissions. (The generator *must* be run outdoors and away from the house, to avoid carbon monoxide poisoning.)

If the average power you need is about 500 W for 24 hours a day, then you would need about 3 gallons per day. But here is where efficiency comes in. A conventional generator is not going to be efficient at light loads. In fact, it will still consume gasoline even with no electrical load, since the engine has to spin the generator at exactly 3600 RPM to maintain the 60 Hz output even if there is no load. This is terribly inefficient when the refrigerator compressor cycles off, and you are not using any lights in the daytime. The generator engine still has to run at 3600 RPM to provide power for even the smallest of loads. So the generator actually consumes maybe four times the gasoline actually needed to meet the load requirements, due to all the time that full power is not being used. This is where you have an opportunity to make a smart generator investment, and not just get the cheapest one.

Inverter Generators

Inverter generators have revolutionized portable generator technology. They are much more efficient and run much more quietly because they do not have to spin always at 3600 (or 1800) RPM to maintain 60 Hz power, but these benefits come at a significantly greater initial purchase price. Several examples are shown in **Figure 9.5**. The 120 V or 240 V, 60 Hz power from these inverter generators is generated electronically by a dc-to-ac inverter. The generator can idle down to low RPM when the load is light, and then speed up as the load increases. Inverter generators are ideal for longer term power because they consume less fuel while loads are lighter. (For example, see the EU2000iA later in Figure 9.14.) Be sure to check the noise spec before purchase to make sure you are getting a very quiet model. There is nothing worse than being on emergency power and having to put up with the screaming noise of a generator engine!

Figure 9.5 — Inverter generators vary their speed depending on load since the 60 Hz ac is electronically generated from an inverter. They are available in a wide range of sizes from many manufacturers. Examples shown here are a portable 1000 W unit from Yamaha, a 2000 W unit from Champion, and a 7000 W unit from Honda that provides both 120 V and 240 V ac.

Other Considerations

I say that portable generators are a very economical source of *temporary* power because after about a day of any significant region-wide power outage you will probably have used up the gas on hand, and many gas stations cannot pump gas without electricity. Even though generators are 10 times worse than an automobile as far as toxic emissions are concerned (because they do not have modern emissions control technology such as a catalytic converter), we run them very rarely. However, rare usage brings about another problem.

In the last five years since I bought a big emergency backup generator, the power has *never* gone out longer than the time it takes me to get up off the couch, find a flashlight and think about getting around to going outside and digging out the generator and finding the gas and getting around to starting it. This year, since the generator is five years old and has never been used, I decided to crank it up in anticipation of a coming storm. It would not crank. I gave up.

Fortunately, we never lost power. But, because of the continuing rain, and the lesson learned about leaving a generator unused for years, I ended up putting a tent over it and working on it every night for a week before I finally got it to run. Yes, it is my fault for not taking care to have fresh gas and not using a stabilizing additive in the tank, and especially for not running it an hour or so every month for the last five years as any good homeowner would do.

But if the point is to reduce emissions, it is an anathema to me to run a gas generator for an hour every month *just-in-case*. Especially since such a portable engine without emissions controls is 10 times worse than an auto, making that one hour "test" per month the same as *10 days* of average commuting in a modern gas car. It is even worse than that because during warm-up, any engine is even worse than it is at steady state. Fortunately, with the rise of solar and hybrids and EVs, there are better and more reliable ways to generate power at home.

Co-Generation

Since more than 65% of the energy consumed in a gasoline generator is lost as waste heat, there is potential to use that waste heat in the winter to heat the house. This is called co-generation, and can bring the efficiency of such a generator up from maybe 18% as a generator of electricity only, toward 83% if all that waste heat can be captured and used for backup heat. For example, if your generator is 1500 W, then about 18% of the energy in the fuel, or about 5,000 BTU, enters the house as electricity. But that other 65% in the waste heat can represent about 18,000 BTU, which is more than three space heaters on high.

Recovering heat from the exhaust would make use of about 35% of the gasoline energy normally lost. Recovering heat from the air that cools the engine would make use of another 30%. The challenge would be to safely capture this waste heat without introducing poisonous carbon monoxide (CO) into the house, and I would not recommend attempting this.

In some commercial micro-grids, making use of the waste heat of a gas turbine generator can greatly improve efficiency, but only in the winter when the waste heat is useful. In the summer, when we need added electricity for air conditioning, there is no added benefit from capturing waste heat unless it is used to heat water for other purposes.

A Modest Battery for Grid-Out

In spite of the other ideas for short-term and long-term power when the grid is out covered in this chapter, it is nice to have a modest battery system to be able operate a ham radio station for a few hours, or to turn off the generator overnight and still be able to run the refrigerator and some lights until the next morning.

One simple solution is to add an inverter to your hybrid or EV as described in the next section (cost about $150). That needs the car in *ready* mode, and it ties the car to the house and leads to inconvenience during long power outages. So I do admit, it is nice to have to have a minimum battery system even for homes with grid-tie solar. I use two marine batteries (cost about $200) wired in parallel to drive a 1500 W inverter ($150), plus a common 12 V battery charger ($50) to charge them during the day. I calculated that my refrigerator needs about 250 W, but it only runs about 50% of the time for an average power need of about 125 W over the worst-case 16 hour winter night. This totals about 2 kWh, which equates to about two 12 V deep-cycle batteries. This DIY emergency battery system should cost under $500 and is a bargain compared to the typical $10,000 whole-house battery backup system or whole-house generator.

For typical outages of several hours, recharging the battery from the mains is the simplest way to go. In that case, consider getting a battery charger that is not constrained to 60 Hz ac. As noted in Chapter 2, there are now lots of sources of universal power from 100 to 240 V ac and up to 330 V dc. So this is where you need to be selective in finding a battery charger. Look for one that is very light weight compared to other chargers (does not have a 60 Hz transformer) and that it is likely to be rated for operation on 100 – 240 V ac. If this is the case, it likely uses modern switching power supply circuits to convert from the higher line voltage (120 V) down to the voltage needed to charge the battery. This means it can probably run on dc power directly from the solar panels, or from your hybrid or your EV battery as described in the next section.

Another solution, described later in this chapter, is to have a solar grid-tie inverter with a grid-down backup secure power outlet. In that case, you can just plug in any battery charger there and charge from the sun.

Hybrid or EV Power

As the electrification of transportation evolves, your hybrid or EV will be your most readily available and reliable source of backup power, as shown in **Figure 9.6**. The use of hybrids or EVs for backup power is a huge untapped resource (see **evadc.org/2012/10/31/using-an-ev-to-power-a-home/**).

The powertrain in every Prius or other hybrid, for example, contains a very efficient engine and at least a 50,000 W generator as shown in **Figure 9.7A**. Not only that, but the engine has extremely low emissions because it meets modern federal guidelines. It's reliable, because it is used almost every day for transportation — you know it will work when called upon. As discussed before, the toxic emissions from a car engine with a catalytic converter are far less than emissions from a small generator gas engine, and in a hybrid, the engine only runs when needed.

Although this 50 kW generator in every hybrid is enough to power an entire neighborhood, it can only do that when running wide-open. A more modest level might be about 10 kW. So far, the auto manufacturers have not

Figure 9.6 — Power for ARRL Field Day: 200 W of solar panels on the car roof; 300 W of solar panels on the trailer; a 1500 W, 60 Hz inverter that operates from 12 V; and a hybrid 10,000 W generator at 200 – 240 V dc. There's another inverter in the trailer.

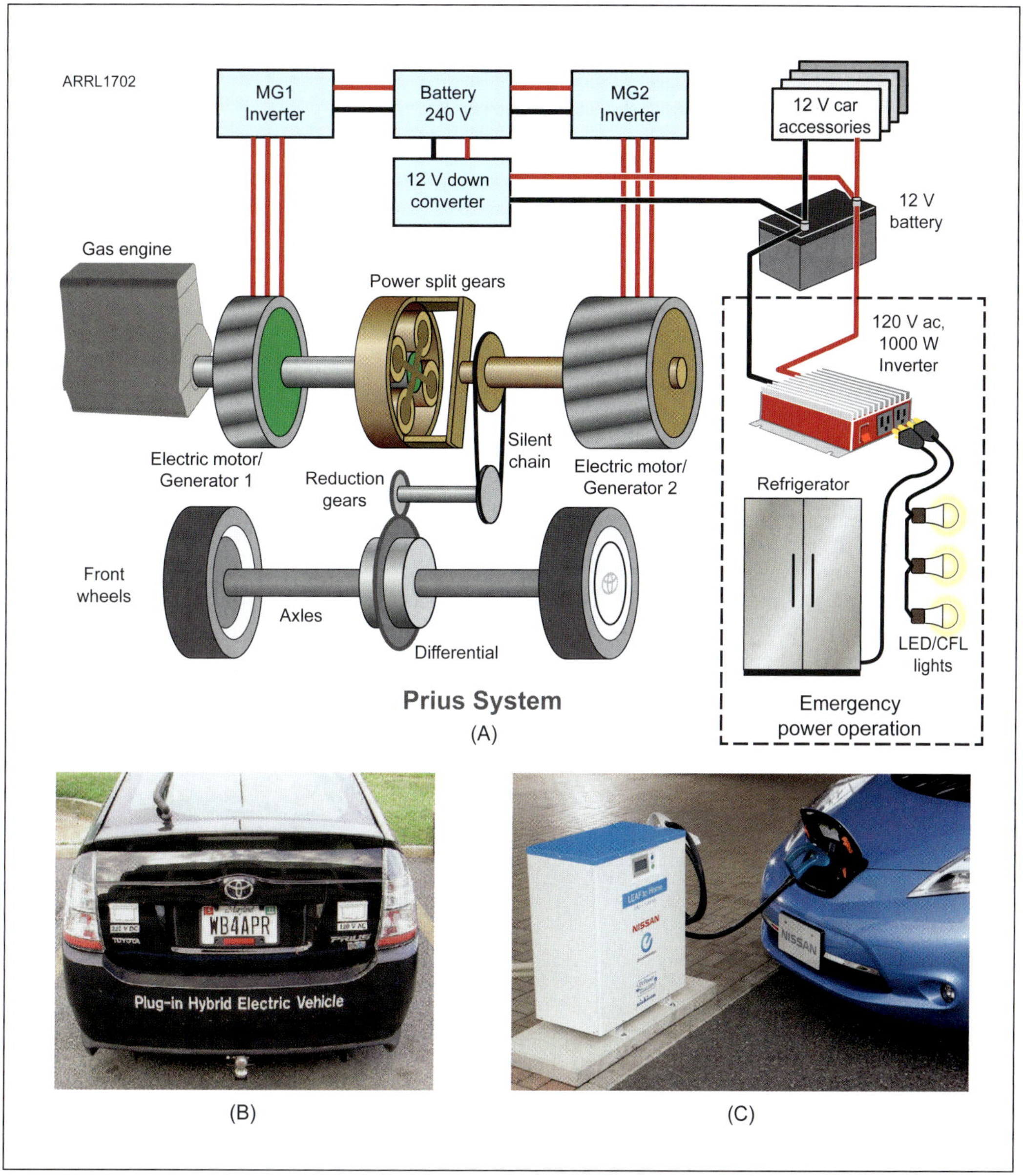

Figure 9.7 — A hybrid can provide tens of kilowatts at high voltage dc, or about 1000 W of 120 V, 60 Hz ac from the 12 V battery that the hybrid system maintains (A). At (B), my Prius has a 10 kW outlet for 220 V dc on the left, and a 1 kW outlet for 120 V ac on the right. Nissan has demonstrated the Leaf-to-Home system that can power a home from the Leaf EV's battery during a power outage (see www.nissan-global.com/en/zeroemission/approach/comprehensive/ecosystem/).

yet capitalized on this vast potential and developed a safe way to provide this power for use by the average car owner.

Both Toyota and Nissan have demonstrated systems to provide whole-house power from cars to test markets in Japan, but so far have not offered it in the US (Figure 9.7B). These home interfaces allow the house to draw power from the hybrid or EV car battery. If the battery is rated at, say, 32 kWh, and the 24 hour average draw of a home during emergency outage conditions averages around 200 W, then the EV battery can run the house about a week before the EV must be recharged from some other source of power (such as solar).

Plug-in-Hybrid Example

In the June 2018 issue of *QST*, Dave Treharne, N8HKU, described how he used his Ford Fusion Energi plug-in hybrid to power Amateur Radio operations for almost six hours during the 2017 solar eclipse operating event (see **Figure 9.8**). He ran the 120 V ac station items from the built-in inverter (such as the one **Figure 9.9**) and the 12 V items direct from the battery via Anderson Powerpole connectors as shown in **Figure 9.10**. He included the

Figure 9.8 — In the June 2018 issue of *QST*, David Treharne, N8HKU, wrote about his group's experiences while operating an ARRL Field Day station for six hours from a Ford Fusion Energi plug-in hybrid. At the end of the operation, they still had 62% of the battery capacity remaining.

Figure 9.9 — Built-in 120 V ac Field Day power is now found in many plug-in hybrids, EVs, and other vehicles, although the capacity is usually only 100 W or so.

Figure 9.10 — N8HKU's 12 V tap with Anderson Powerpole connectors for dc loads. The 12 V battery in most hybrids and EVs in the back, since it is not used for engine starting.

plot shown in **Figure 9.11** to show the total 2200 Wh drawn from the high-voltage battery down to a 62% state of charge without the gas engine ever starting. In fact, he could have operated maybe another six hours before the hybrid engine would have started to begin replacing the battery charge. When Dave stopped operating, he still had enough battery remaining to drive 12 miles home where he could have just plugged into his house to recharge the battery, and the hybrid gas engine would have never needed to start.

This example used a plug-in hybrid with a 5.5 kWh battery (20 mile EV range), so the engine never had to run at all. But for a conventional non-plug-in hybrid, the battery is much smaller, typically only 1 kWh in the Prius, for example. When I use hybrid power from my Prius (**Figure 9.12**), it likes to keep the high-voltage battery up near 80% state-of-charge, so during a five-hour event, it would have run the gas engine on and off periodically to maintain the battery state. Even using the engine periodically, the gas consumed per kWh is comparable to that of a good quality gas generator, with about a tenth of the noxious emissions.

When I use my 1500 W inverter connected to the Prius as shown in Figure 9.12, it is limited to a long-term average power of around 1 kW by the capacity

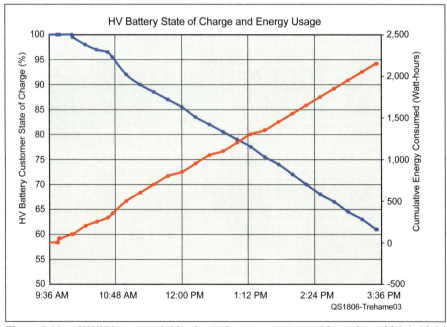

Figure 9.11 — N8HKU prepared this chart of energy consumed from the vehicle's high-voltage battery during Field Day operation versus the battery's state-of-charge over time, ending at 62% and 12 miles range for the drive home.

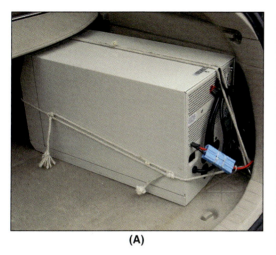

Figure 9.12 — Drawing 60 Hz power from the car's high-voltage battery via a modified 3 kW UPS supply connected to the 220 V battery (A). At (B), a typical 1500 W inverter connected to the car's 12 V battery system in the rear.

of the 12 V battery and dc/dc converter in the hybrid, and takes no advantage of the large high-voltage hybrid traction battery. On the other hand, it is possible (but not easy) to wire directly into the car's high-voltage battery to get power without having it first downconverted to 12 V. An aftermarket has arisen to sell converted high power uninterruptible power supplies (UPS) for the kind of input voltages that match the hybrid 200+ V batteries.

With about eight gallons of gas in the tank, and only drawing about the same 200 W overhead plus, say, 200 W average home power, the Prius can run the house under emergency minimum loads for about a week. This only works for hybrids, and not for normal gas cars, because the hybrid will only run the gasoline engine when it is needed to recharge the battery that is sourcing the power. The car just takes care of itself.

You can even leave it like this in the "ready" mode overnight and never have to go out in the rain or cold to turn the car on or off. Of course, if you do go out and turn off the car when power is not actually needed, you can save that 200 W overhead power and run for much longer. Although the 1500 W inverter can easily provide 1500 W from the 12 V battery, and instantaneous peaks maybe as high as 2000 W, it has been shown that the Prius only replenishes the small 12 V battery from the high voltage battery and engine at about an 800 W average rate from its dc/dc converter. So long term, the average power should not exceed about 800 W continuous. This is plenty for the average house under power-outage conditions where the average load is between about 200 and 500 W, and peak loads last less than a few minutes each.

Rather than hardwiring the 12 V inverter permanently in the car, the easiest method to draw 60 Hz ac power from the hybrid is to use an inexpensive inverter plugged into the cigarette lighter socket as shown in **Figure 9.13**. Such a simple inverter can provide up to about 120 W, enough to power more than 20 LED light bulbs at a time. If more power is needed, a larger inverter that clips onto the battery terminals and can be used with any car at any time is a good investment.

A Prius Week-Long Example

On an online Prius technical discussion group, Bob Wilson shared some significant testing he did when using his Prius to provide emergency power (see **hiwaay.net/~bzwilson/prius/priups.html**). His external 12 V-to-120 V ac inverter connected to the Prius battery was running at the maximum 1 kW that can be drawn from the 12 V battery system. It produced power at 4 kWh per gallon of gas, and **Figure 9.14** shows how that compares to a number of Honda portable generators of different sizes.

In this condition, the Prius gas engine is cycling on and off at about a 50% rate. The lower overall efficiency is because of the 200 W overhead power of all the other Prius static loads. If we can draw the power directly from the high-voltage battery, the efficiency can go up as the ratio of user load compared to the fixed overhead goes up.

In follow-up emails, Bob Wilson provided these additional comments on his testing not included on the above web page:

1) The maximum sustained draw on the 12 V system seems to be about 70 A. Above that sustained load, the voltage from the dc/dc converter cannot maintain the battery above 13 V. The car will operate 24×7 at that rate as long as it has gasoline for the engine. Testing was done with a resistance space heater at the 1 kW setting.

2) Undocumented on the web page, he ran a 1.5 kW pure sine wave inverter on a Gen-3 Prius. However the lower efficiency of the pure sine inverter meant the net power was slightly lower at ~850 W compared to a modified sine inverter.

3) This lower efficiency is not such a bad thing because the voltage drop through an extension cord is less for the pure sine inverter compared to the

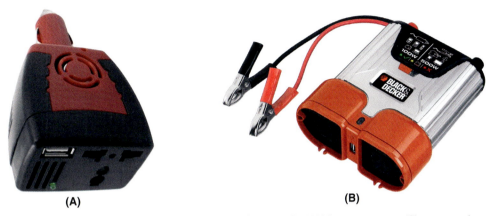

Figure 9.13 — There are lots of options for inverters using a car's 12 V battery system. They range from a 140 W unit plugged into the cigarette lighter (A) to a larger inverter clipped directly to the battery (B).

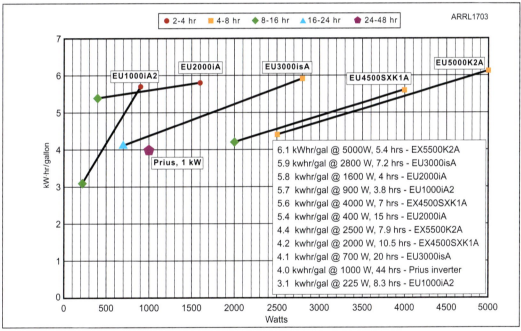

Figure 9.14 — Energy production in terms of kilowatt-hours (kWh) generated per gallon of gas consumed and run time on a full tank of gas for a number of Honda portable generators at various loads, compared to the Toyota Prius. The light-load and full-load consumption values are connected by lines. For example, the popular EU2000iA portable inverter generator produces 400 W at 5.4 kWh/gallon (light load) versus 1600 W at 5.8 kWh/gallon (full load). The EU4500XK1A, a larger, conventional generator, produces 2000 W at 4.2 kWh/gallon (light load) and 4000 W at 5.6 kWh/gallon (full load). Gas consumption for the Prius was comparable to the generators running at light load, providing 1000 W at 4 kWh/gallon. (Testing and data provided by Bob Wilson; seehiwaay.net/~bzwilson/prius/priups.html.)

losses for the quasi square waves of a modified sine inverter. The sharp edges of the modified sine treats the extension cord as a capacitor, giving greater peak currents and wire losses.

4) The advantage of the pure sine inverter is that it will always work safely and properly with any electrical appliance in the house because its output is identical to utility power.

5) The "surge" capacity rating on most inverters is not worth that much because it lasts less than 300 ms, or only about 20 ac cycles. A better solution is choosing over-capacity in the inverter and letting the battery provide up to about 10 seconds of extra power to handle spin up of motors or inrush loads.

6) One can add an inrush thermistor to handle inrush current into traditional power supplies. Oversizing an inverter is a much better approach because it eliminates the parasitic load of a thermistor.

7) After a couple of years, most 12 V batteries in hybrids are way down in capacity but that is never noticed by the owner because they don't see a peak load to crank the engine. A reduced capacity battery will limit how many seconds it can handle a peak overload.

8) Use a quality, 20 A rated extension cord. The cheaper 12 A extension cords should only be used at $80\% \times 12$ A = 9.6 A. The cost difference is not that great and you'll get decades of usage without having the expense and delay of replacing melted sockets and plugs.

Figure 9.15 shows a similar arrangement with a 1 kW inverter installed in a Chevy Volt. The typical cost of 12 V inverters is very low — about 10 W per dollar. So a good price for a 1500 W inverter is about $150. These are all "modified sine wave" inverters because they do not produce perfectly pure sine waves, but instead produce a 60 Hz "blocky" or "chunky" waveform. This provides all the power of a 60 Hz sine wave but is noisy, and there may be some electronics systems that do not operate properly with them. On the other hand, if you pay about twice as much, you can get a "pure sine wave" inverter that produces clean power indistinguishable from the power company. The only disadvantage is the cost, and they are usually just a tad bit bigger.

More Power Scotty!

(Apologies to anyone too young to remember this phrase from the 1960s TV series, *Star Trek*. Mr. Scott, the Chief Engineer, was always able to somehow come up with extra power to save the day.) There are lots of high-power uninterruptible power supplies in data centers, and a small number of them run on sixteen 12 V batteries. This is 192 V nominal, which is just fine to run from the Prius 208 V dc nominal battery. The installation in **Figure 9.16** by Doug Gaede shows his 6 kW UPS on the left, Because most of these

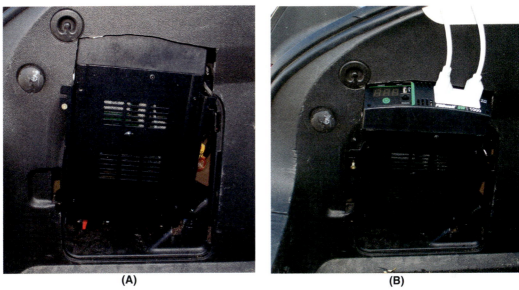

Figure 9.15 — A 1 kW pure sine inverter hacked into back of a Chevy Volt. The inverter fits in flush (A) and tilts out for use (B). The tilting cover panel and hinge are not shown.

Figure 9.16 — The 6 kW UPS on the left can wire directly to 200 V Prius battery and generates 208 V ac. The box on right is a 208-to-240 V ac split phase transformer to make the 208 V ac UPS output compatible with the requirements for whole-house power. (Courtesy Doug Gaede; www.priups.com/others/Doug/index.html)

UPS output at only 208 or 240 V, the box on the right is just a transformer to convert that to 240 V ac split phase for direct connection to the house. He says that any of the APC models SURT3000, SURTD3000, SURT5000, SURTD5000, SURT6000, or SURTD6000 will do (see **www.priups.com/ others/Doug/index.html**). Above 6000 W, they take 384 V dc input instead of the 192 V. He says "there are 2 rare models which will output 120/240 V split phase natively, but don't expect to get a cheap deal on eBay."

Doug reports that his system ran for 12 hours with moderate loading for 1/3 of that time and baseline loading for the rest of the time (two refrigerators, one freezer, and various minor loads). According to the gas pump the next day, it only used 1.6 gallons. That's about 0.13 gallons per hour, which puts it in the same ballpark as the 1 and 2 kW Honda or Yamaha portable inverter generators. At that rate, the Prius should run continuously for 2.5 to 3 days on one tank of gas, longer if he took some steps to conserve.

Powering from the high-voltage battery directly is more efficient and can draw much more power than going down to 12 V first. But closer analysis suggests that there might be a limit on how much power we can draw. Presumably, the Prius will only produce the full specification 50 kW to drive the motor and wheels at full throttle under maximum load under the control of the hybrid system when the throttle and road demand it. Many tests have shown during average driving that the typical peak power going into and out of the battery is around 20 kW.

When we tap into the 220 V system and draw power from the bus for external loads, the car still thinks it is sitting still and will probably not command the engine to run near this power level. What it will recognize is that the voltage of the high-voltage battery is going down, and so it will start the engine to make up the charge. No one seems to know what this rate of replacement officially is. But it is certainly a limit set to protect the battery, and is not the maximum power 50 kW by any means. Although the Prius has been shown to dump more than 100 A (20 kW) into the battery during braking, that is a short term process, and again, is a different algorithm than the Prius just deciding to use gas to make up for lower battery voltage. So how much power can be drawn and sustained from the hybrid system is still open for experimentation.

Excellent coverage of this topic was provided by Richard Factor, WA2IKL online at **www.priups.com/sitenav.htm** and his summary page at **www.priups.com/tests/summary.htm**. There he did sustained testing at 2.4 kW for a half hour and observed a 41% engine duty cycle of 3 minutes on and 4 minutes off. He provides another plot in **Figure 9.17** for tests of the Prius battery by itself without being connected to the car at 4 and 6 kW loads,

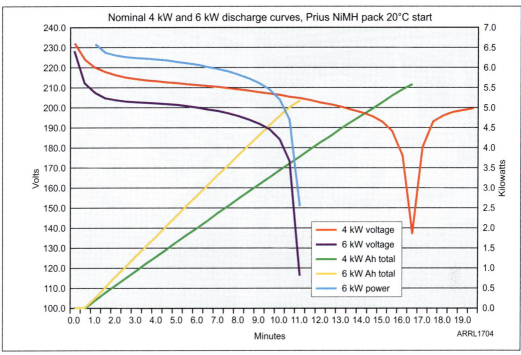

Figure 9.17 — A stand-alone Prius battery (only 6 AH capacity) discharged at 4 and 6 kW. (Courtesy Richard Factor, WA2IKL; www.priups.com)

and suggests a peak power limit of about 20 kW due to the 120 A fuse in the high-voltage battery. The plot shows about a 15 minute discharge at 4 kW.

Engine Running Considerations

Since the Prius computer strives to maintain its small battery between 80% full and 20% discharge, the engine will cycle much more frequently than a plug-in hybrid or EV. But this is no additional wear-and-tear because a hybrid does not use a gear-crunching starter motor. Engine starts and stops are as common as normal driving on every press and release of the accelerator. At these higher power levels, it is still doing significant deep cycles of the battery every few minutes. One possibility to reduce battery wear is to put the Prius in engine-maintenance mode (see the Prius manual) that will keep it idling continuously, but I do not know how long it will stay in this mode. Another idea might be to turn on the heater in the Prius because we know it will run the engine to provide heat even if the electrical load does not demand it. Hmmm, duct that heat into the house and get free heat too!

Richard, WA2IKL, also provides links to web pages for other DIY Prius backup power systems (**www.priups.com/others/index.html**). When the inverter is small and fits into the back of the car, it is nice to have around all the time for power anywhere. But when seriously providing power at higher power levels, some of these designs just provide a 220 V dc power connector that then runs to the inverter permanently mounted in the house. Even at 4 kW, this line only carries 20 A and can use #12 AWG wire to the house.

Richard also found a reference that Toyota's vehicle-to-home (V2H) converter offered only in Japan runs at about 3 kW. Presumably this is a design decision to match the electrical load of a typical Japanese house during power-out conditions and not an indication of the maximum that Toyota wanted to draw from it.

Hybrid Engine Mode

It should be noted that another owner of a plug-in hybrid (not a Prius) reported that his hybrid would not provide significant high-voltage battery-to-12 V circuit charge current while the car was in park. This makes some sense. Why would the computer think that a car sitting and doing nothing in park would need more than a few amps to run the radio and fan? This person had to chock his wheels and put the car in drive before it would provide full amperage to the 12 V battery system to meet the loads being drawn from it by the add-on inverter.

On the one hand, maybe chocking the car and putting it in drive is a clue as a way to get more charge current from the high-voltage battery available for either high- or low-voltage emergency power inverters. On the other hand, one would think that the very sophisticated computers in a hybrid would still not expect the car to be consuming very large amount of energy (kWs) if the wheels were not also spinning. Putting the car in chocks in drive, much less jacking up the wheels so they spin, verges on the insane and certainly is not safe. We hams should keep a list of hybrid models that will sustain external loads while in Park for future purchases. (See **aprs.org/ARRL-power.html** for updates.)

The Value of an EV During Power Outages

Many people think that the last thing of any value in a power outage would be a battery-only electric vehicle. But in fact, the most vulnerable mode of transportation during an extended outage is a gasoline car standing in line to get gas when all the gas stations have either run out of gas or don't have any electricity to pump it out of the ground (**Figure 9.18**). This is

Figure 9.18 — Surprisingly, gas cars are much more vulnerable than EVs during power outages when fuel supplies run short or gas station pumps are out. EVs can recharge anywhere there is power (such as solar, or an area not affected), and they don't wait in gas lines (A). They can also provide power for your home, as discussed earlier in this chapter. At (B), as part of the Toyota City Low Carbon Project in Japan, starting in 2011 Toyota demonstrated that a model home could be powered from a Prius hybrid via a Vehicle-to-Home (V2H) interface for power during outages.

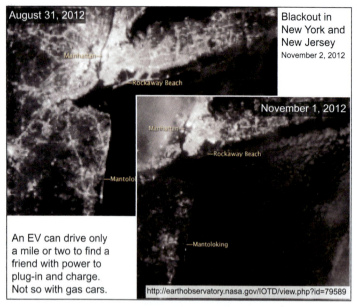

Figure 9.19 — Before and after NASA satellite images of New Jersey and Long Island showing the extent of power outages after Hurricane Sandy in 2012. There are still plenty of areas with power suitable for charging EVs. An EV can drive a mile or two to find a friend with power to plug in and charge the car. (From earthobservatory.nasa.gov/IOTD/view.php?id=79589.)

counterintuitive, but it is true. The horror stories of gas lines and gas shortages during the aftermath of Hurricane Sandy in 2015 are legion. And both Toyota and Nissan have announced ways to power a home from an EV for backup power, as mentioned earlier in this chapter (Figure 9.18B). So, the EV is valuable in several ways when the grid is out.

After Hurricane Sandy, there was still plenty of power available for the EV driver. As shown in the satellite images of New Jersey and Long Island in **Figure 9.19**, under normal circumstances there is lighting (power) everywhere. After Hurricane Sandy, satellite imagery shows that although about half of the utility customers were without power, the actual outages were somewhat scattered. That meant power was still available to half of all homes or half of all neighborhoods, and so the EV driver only needed to drive to an area where the lights were still on and ask to plug in to any available 120 V outlet at a friend's house. The cost is still the same 20 cents an hour, not much to ask of a Good Samaritan during an emergency. It beats sitting in gas lines for hours.

Home Solar Daytime Power Backup

Of course, anyone with home solar has thousands of watts of power available during the day, not only for use in the home, but also to charge up all the EVs and portable battery equipment during a power outage. And even when the sky is overcast, the typical array is producing about 10% of rated power. For a 10 kW solar system, this can be about 1,000 W on cloudy days. The problem is that the grid-tie system stops producing on those rare occasions when the grid goes out.

In the past, a grid-tie system could not produce *any* power when the grid is down for safety reasons. The good news is that more recent grid-tie inverters such as the Sunny Boy series from SMA include a 15 A backup power outlet built into the inverter as shown in **Figure 9.20**. This "secure power outlet" as SMA calls it has no battery backup, but does provide about 1500 W of emergency 120 V, 60 Hz ac power via that outlet when the grid goes down and there is still sun. That should be enough to charge any EV through its standard charge cord and is an excellent investment.

Grid-Down EV Charging

Richard Factor, WA2IKL, tried charging his EV from the secure outlet on his grid-tie inverter and found that the inverter would trip off as his 2012 Prius charger ramped up to the nominal 12 A charging current, just at the threshold of the solar supply. So he solved it by wiring a 12 V, 12 A

Figure 9.20 — The Sunny Boy series of grid-tie inverters from SMA also provide a backup secure 120 V power outlet to provide backup power while the grid is down and the sun is up. I installed this one at my church. Note the secure backup outlet at the right.

transformer in buck fashion that lowered the output voltage to 108 V, and that was enough to let the inverter continue to operate. Another simple solution is that some EVs such as the Prius Prime and Chevy Volt allow you to select an 8 A charge rate instead of the default 12 A, which would draw only 1 kW from the 15 A outlet and will not trip the secure outlet.

So to anyone thinking of investing in a home grid-tied solar system, be sure to get an inverter with this secure backup outlet. The added cost of this feature is insignificant compared to other models without it. The obvious problem is that you can only use this backup outlet during the day. At night if you still need power, you will have to use any of the other methods we have discussed for backup power, or just go to sleep.

Using Grid-Down Secure Power at Night

One thing to note is that the input of this SMA inverter, like all string inverters, can probably be any dc voltage from around 200 V to almost 600 V. This means its 120 V, 60 Hz "secure power" outlet can be used as a source of grid-down power even at night from almost any high-voltage dc source such as a hybrid or EV. This is the type of all-around universal dc input inverter we would all like to have for emergencies and backup. The secure outlet provides only 1500 W, but if you have a typical 6 kW to 9 kW solar array, you could have two or three of these SMA inverters, and thus have a total of 3000 to 4500 W of grid down power. In addition, when running the inverter input from, say, the 220 V dc from a Prius, the wire out to the car needs to carry only 7 A and can thus be almost any inexpensive #16 AWG extension cord while still delivering 1500 W at the secure outlet.

Brute Force Approach to Solar Backup Power

Another way to directly convert sunshine to 60 Hz home ac when the grid is down is to find a high-voltage dc power supply that is capable of producing 100 A or more at 12 V dc. Then just use this supply, driven by the high voltage dc of your solar arrays, to produce the 100 A at 12 V to power a typical 1000 W, 12 V dc-to-60 Hz ac inverter.

Interestingly enough, such a very high-amperage 13.8 V dc converter with high voltage dc input is found in every hybrid car. In most cars (including the Prius), it is integrated deep in the hybrid engine system and usually not separable as a separate box from the 50 kW engine drive inverter system. But in the Toyota Camry and Nissan Altima, it was a separate box easily reachable from the trunk area as shown in **Figures 9.21**. These can be had from any salvage yard, but last time I checked, the price was over a hundred dollars.

Figure 9.21 — The Camry Hybrid 13.8 V, 100 A converter is located behind the battery shown above left. It can make a great backup ham radio station power supply from any source of 200 – 250 V dc.

Batteries with Solar GT Inverters

As noted earlier, high-voltage-input backup inverters or UPSs are as rare as hen's teeth, but on the other hand, virtually every grid-tie string inverter is designed for any voltage from about 200 to 600 V dc input. So it is trivial to connect your hybrid or EV high voltage generator or battery directly to the input (via a high-voltage dc fuse) to provide an energy source. The solar inverter will adjust automatically because the maximum power point tracking algorithm (MPPT) will adjust the inverter to derive maximum power from the battery. This can provide emergency power in the case of the SMA inverter with backup secure power outlet, or it can be used to back feed the grid to sell power back to the utility.

But, alas, neither of these make practical sense under normal conditions. All you will get out of the big solar inverter with the secure power output when the grid is down is the same 1500 W you could get from the 12 V battery and a common 60 Hz inverter. And there is no sense to use the hybrid gas engine to drive the grid-tie inverter to sell power back to the utility when the grid is up, because the cost of gas is far more than the cost of electricity.

In Maryland where they pay $1.25 per kWh on peak summer demand days, you could do it and make a few dollars a day. The Prius can produce the power from gas like most generators at about five times the nominal utility cost, but on these peak solar days when they are paying 10 times the normal rate, then you are making about 10 cents per kWh profit over the cost of gas. That's not worth it, and you would be running an unnecessary gas engine, but it can be done.

    I only went through that analysis to better understand all the possibilities of interconnecting my power and energy systems to discover what makes sense and what doesn't. But, although there is no sense in doing this generation for now, in the future case covered in Chapter 10, when the metering and billing of the grid begins to buy and sell power at variable rates depending on instantaneous demand, then it is good to understand the interconnectivity of your power sources so that you can buy power when it is cheap and push it back when the grid is paying more for it.

10 High Voltage DC Emergency and Backup Power

Simple Solar Power for Electronics

As noted in Chapter 2, for the last few decades there has been a subtle revolution in consumer electronics power supplies. We older folk clearly remember when all wall transformer power supplies for portable electronics were much heavier and larger than they are now. The same goes for televisions, stereos and home theater receivers, media players, laptop computers, and just about any other modern electronic device. A cell phone charger now is as small as a golf ball, yet still plugs into the 120 V wall outlet.

What has happened is that the old iron-core 60 Hz power transformer is obsolete, as described in Chapter 2. It has been replaced by modern switching power supplies that use transistors and ICs instead of the bulky and heavy transformer. These modern power supplies can run on dc just as well as ac — exactly what the home solar power system and modern EV can produce.

Of all my electronics rated for 100 – 240 V ac, I have not found a single one that does not also work on similar dc voltage as well. This means that one of the simplest sources of power when the grid is down is to simply tap off at the 150 or 300 V dc point on any solar array to drive these modern universal supplies.

What I did was to split my 500 V dc arrays in half and install a pair of 10 A diodes and a cutout switch as shown in **Figure 10.1**. I can either operate the panels in full series to drive the grid-tie inverters normally for feeding the grid, or I can remove the pullout. This effectively wires the two half-arrays in parallel to give me about 250 V at double the current, about 15 A in full sun.

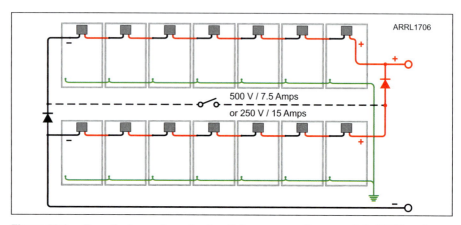

Figure 10.1 — Two diodes and a cutout switch can reconfigure an 8 A, 500 V series solar string to a 16 A, 250 V string for direct operation of almost all universal supply electronic systems.

Caution

But first, a word of caution. See the sidebar in Chapter 1 on dc safety ("High Voltage DC is Now Everywhere"). Never operate any device that has an on/off switch on the *input* side of the power supply on dc. The switch will arc over and fry the first time you try to turn it off. The dc electrons will just jump the gap in the switch and burn everything around it. This does not happen on ac since the electrons reverse direction 60 times a second and self-extinguish any arc in less than 16 milliseconds.

Fortunately, most portable universal power supplies and devices do not have an input power switch. They just plug in all the time, and the switch then can be lower quality on the low-voltage side of the circuit. More often than not, these days, it is just a push button to tell the transistors when to start and stop their power. When you plug in or unplug these devices, the small 1/60 second arc at the tip of the plug is not noticed. But if you do use one of these universal power supplies or devices on high voltage dc, be sure to unplug it quickly so the longer arc will extinguish quickly.

The High Voltage DC Snubber

Of course we switched high-voltage dc all the time in our old tube-type power supplies. All it takes is a capacitor and resistor across the switch to absorb the transient dc current and let the arc extinguish. But the choice of resistor and capacitor and the details of the switch contacts are important. Again, see the sidebar in Chapter 1 for more information.

The High Voltage Solar DC Conundrum

So, on the one hand, almost every modern electronics device is manufactured with a universal power supply that can run on dc, as shown in **Figure 10.2**. And a solar homeowner has thousands of watts of high-voltage dc solar power available during the day (as well as an EV in the driveway with a huge dc battery capacity). So it would seem that we have all we need for emergency backup power.

The problem is, almost everything that you really need in a serious emergency, such as your refrigerator, well pump, furnace, or air conditioner — almost everything that is non-electronic in your house — cannot run on

Figure 10.2 -- Most modern electronics have universal power inputs of 120 to 240 V ac. Typically, they can run on any dc input from 100 to 330 V dc as well. PC and monitor power supplies are shown on the left, with some laptop supplies on the right.

dc. They have motors and heavy transformers that must have 60 Hz ac. The things that *can* run on dc — the cell phone chargers, and laptop chargers, LED bulbs, and so on — take so little power as to be insignificant.

You could ask your solar installer to add a 120- to 330-V dc tap on your solar panel array as suggested in Figure 2.5 in Chapter 2 and wire it to an outlet labeled in big red lettering: *Universal Power Supplies Rated at 100 – 240 Volts DC Only*. However, about all you can do with all that power when the grid is down is to charge your cell phone, laptop, tablet, and other toys. You cannot run most of the essential 60 Hz home systems you actually need with it.

We are only at the beginning of these new energy concepts. Although for more than a century the power grid has consisted of poles and transformers and 60 Hz ac, things are changing. We can generate our own solar power at home (which starts as dc), and we can drive EVs that can store huge quantities of dc power or hybrids that can generate huge quantities of dc power, and most of our modern electronics can run on dc power.

Fortunately, some major appliances are beginning to follow. Many appliances that operate under variable loads can be more effectively controlled by operating the motors at variable speeds from an inverter controller. This is so much more efficient that more and more traditional appliances and large systems are beginning to also switch to variable speed motors. This includes some of the very latest air conditioners and heat pumps with variable speed compressors that internally run on dc controlled by transistors. We'll discuss that in more detail in later chapters.

So the trend lines all clearly point to a resurgence of dc in the home, though its presence will likely remain out of view and out of touch to the homeowner. It is likely decades from becoming an everyday reality since our entire National Electrical Code will have to be rewritten and everything rewired. For example, dc circuits must be in metal conduit and have special circuit breakers since a bad connection in the wiring will always burn with a plasma arc and destroy everything near it

Converting a 12-V-Input Inverter for Higher-Voltage DC Input

Many of the ideas in this book explore ways to use dc power at high voltage because there simply is not an inexpensive, mass-produced, 60 Hz ac inverter that can run from high voltage sources. So, this next topic is a possible DIY path to low-cost conversion from high-voltage dc to 60 Hz ac. The approach suggested is to take one of the readily available low-cost 12 or 24 V dc input 60 Hz inverters for backup power such as shown in **Figure 10.3** and modify it for high-voltage dc input. This might be easier than it might appear.

Figure 10.3 — A typical low-voltage pure sine-wave inverter internally upconverts the 12 V dc input at high frequency to 170 V dc, then chops it to a 60 Hz waveform for the 120 V ac output. It should be possible to directly feed this type of inverter internally from a solar array at 170 V dc.

Although this simple hack might be easy, there is still no commercial market for such high-voltage input because there is no consumer-safe connector or standards for high-voltage dc. But it should be easy to make such a conversion. Almost all inexpensive 12 V dc-to-120 V ac inverters these days no longer use 60 Hz inversion with a big, heavy 60-Hz-core transformer. Instead, since the input is already dc, they use typical high frequency dc/dc switching inverter circuits to first boost the 12 V dc to a fixed 170 V dc. Then the output section is simply a quad of high-voltage MOSFETs to pulse-width chop that 170 V dc into 60 Hz, 120 V ac with pulse-width modulation as shown in **Figure 10.4**. And they can do this with the 95% or so typical efficiency. Students at the Worcester Polytechnic Institute published a detailed paper on this technique, available online from **web.wpi.edu/Pubs/E-project/Available/E-project-042507-092653/ unrestricted/MQP_D_1_2.pdf**.

Since the inverter is working internally at 170 V dc prior to the modulation to ac, it should be easy to bring in an external 170 V dc supply directly from a solar array or EV battery tap to provide thousands of inexpensive watts to the ac inverter for emergency backup power. Five home solar panels in series should put out 150 to 180 V dc depending on load and provide over 1 kW of power. This would translate to 106 to 127 V ac even

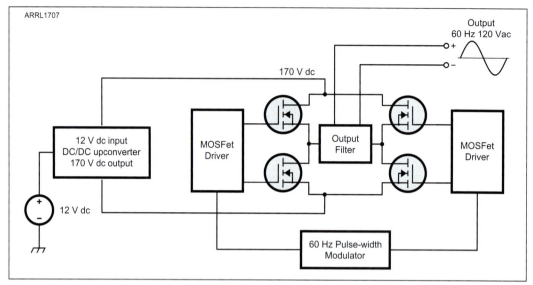

Figure 10.4 — Block diagram of a typical dc-to-60 Hz ac inverter. It should be possible to bring in external 170 V dc to the H-bridge MOSFET circuit, which then chops the dc to 60 Hz via a pulse-width modulator to get pure sine-wave 120 V ac.

without regulation. But these inverters also watch the output voltage and feedback to a pulse-width modulator (PWM) that regulates the output. So hopefully this will be an easy conversion. To keep the inverter circuits happy and operating, of course, it will still be necessary to be connected to a 12 V input source so it keeps running. It is just that the bulk of the power can come from an external source at the 170 V dc level.

While the Prius hybrid battery voltage is 208 to 240 V dc and might work depending on the range of regulation of the inverter, it is doubtful that higher voltages such as the 300 to 370 V for the Chevy Volt should be tried. This will exceed the voltage ratings of the inverter components with disastrous results. The good news is that now, in the 10th year of modern EVs, there are plenty of inexpensive salvage high-voltage batteries on the market. Just take out the number of cells that add to approximately 170 V dc, and there you have your home backup high-voltage battery at hobby prices.

Universal HV DC Power Connectors

One of the first issues with conveniently distributing high-voltage dc power is finding a safe connector that is inexpensive and readily available yet, cannot be confused with any other electrical connector. This connector must be unique to prevent anyone from plugging in an device that is not set up for "universal" high-voltage dc. The connector we came up with was a standard 15 A, 120 V ac power plug but with a *prevention device* to prevent inadvertently plugging in other existing plugs. The connector is shown in **Figure 10.5A**. Although we normally used these plugs at 120 V, they are rated for 600 V in most cases, as are most common electrical parts.

A standard two-prong 15 A, 120 V receptacle is shown, but it can also be a three-prong receptacle with ground. What makes it unique is a ³⁄₁₆ inch nylon pin fixed to the center of this receptacle in between the two power prongs. This blocks the use of any existing standard plugs. To make a mating plug, we use a standard replacement plug with the center drilled out to pass this blocking pin as shown in the photo.

Plugged into the outlet on the right side of the photo is a plug with the cover removed. The center pin protrudes into a hole drilled in an unused and isolated area of the hard plastic plug shell, between the two conductors. These connectors cost less than $2 each for both the plug and the receptacle.

Lightweight Power Cords

With wire loss proportional to the square of current (I^2R losses), the much lower current demand at 240 V than at 120 V (for example, high voltage dc from the Prius hybrid battery) can result in the same power delivery over smaller wire. In this case, AWG #18 zip cord (two conductor lamp cord) can easily carry a kilowatt or so of power over hundreds of feet because the loss in the cord is ¼ the loss at 120 V.

In Figure 10.5B, the original 25 feet of large orange extension

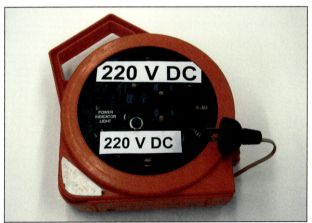

Figure 10.5 — My cheap high-voltage dc connector does not match anything else. A post-and-hole combination makes inexpensive 120 V connectors unique to block inadvertent use with 120 V ac equipment. This from my web page, www.aprs.org/FD-Prius-Power.html.

cord was removed from the convenient plastic spool, and replaced with about 100 feet of #18 AWG lamp cord. The current carrying capacity of #18 AWG wire in air is as high as 10 A, but I limit mine by fuses to only 5 A. Even at 5 A, this cord can still deliver over 1 kW at 220 V dc from the back of a Prius. Again, the high-voltage dc outlets are blocked from inadvertent use with standard 120 V ac devices by the post-and-hole blocking system. Only universal switching power supplies or other loads that can operate on the high-voltage dc are provided with these matching plugs.

Long Distance Power Distribution (SWER)

For much longer distances, power can be distributed using a Single Wire Earth Return or SWER system. Using a 140 W power inverter that plugs into an automobile cigarette lighter socket, a very long (but compact) spool of #22 AWG wire, and a few ground rods, a few hundred watts can be delivered over nearly a kilometer to power a typical emergency or portable Amateur Radio station as shown in **Figure 10.6**.

Although SWER distribution from the grid is not permitted in the National Electrical Code in the United States, the NEC does not apply to systems independent from the grid such as used here. The SWER technique is used in other countries to distribute hundreds of kilowatts over hundreds of miles using a single wire on poles.

In this example, the need was to deliver 100 W to my station more than a half mile away, up several hundred feet from the parking lot, and then up an 80-foot tower for operating during the annual Golden Packet Event (see

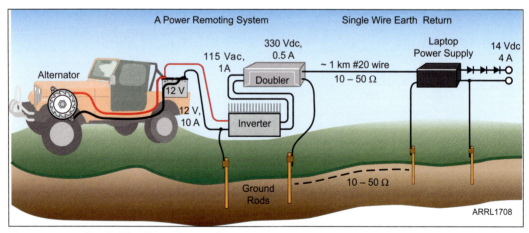

Figure 10.6 — Single Wire Earth Return (SWER) method of distributing power over great distances from a car.

aprs.org/at-golden-packet.html). My station is the middle station out of 15 stretching the entire length of the Appalachian Trail from Maine to Georgia to demonstrate communications via APRS packet radio. My station is shown in **Figure 10.7** operating from the top of the observation tower with only one end of the 3200-foot piece of #22 hookup wire connecting me to the Prius

(A)

(B)

(C)

Figure 10.7 — Bob Bruninga, WB4APR, and sherpas AJ Bruninga, WA4APR, and Bethanne Albert Bruninga, WE4APR, operating the Golden Packet Event from the top of the Governor Dick tower in Lebanon County, Pennsylvania. The equipment was powered by a Prius in the parking lot, more than half a mile away, via a single strand of #20 AWG hookup wire.

Figure 10.8 — This entire 3200-foot power distribution system fits behind the car seat in a laptop bag. Wire length can be adjusted shorter or longer as needed for each location.

parked down at the bottom of the hill in the public parking area. For this first use of SWER power, we had to power the 50 W APRS radio plus two laptops and a few handheld radios. Since we were not sure if it would work, the WA4APR and WE4APR sherpas shown also lugged up several pounds of gelled electrolyte batteries as well.

The complete SWER package is shown in **Figure 10.8**. The 3200-foot spool of wire is in the center. On the left are the 140 W cigarette lighter inverter and a box containing the two-capacitor/two-diode voltage doubler. This box has a high-voltage binding post on the top and four ground clips. To the right of the wire spool is another small box with another binding post and four more ground clips to house a standard 120 V ac duplex outlet into which the universal laptop supply (far right) and other devices at the remote location could be plugged.

The reason for the multiple ground clips is twofold. First, the more ground rods you use, the lower the ground resistance will be, and the shorter the portable rods can be for the same resistance. Second, having multiple parallel ground connections reduces the risk of shock while dabbling with any single one of them as long as one remains connected. It turned out that we did not need to use the remote ground rods because we could just clip to the steel cage of the observation tower, which was very well grounded for lightning protection.

Location, Location, Location

As you can see in the soil-resistance chart in **Table 10.1**, SWER distribution works best in damp soils and does not work at all in dry or rocky areas. The resistance is nearly constant with distance because the farther you go, the more ground volume is conducting the current. In good soils, the wire resistance can actually dominate the loss. For my 3200 feet of #22 AWG wire, the ground resistance might have been 50 Ω, but the wire resistance at 3200 feet is also about 50 Ω. In this case, the power delivered before the voltage dropped to half (240 V from Prius down to 120 V at load) could still be almost 300 W or so and plenty for any 100 – 240 V ac universal (and dc) power supplies. Although half the power (another 300 W is lost along the way, the power delivered is still more than adequate. In addition to the laptop power supplies plugged directly into the high-voltage dc, we had a universal dc supply providing 14 V to keep a small battery charged to provide peak 12 V, 10 A transmit currents.

Danger, Will Robinson!

(Apologies to anyone too young to remember this phrase, made famous by the robot in the 1960s TV series, *Lost in Space*.) Of course anything over 60 V or so is considered unsafe for handling. Take extreme care to protect the power line from all humans and animals that might cut through the wire insulation and make contact with the wire while standing in direct contact with the ground return path.

Table 10.1
Resistance of Various Soils

Type of Soil	Earth Resistance (Ohms)		
	3 Meter Ground Rod	6 Meter Ground Rod	10 Meter Ground Rod
Very moist soil, swamplike	10	5	3
Farming, loamy and clay soils	33	17	10
Sandy clay soil	50	25	15
Moist sandy soil	66	33	20
Concrete 1:5	—	—	—
Moist gravel	160	80	48
Dry sandy soil	330	165	100
Dry gravel	330	165	100
Stony soil	1000	500	300
Rock	—	—	—

Trail Lighting

Another use of SWER techniques is for long wire trail/driveway lighting. My brother-in-law has a 1200-foot driveway that winds through the woods. We used a transformer with a 48 V secondary to keep the voltage within the low-voltage spec of the National Electrical Code and ran a single string of #22 AWG wire through the woods to about eight well-spaced lights.

Each light was a modern dimmable LED light bulb inside a piece of PVC pipe, with one wire of the bulb going to a drop line to the SWER line, and the other dropping to ground and attached to a thin 2-foot ground rod. The 40 W equivalent lamps were operating at much less than normal brilliance, but he did not want bright lights anyway. It was just enough to mark the driveway at the curves. The LED bulbs in this kind of high-resistance, low-voltage application have to be dimmable, or they simply cycle on and off as their internal switching supplies try to start over and over again through the high resistance.

SWER Wire Considerations

It is trivial to string the wire, but some form of stress relief should be considered. In a woods environment, you know there will be sticks and limbs falling, and they will snap the line unless stress relief is considered. My approach was to make sure the supports were high enough to allow enough sag between each support, but still above head and arm height. That allowed enough excess length in the entire run so that a limb could fall and take one section all the way to the ground, and yet not break the entire length as it adjusted to the tension. The 120-to-48 V transformer was plugged into a regular outlet in my brother-in-law's shop so that it was not a permanent installation requiring an electrical permit. It provided isolation from the grid and was thus not prohibited by the NEC. (The NEC prohibits lines and lamps supported by trees.)

11 The Powerwall and Grid Battery Storage for Home

Although the number one problem in the adoption of renewable energy has been energy storage, as discussed in earlier chapters in this book, using batteries for daily local storage of energy generated from solar is simply not even close to cost effective in today's utility climate. With the exponential growth of solar in the past decade, the energy storage problem has been easily and inexpensively solved with energy storage in the grid. Once the owner is grid-tied and has a net meter, energy storage is essentially free. The homeowner can pump a full year's worth of energy into the grid, pushing the home electric meter backward, and then get it all back at any time during the year at no additional cost when the meter moves forward, counting the kilowatt hours of demand. This is a benefit not only to the solar homeowner, but also to everyone else in the neighborhood who is using the locally produced solar power during the day at no additional cost to the utility. But there is an upper limit to this balance.

When even a quarter of all utility customers eventually are producing all their own power during the day, plus sending excess to the grid to cover all that they will need at night, there won't be enough other customers to absorb all that daytime power in real time. Some type of large-scale storage will eventually be needed. This is one reason to get into solar now and be grandfathered for the next 20 years, and not wait! Because this current net-meter grid storage is essentially free, it would seem that the cost of battery storage will have to come down to practically nothing in order to compete.

The Cost of Electricity

There is a whole lot more to the typical 12 cent per kWh national average cost of electricity than customers see on their monthly bills. The instantaneous and widely varying costs in production, transmission, distribution, and use of electricity normally is not visible to the average utility customer. Taking all of these factors into account, the future of battery storage will see huge growth in the next decade. At this writing, there is much talk about the Tesla Battery GigaFactory that will produce big batteries at 1/8 the cost of what the initial batteries for EVs cost in 2007. There is also significant promise of home battery storage units such as the Tesla Powerwall (**Figure 11.1**) which is designed for such future home energy storage.

The key to understanding the implications of battery storage for solar energy is to understand electricity supply and demand and to understand the high variations of the price of electricity as mentioned earlier in Chapter 4 and shown in Figure 4.7. Although Figure 4.7 shows that hourly average pricing varies as much as 5 to 1, the actual minute-by-minute instantaneous price can see the 10:1, 20:1, and in extreme cases, 50:1 fluctuations in instantaneous wholesale electric pricing as the grid managers buy and sell electricity minute-by-minute throughout the day to meet the load. In many grids, this live data is available online. Although instantaneous pricing swings wildly, most consumers simply pay the fixed average price on their monthly bill of say 12 cents per kWh. This price is negotiated between the various public service commissions and the utilities to cover the average annual cost of electricity, plus the cost of transmission and distribution, billing, and profit.

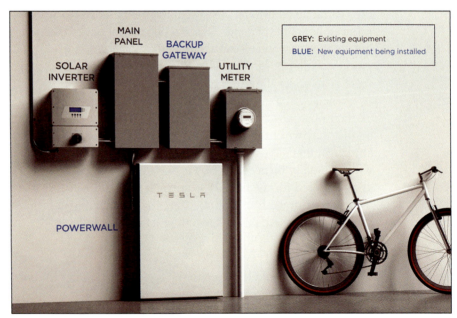

Figure 11.1 — A huge new disruptive spinoff of the electrification of transportation is the availability of big batteries such as the Tesla Powerwall for home storage. (Courtesy Tesla)

Off-Peak Electricity Cost

Historically for the last century, the least expensive electricity was at night when usage was low and power was being provided by base-load coal and nuclear plants that had to keep running anyway due to their very slow response times. They could not ramp-up and ramp-down easily, whereas the grid demand can change instantly. The typical overnight price was around 2 to 3 cents per kWh wholesale. But then during peak air-conditioning days, this price could jump to 20 cents, 50 cents and even as high as $1.25 per kWh or more as demand exceeded supply at any given instant.

Customers in the Maryland market, for example, could get proof of this variability on their bill as everyone was offered a "peak reward" of $1.25 per kWh for any electricity they *did not use* on a peak summer air-conditioning day. They were promised up to five such peak reward days a summer. At that price, a ham friend of mine would fire up his natural gas home backup generator and make $30 or so a day selling his power back to the utility. Of course all this inefficient carbon produced energy was exactly opposite of the intent of this incentive program, but then people will do what they are gonna do. But this $1.25 per kWh offer to all customers proved in writing how much electric prices can vary during the day, and how much the grid is willing to pay on a peak-demand hot summer day.

Day Will Be the New Night

But then came solar. Now in 2018 we have so much solar in some progressive areas, such as Hawaii and California, that produce so much daytime electricity that it affects the price dramatically. During a spring or fall day when the sun is maximum and air conditioning and heating are minimal, the supply of electricity can actually exceed the demand, and the wholesale price of electricity can even go negative. This means that the utility is not only willing to give away power for free but is actually *paying* large customers to take it. Remember this when you think of buying an electric car, and utilities will be willing at some times of the day to *pay you* to let them dump energy into your car battery.

Figure 11.2 shows this mid-day overproduction effect for a day in March 2017 in California. Notice how the wholesale price for electricity was negative from 7 AM to 3 PM on this particular day because of so much solar production and relatively modest grid load in the spring.

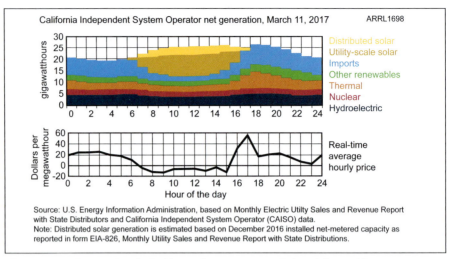

Figure 11.2 —**Demand satisfied by various sources of electricity and instantaneous cost of electric generation over the course of a spring day in California.** For more on this, see the US Energy Information Administration website at www.eia.gov/todayinenergy/detail.php?id=30692.

The Duck's Back Curve

There is also something else to learn from this situation. Not only does solar now help provide almost all the peak daytime energy in some areas on some days, it also creates a significant challenge for the utility when the sun begins to go down. The evening around 6 PM becomes the peak load time because many businesses are still open, and many consumers go home to turn on their air conditioning units and lights, and plug in their EVs to charge.

That can be seen along the top of the overall curve in Figure 11.2, with the peak around 1800 hours (6 PM). As shown in the figure, much of the power during the day is being provided by solar, from 8 AM to 4 PM. When the sun angles begin to wane at about 4 PM, moving away from south-facing arrays, solar power begins to drop off rapidly. At that point, the demand from other sources surges 10 times or more, and it does so at such a rapid rate that the utility is seriously challenged to meet that very rapid rise in demand from about 4 PM to 6 PM.

This problem was first documented by the California Independent System Operator (CAISO, **www.caiso.com**) in the now-famous plot shown in **Figure 11.3** that plots the net load on utility-generated electricity over the course of a typical spring day in California. In the years before the widespread installation of solar arrays, you could see a traditional smooth rise in demand for utility-

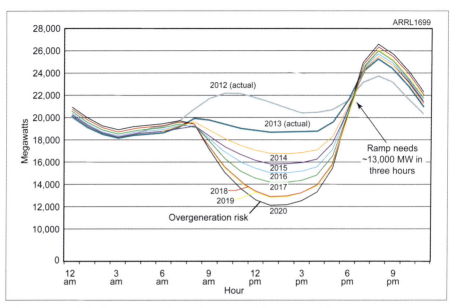

Figure 11.3 — The famous duck's back curve originally published by CAISO in 2013 that portends the future of solar power. For more information, see the National Renewable Energy Laboratory website at www.nrel.gov/news/program/2018/10-years-duck-curve.html and also the CAISO website at www.caiso.com/Documents/FlexibleResourcesHelpRenewables_FastFacts.pdf.

generated power from about 8 AM to a late afternoon peak, and then a slow decline toward midnight. By 2012, there was enough solar on the grid to start driving up the supply during the day and driving down the net demand for utility-generated power in the afternoon. That trend is shown in the curve shown for 2012 in Figure 11.3, where load on the utility dips during the day and rises sharply in the late afternoon/early evening hours. By 2013, the solar supply roughly equaled the demand on these spring/fall days, and that is when system operators began to predict future demand through the year 2020. The resulting curve begins to look like a duck's back and hence the name.

It is starting to be clear that in the future, *day will be the new night* as far as electricity cost and demand is concerned. With the growing supply of solar electricity leading to oversupply during the day, a new problem is developing. And that is the significant ramp-up of traditional generation (coal, nuclear, natural gas/propane) from 4 PM to 9 PM. Meanwhile, the residential consumer sees nothing of this wildly fluctuating supply and demand and just pays the nominal 12 cents per kWh. This cannot last as the regulatory bureaucracy and existing public service commission rules slowly begin to price electricity to the end customer at what it really costs in real-time to produce.

Battery Storage for the Afternoon

The earlier chapters in this book discussed how uneconomical batteries were for self-storage of solar power for people wanting to store all of their energy in batteries to be "off-grid" or independent of the grid. The estimated cost of adding self-storage instead of grid storage would typically triple the cost of the solar system over its several-decade lifespan.

Looking at the duck's back curve in Figure 11.3, however, there is a great opportunity for simply storing enough daytime energy to help the grid meet the 4 to 8 PM ramp-up. Of course the grid operators can easily anticipate this ramp-up and meet most of it, but the spike in pricing shown in Figure 11.2 just for the two hours between 4 and 6 PM shows that it is worth maybe 5 to 10 times the average cost of electricity to meet that surge.

Recognizing this very predictable but brief demand surge, battery storage for home customers starts to be attractive and cost-effective to pay off the cost of the battery — but *only if* the utilities, public service commission, politicians, and grid operators are willing to push that real-time pricing out to the individual customer's electric meter and actually pay the customer with battery storage what that battery electricity is worth at peak ramp times.

It's important to note that this peak ramp value means that a solar customer does not need enough battery capacity to store enough solar energy to run through the longest 12-hour winter night, but only needs to supply power for the two hours from 4 to 6 PM when he can sell it at the highest price back to the utility. This two-hour window reduces the battery investment to only 1/6 of what would be needed for full off-grid storage. It is this five times energy value during peak hours, in conjunction with the six times lower investment because of the limited time when power is needed, that now could make home battery storage practical and cost effective.

Tesla Powerwall

Some progressive states are recognizing this potential. Beginning in 2018, Maryland is providing 30% credits and rebates for customers that install home battery storage. Of course, Elon Musk, the Tesla pioneer, is aware of this. Not only has Tesla developed EVs for the new energy economy and merged with Solar City to build solar in homes all across America, but they have also invested billions in the Tesla Battery GigaFactory to meet this future market demand for batteries. At this writing (late 2018), a Tesla Powerwall battery (**Figure 11.4**) with 13.5 kWh usable energy rating is priced at $6,700 plus supporting hardware of $1,100 to integrate with the home, plus typical installation costs of $1,000 to $3,000 according to Tesla. That gives an overall investment of $8,800 to $10,800. Notice that this 13.5 kWh battery matches nicely the average home solar output of about 7 kW for the needed two hours when electricity prices spike.

To analyze this investment, let's take 13.5 kWh per day times 365 days for a total energy supply of about 5,000 kWh per year. At 12 cents per kWh, that gives an average customer electricity value of about $600, and it would take 15 to 18 years to amortize the cost at today's net-metering rates. But what if the utility were paying five times the average rate for those two peak hours every day? Then the payoff is $2,500 per year, and the battery has paid for itself in about four years. (Note that the Powerwall design calculator on Tesla's website seems to always recommend a minimum of two batteries.)

Then the only question becomes the battery life. As long as the battery lasts more than four years before replacement, then it's breakeven. Tesla's warranty is 10 years, giving an idea of expected battery life. Fortunately, battery and solar costs will continue to go down, and the value of storage to the grid in the evening ramp-up will only rise. So as soon as the public service commission, utilities, politicians, and bureaucracy catch up to this new reality of electricity supply and demand in the age of solar, and pass it along to the end consumer, then home storage will definitely be in our future.

Figure 11.4 — Tesla's Powerwall measures 45.3 × 29.7 × 6.1 inches and weighs 276 pounds. It includes a battery and inverter, with a rated usable capacity of 13.5 kWh. Up to 10 Powerwalls can be used in a single installation, and the units can be used indoors or outdoors. (Courtesy Tesla)

Peaking Batteries for Anyone

It should also be noted that this peak-demand battery storage and sell-back idea does not even need to be integrated with solar. This can benefit those customers with shade and without solar, because they can still charge up the battery with cheap daytime electricity from the grid and sell it back at a profit during the two-hour peak demand. This is the big picture for the future. Only time will tell how and when we get there.

Also remember that if you own an electric car, you already have a huge battery that you can use to charge on cheap electricity and sell back when the utility is paying the most. Notice that the battery in a Tesla Model S is at least six times larger than this nominal home battery need.

A Side Benefit: Battery Backup

Now that we have made the case for the home battery solar storage system to finally, possibly be economically viable in the overall grid to meet peak demand at a net benefit to the battery owner, we can finally realize a free side-benefit: battery backup power at no additional cost. This 13.5 kWh Powerwall battery not only would pay for itself by selling peak power back to the grid, but it can also provide all the power your home needs during an outage.

A single Powerwall can provide energy for several hours of normal use of everything in a home. An installation is scalable up to 10 Powerwalls if greater energy storage is needed.

For long-term emergency situations, running just LED lights, Energy Star refrigerator, and nominal electronics as described in Chapter 9, and drawing a 24 hour average of only say 200 W, a single Powerwall could provide sufficient power for almost three days. That can easily increase to a week if the solar system inverter has the small 15 A secure outlet that provides 120 V ac from the solar system during the day as discussed in Chapter 9, so that these essential loads need to run off the battery only at night.

Home Battery Around the Corner

To finish the battery question, notice that the home-storage battery system can be added at any time and is mostly an economic decision independent from home solar. So invest in solar based on the current value of solar in your area. At any time you can add a peak-load-sharing battery system when the specific local variables, pricing, and politics all align to make that a good investment too. Just be wary of adding an expensive battery for whole-house energy storage or battery backup just because of legacy thinking that equates solar with battery storage. That does not apply anywhere that a home has access to the grid. But it will surely apply as we approach a clean energy economy and the true value of solar and the true value of battery storage reaches the end consumer — you.

It will never be cost effective to go off-grid if you have grid access already. The grid is our local community's way of sharing resources for the good of all. As long as we view the grid as a beneficial community property for all of us, the future is very bright.

12 Life's Major Energy Milestones

It turns out that, on average, we are never more than a year or so away from having to make a major personal energy or lifestyle decision, and each of those events presents an opportunity to choose a cleaner solution. Almost everything we do demands energy, yet we take the source of that energy for granted and do not usually think of the long-term impacts and costs of our energy decisions. If we do our homework in advance, we can be ready to switch to clean energy at these milestones, while also achieving lifelong savings in energy costs and improvements in our environment.

On the other hand, if we do not consider our options in advance of these inevitable decisions, we usually end up making quick, convenient, short-term choices, and opting for the least-expensive immediate solution that may cost more in the long run and be worse for the environment. For example, a gasoline car bought today will be on the road for nearly two decades through multiple owners, and an oil or propane heating system repaired today will still be burning fossil fuel for another dozen years, when we could be using cleaner, cheaper energy.

Energy Decisions We Face

Figure 12.1 shows some of the major energy milestones and choices we may face. We can anticipate most of these, and with preparation can be ready to seek the best long-term path.

Energy Supplier

In a number of states with progressive energy policies, the utilities offer consumers a choice in energy supplier (see **Figure 12.2**). The choice is to continue to purchase electricity from the local grid mix, which can include as much as 40% coal in some areas, or to subscribe to utility solar or utility wind energy at only fractions of pennies additional cost. At Maryland's nominal 14 cents per kilowatt-hour (kWh) electric rate in 2016, the difference

Life's Major Energy Milestones

Every few years we face a major energy milestone.

Our decision will have a *decade of consequence*.

Are you prepared to make the right choice?

- Every 20 years: A new roof — why not solar?
- Every 6 years: A new car — why not a Plug-in?
- Every 8 years: A new water heater — why not a heatpump?
- Every 15 years: A new heating system — switch from gas or oil
- Every year: Your utility offers energy choice — choose wind
- Every 12 years: New job/move/retirement — all of the above

Figure 12.1 — On average, we face a major energy decision every few years.

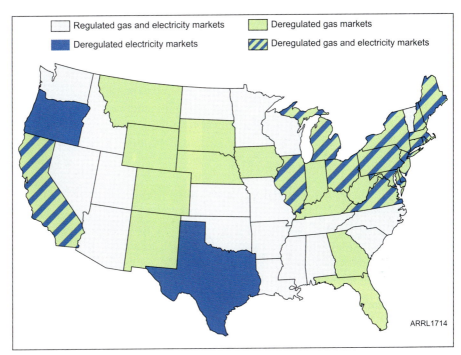

Figure 12.2 — As of 2018, many states offer energy choice. Choose wind or solar if available in your area. (For more information, see www.electricchoice.com/map-deregulated-energy-markets/.)

to switch our selection from standard grid mix power to 100% renewable wind power was about a half-cent per kWh. It's as easy to do as checking a box on your utility bill, and anyone in a state with energy choice policies and utility deregulation can do it.

Wind Power

Wind is a vital component of clean, renewable energy. As described in Chapter 1, virtually no homeowner has enough wind to make a system practical. Unless your hat blows off your head almost every day you go outdoors all year long, you don't have enough usable wind. I enjoyed the quote I once heard from an enlightened engineer, "Just because something spins in the wind does not mean it is generating any usable power under load."

On the other hand, wind is entirely viable on large-scale utility projects that are well underway, and is definitely something to support. In fact, investments in large-scale wind generation are exploding, and by 2016, large-scale wind was coming in below the cost of coal. In 2017, even oil- and gas-rich Texas saw the first day where 100% of utility energy demand was being met entirely from wind and solar. Although it was a unique day, and a Sunday when the overall load is less, it still demonstrated that the grid can now tolerate the variability of wind even up to 100% while also taking advantage of free energy fuel when it is there.

Signing up for wind power from your utility is an easy step toward a personal investment in our sustainable future.

Roof Replacement

Typical shingle roofs need care or replacing about every 20 to 25 years, and they may be our most important energy asset. Any decision to repair or replace a roof should fully consider the roof's potential for life-long solar energy production. In addition, once a solar array covers a roof, not only does it generate energy, but it also greatly extends the life of that roof since the shingles are no longer directly exposed to the elements.

Your roof is not the only place for solar panels. At my house and my church, we chose to install our panels on the ground for a variety of reasons. First was to avoid the shade on the roof, and second was simply to avoid the issue of the present condition of the roof and its unknown remaining life. A new roof would have cost more than the solar panels, and it seemed to be in good shape, even though it was 20 years old. We decided that it had plenty more years before it would need to be replaced. Ground mounting the array avoided the shade from trees and also gave us flexibility in solar panel array location and pointing direction, as well as flexibility in any future decisions about the roof.

An often overlooked value of solar panels is a degree of weather protection to an existing roof. The roof on my 90-year-old garage was damaged and leaking badly. It even had a 6-inch hole right in the middle being used by a possum to live in the attic (**Figure 12.3**). So rather than spend several thousand dollars for a new roof, I just slipped a few shingles over the possum hole and covered the entire roof with overlapping solar panels instead. Also shown in Figure 12.3 is a horizontal steel cable zipline tied to a tree to the right, then over the roof and hooked to my car bumper to pull it taut on the left. With a pulley and uphaul/downhaul line, my son on the ground sent up the solar panels to a spot where I could unhook and install them. Twelve panels at $120 each was about $1500, much less than installing a new roof while providing another 3 kW of free solar power.

You can see the rain-directing overlap of the panels in **Figure 12.4** with the 2×6 rails and long notch for the lower panels. That particular 2×6 was

Figure 12.3 — The patch over the possum hole and the ropes and cable used for lifting panels.

Figure 12.4 — Solar panels are mounted on 2×6 rails that are notched to provide a 1 inch overlap.

badly warped, so I had to cut a lot of saw kerfs to get it flat rather than get down off of the roof and go back to the store for another one. I just screwed the rails directly into the roof with deeply countersunk 4-inch screws and used homemade fasteners from under the panels so that there was no gap at all between them.

The upper row of panels was installed first so I could reach underneath to complete the four hidden fasteners on each panel. Then the lower panel was slid under the overlap to hold the top edges down and I could complete their lower fasteners from below the lower edge.

Without the vertical gaps seen in most installations, and with the horizontal overlap of panels, water will not reach the roof, and so I did no caulking or any kind of weatherproofing. The water just runs off. If I were really paranoid about water, I could have run a bead of caulk down the vertical joints, but they are raised slightly and so the only water that can get in there is so miniscule as to be nonexistent.

In **Figure 12.5A** you can see the deplorable condition of this structure with peeling paint. That is why the panels overhang the eaves — to keep water off the aging wooden siding, which will be repaired or replaced as a future project. See more photos, including the DIY hidden fasteners, on my website at **www.aprs.org/garage-array.html**.

Roof Access Trolley

Since this garage roof project took a while to figure out and develop and was more than two stories off the ground, I did take some time to develop a horizontal trolley system with a moving platform so I could zoom back and forth below the panels easily without having to go up and down ladders to move them every 4 feet while working.

The upper wheels visible in Figure 12.5B are 3-inch V-belt pulleys running along a 1-inch angle track. The lower wheels are perpendicular and are rubber wheels that run along the siding. For safety, I added a second 1-inch angle bracket above the 3-inch V-belt wheels so they could not possibly jump the track (not shown in this photo). The back of the garage needed many more repairs and siding as well, so this investment in the trolley system was worthwhile and allows me to scramble all over the three separate roof areas of this garage upper floor. This will be my permanent ham station location after I retire, and so access to every bit of roof area for antennas is a must. The trolley will also be used for replacing all the siding high up on this structure.

Shade Trees

Although we love shade trees and their shade has significant value in

Figure 12.5 — A trolley for rolling across the back of the two-story garage (A) not only gave me access to the solar panels on the rooftop, but also will provide easy access for the siding replacement to cover the deplorable peeling paint. At (B) you can see the pulleys used in the trolley. As described in the text, I added another rail on top of that so that the V-belt wheels don't jump the track and throw me off.

reducing air conditioning costs and improving quality of life, shade can also detract from our solar potential. In Chapter 15, I will show how replacing one tree with a solar array removes as much carbon from the atmosphere (by reducing the burning of fossil fuel for the same energy) as 36 full-size trees remove by photosynthesis! Further, solar arrays mounted on the roof with sufficient spacing to allow some air movement can also reduce summer solar heat gain just like a shade tree and can also reduce nighttime radiant thermal heat loss in the winter.

Community Solar

In areas with abundant trees, such as here in a mid-Atlantic state, only about 20% of homes have good solar exposure. That leaves most homeowners with little access to the solar boom without doing some tree removal. Similarly, apartment dwellers and condo owners in multi-unit buildings usually do not have access to the roof or the adjacent land on which to invest in their solar future.

In some states, the concept of *community solar* is taking root. Homeowners without good solar prospects can simply invest in solar panels in community solar projects where their panels will produce power, and that power will be subtracted from the homeowner's bill. In Maryland, signing up for community solar brings a guaranteed 5% savings off the normal utility rate with a commitment as short as 3 years or as long as 25 years. Subscribers can even carry the credit through to any other home in the same utility service area, or they can sell out if they have to move.

Community solar projects bring solar energy to everyone, not just the 20% with good solar exposure. Five percent savings may not seem like much, but a real value is in knowing that you are no longer participating in the generation of high carbon emissions from burning coal and getting a financial benefit from doing it.

Hot Water

Next to heating and air conditioning, water heating is the largest household energy use in the typical American home. On average, the typical water heater only lasts about eight or nine years, and if your heater is straight electric, it costs about 10 times its original purchase price in electric consumption over its life.

Fortunately, a modern high-efficiency heat-pump water heater that may cost three times as much initially will operate almost three times more efficiently and will save thousands of dollars in energy cost over its lifetime. In addition, if the heat pump water heater is in the basement where humidity is a problem, its operation serendipitously collects water on its condenser coil and acts as a dehumidifier at no added energy cost. Also, because it is electric, the heat pump is ready at any time to be powered from clean renewable electricity from solar or wind or other sources of renewable energy available from the utilities.

Lighting

In the past few years, the wide availability and declining prices of LED and CFL (compact fluorescent) light bulbs have offered dramatic energy savings compared to incandescent lighting. When faced with a burned out light bulb, do not replace it with the same horribly inefficient incandescent bulb (under 5%

efficient) developed over a century ago. The incandescent bulb may only cost $1 initially, but will cost more than $60 in energy over the next few years.

Replacing an incandescent bulb with an inexpensive LED bulb will only cost $10 in energy over the life of the bulb and result in one-fifth the carbon emissions needed to power it over the same time frame. A typical suburban home with about 50 light bulbs can save almost $3000 in energy costs over the life of these LED bulbs with this simple energy decision — a huge return on investment. A representative of our local utility told me that the change to efficient lighting has caused a 20% overall reduction in the entire local grid generation requirement over the last several years.

Although LED bulbs are touted to last 25 years or so, do not be surprised at failures. The LEDs themselves will last, but it is their cheap dc/dc switching circuitry that goes when there are damaging transients from local thunderstorms or electrical events. I have now retrieved at least six such damaged bulbs, and every one of them has good LEDs. The plastic ping-pong-ball globe is easy to cut off with a hack saw or even hot soldering iron, and I save these LED disks for other low voltage lighting projects (**Figure 12.6**).

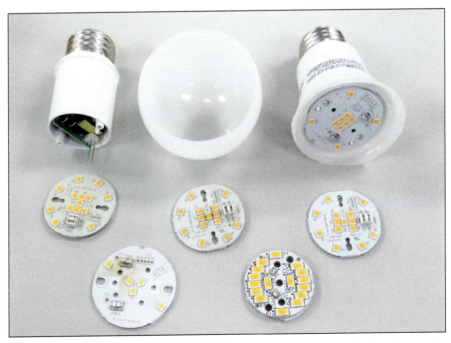

Figure 12.6 — The LEDs in damaged bulbs always seem to be good and make great lower-voltage lighting projects.

The LED chips themselves seem to take about 5 V, and of course must have a current limiting resistor. By calculating back from the original ac power rating of the bulb, it is easy to calculate the actual wattage for each LED. And from that you can estimate the current. The five LED disk in the lower left of the photo needs only 25 V to begin to light, with each LED being a 1 W chip. The disk on the lower right has 16 LEDs, and they work out to be four strings in parallel with each chip being a 0.5 W LED that lights around 20 V. The three disks along the upper row all use 14 LEDs in series, needing about 70 V to light the string. Choose an external series current-limiting resistor based on your available voltage and the needed current limit.

Heating, Ventilation, and Air Conditioning (HVAC)

In most climates, HVAC is the largest and most expensive home energy system and historically the most dependent on fossil fuel. These systems typically have an average life on the order of 15 years or so between major energy decisions. Historically we burned wood, then coal, then oil, and more recently natural gas and propane for heat. Of all these, the biggest financial opportunity for the reduction of cost and carbon emissions is to switch from oil or propane to a heat pump. When you think about it, it is the ultimate travesty to be burning a high-carbon, limited resource just to produce heat with no meaningful work being done.

When the price of heating oil rose above $2.80 a gallon in 2015, the cost to heat with oil actually exceeded the high cost of straight electric resistance heating (at the national average of 10 cents/kWh). The initial cost of a new heating system is big, but it is dwarfed by the lifetime energy costs required to operate it.

Although natural gas is considered a cleaner fossil fuel with half the carbon emissions of coal for the same heat, it is still burning fossil fuel into the atmosphere and contaminating ground water due to the rise of hydraulic fracking to extract it. Historically, the price of natural gas has been anything but stable and consistent. Despite the historically low prices in 2016 due to the rise of hydraulic fracking, the instability and controversy surrounding that extraction method make the long-term price vulnerable to change. In addition, the volatility of gas pricing is inherent in the fact that gas is not a commodity that can be easily stored. It has to be produced and used in real-time. This also makes pricing highly dependent on instantaneous supply and demand.

Heat Pump HVAC Units

The clean renewable HVAC alternative to these fossil fuels is the heat pump which is two to three times more efficient. Heat pumps run from electricity, so they can be powered from any source including renewable as the grid gets ever-cleaner over time. For example, between 2008 and 2012, the impact of coal on our air quality finally began to be widely recognized and was punctuated by the gray images of unbreathable air at the Beijing Olympics.

During this period, the use of coal driving the grid saw a 20% drop, resulting in a cleaner grid. During the same time, the growth of solar and wind energy have been phenomenal. Switching to a heat pump for home heating can be done by almost anyone. It does not need to be a whole-house installation in many cases. **Figure 12.7** shows the variety of DIY, easy-to-install units, including window-mounted or portable combined air conditioner/heat pump units and mini-split air conditioner/heat pumps. The mini-splits are gaining in popularity, as they can be installed anywhere and need only a finger-sized hole in the wall for the copper pipe connections to the outside unit. That eliminates installing expensive ductwork needed for a conventional forced-air HVAC system.

Portable AC Units as Heat Pumps

The only difference between an air conditioner and a heat pump is which refrigeration coil is inside and which one is outside. Thus, instead of putting away a portable air conditioner unit at the end of the summer season, consider using it as an effective heat pump in the winter in areas where temperatures are relatively mild. Just put the unit in an unheated basement,

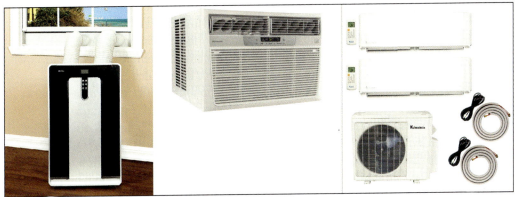

Figure 12.7 — The variety of easy-to-install, bidirectional air conditioner/heat pump units. Left-to-right: portable, window and mini-split units.

or even outside during most mild winter days, and then run the hot air hose to the inside of the house. This will pump heat from a cool basement into a room above, or from a protected or unheated space outside into a room where more warmth is desired. An example is provided in Chapter 13, showing how we provided additional space heating in a classroom at our church by using a portable air conditioner to pump waste heat from the kitchen via a hose through the wall into the classroom.

Never Buy or Repair Another Air Conditioner Unit Again

Another milestone occurs when it is time to repair or replace an air conditioner — whether it is a window unit, a whole-house unit, a portable unit, or a mini-split. If you are still heating with fossil fuels, the added cost of switching a new or replacement air conditioner unit to a bi-directional heat pump is only a small percentage, yet it can provide both heating and cooling from the same unit. Paying just a little more up front to make it a bi-directional heat pump can save thousands in your heating bills over the life of the unit, not to mention reducing your carbon footprint by not burning any fossil fuel during milder winter days when the heat pump is most efficient.

Mini-Split Coil Air Conditioner/Heat Pump Units

These units cost on the order of $1500 or so installed and are becoming very popular for adding highly efficient heating and cooling anywhere in the house without the need for ductwork or a window. The indoor coils of these units can be placed almost anywhere. They are connected to the companion outdoor unit, which houses the compressor and outdoor coil, by a convenient run of two finger-size copper pipes. Mini-splits can be placed in an inconspicuous location to retain the aesthetics of a old house, and there are even models that fit in the ceiling. They look not unlike a simple ceiling duct that is flush with the ceiling, and the bulk of the coils are recessed into the attic between the joists. One outdoor unit can serve two or more indoor units to make sure the conditioned air, either heating or cooling, gets to the right locations.

Solar Powered Heat Pumps

One of the problems with DIY solar is that the only way to get full retail value of all the solar available to you is to either use 100% of the energy as it is being produced or store it at no cost in the grid via a net meter. But this requires the full gamut of permits, approvals, local government and utility inspections, and costs. But there is another way. A new type of mini-split heat pump/air conditioner unit that does both heating and cooling is being built

Figure 12.8 — Today you can buy high-voltage dc air conditioner/heat pumps that can run directly from solar panels. (Courtesy HotSpot Energy, www.hotspotenergy.com)

with variable speed compressors for maximum efficiency. These compressors are driven from variable speed controllers driven from high-voltage dc from the rectified mains. This means that they can also be powered from high-voltage dc from a solar array or from an EV battery connected directly to the same point in the circuit. This allows most of the energy to be provided from the solar panels while the sun shines, but yet continue to run from the mains otherwise.

The mini-split heat pump shown in **Figure 12.8** has been configured with exactly that concept in mind. It can accept dc input of from three to five solar panels providing from 750 to 900 W power directly. And a heat pump/air conditioner unit is something that you can use during the day, even if you are not at home. It can be set on a timer to power on when the sun is up to provide advance cooling in the summer or pre-heating in the winter before you get home. This way you get 100% usage of cheap solar power that is providing useful energy equivalent to full retail electric rates.

The catch is that the heat pump/air conditioner unit is only used in the summer and winter, so these non-grid-tied solar panels will be doing nothing in the spring and fall. You're getting only 50% of the potential value of the panels compared to grid-tie panels which are producing retail value electricity 100% of the time. The solar air conditioner/heat pump does run on dc internally, and so that ties into the overall topic of this book. Other possible sources of dc such as your EV or hybrid can possibly drive it as well.

Geothermal HVAC

Geothermal HVAC commonly refers to a ground-source heat pump. These heat pumps can reduce heating costs three to four times compared to oil or propane heat because they only have to pump heat to or from the constant temperature of the ground (45 °F to 55 °F) instead of the outside air temperature, which might be 20 °F or lower in winter for an outside air heat pump. At this rate, a heat pump system can pay for itself many times over during its 10 to 15 year lifespan, especially when it is time for a new system anyway. Heat pumps are electric, so they can run from solar or wind or any other renewable electricity source.

My old house has radiators, and it originally had a big stinky, smoky, sooty, oily, leaky cast iron boiler. It was costing us about $3000 a year in heating oil (at $3/gal), fed from two old 275-gallon tanks in my basement. Switching to the geothermal-to-hot-water heat pump shown in **Figure 12.9** eliminated all that mess, and getting rid of the tanks gave me 30 square feet

Figure 12.9 — This 6-ton geothermal heat pump replaced my old oil boiler for my radiator heating. The new hot water heat pump tank and old conventional electric hot water tank are also shown on the right.

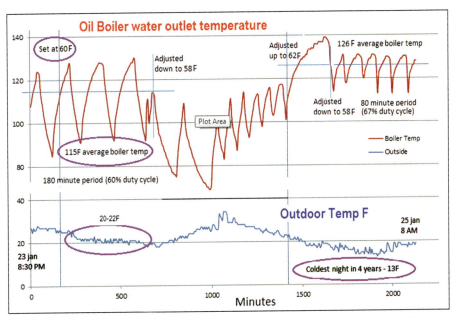

Figure 12.10 — Temperature data for the old oil boiler on the coldest night of the year.

more space in the basement for ham radio stuff. The added electric load was only about $1500 a year for a 50% reduction in heating costs. I added another 8 kW of solar panels to make up for the added load for lifelong free heating in this big ole' leaky house.

To figure out how big a heat pump I needed, I programmed a microcontroller to capture temperatures of the old oil boiler every minute on the coldest two days of the year as shown in **Figure 12.10**. Yes, because of the high cost of oil we got accustomed to miserable 58 °F settings at night and a high of 62 °F when we were home. The left side shows normal cycling when the outdoor temperature is 20 °F and indoor is set to 60 °F. The water reaches a high of maybe 130 °F and rapidly cools when the thermostat cycles off, but with an eyeball average of maybe 115 °F. On the coldest night of four years shown on the right, with the thermostat at a chilly 58 °F, the hot water temperature was about the same on peaks but the cycles were much shorter. By eyeball, I figure the average water temperature was about 126 °F.

When getting estimates for a geothermal heat pump to replace the boiler, the contractors all wanted to install an 8-ton heat pump system based on their calculations from the number of radiators in the house. I argued that the house had the radiators installed 90 years ago, before 2 inches of

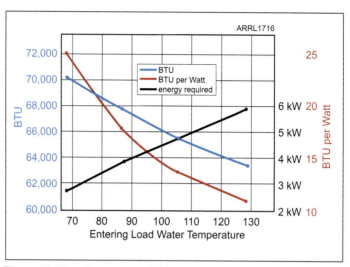

Figure 12.11 — Heat pump efficiency is higher when operating at lower output temperatures.

insulation was blown into the walls a few decades ago. I intended to operate the radiators more efficiently and figured I could get by with a 6-ton unit (the largest available without going to an 8-ton unit and more critical and expensive technology). Normally hot water heating systems assume between 140 °F and 160 °F water temperature circulating to the radiators. Since a heat pump's efficiency goes down as it has to pump to higher temperatures as shown in **Figure 12.11**, the contractors wanted the larger 8-ton unit to guarantee comfort. But I wanted to keep the circulating water temperatures lower to provide more heat at lower cost and use a smaller 6-ton unit.

Their cost estimates for a 6-ton unit came in at $28,000, $38,000 and $45,000 for the same size 6-ton geothermal system. The highest price was from a company with *geothermal* in their name, clearly capitalizing on the explosive growth of geothermal and the availability of 30% tax credits to homeowners who install them. Their well-drilling crew came out and seemed very professional in addressing the constraints of my property for the wells. But this company's system design team seemed to not be even trying to engineer the indoor system to match my house requirements. On closer questioning, the contractor said they have had been doing these for 20 years and they just do them all the same. I dropped them on the spot.

The company with the middle estimate gave me the name of their geothermal well driller, and so I went and looked at a job they were doing nearby. The driller had what looked like a decades-old rusted bucket-of-bolts drilling rig, and I was not impressed.

The third contractor, the one with the lowest quote, said that I would contract with his company for the inside system and with a separate well-drilling company for the wells, and so I would not pay him a markup on subcontracted wells. When his well driller came out, the guy said "wasn't I out here last month?" Turns out they were the same top-of the line drilling professionals used by the first overpriced contractor, but now, contracting with them directly and using the lowest priced contractor for the inside unit, the total system came in at just over half of the most expensive contractor's bid. Plus, the lowest priced bid was from a more local company that was willing to work with me on the specifics of my house and my desire to go with a smaller system than their estimating computers recommended.

All of the contractors were focused only on maximum comfort rather than efficiency or cost. I guess in contracting, satisfaction of the customer is the most important criteria.

Storage Tank Oversell

An example of the lack of any real engineering from all three contractors was their insistence that a very large hot-water storage tank is normally "required" in a water-to-water hydronic heat-pump system. In such typical systems, the heat pump is designed to always maintain the storage tank at a set high temperature and then as the house demands heat, the radiator system water is circulated from this tank, giving a quick response.

What made no sense to me was that the heat pump operates independently to maintain the 120 °F storage tank temperature always at 120 °F, even if the house would do fine with 105 °F water in the radiators during most winter days. Since heat pump performance is inversely related to temperature as shown in Figure 12.11 in blue, this forced high temperature when not needed makes no economic sense. Their justification is that having this high temperature reserve speeds up the response to demand for heat from the radiators. Again, comfort over economy.

The black line in Figure 12.11 shows the increasing electrical power requirement for higher temperatures, and the red line shows the resulting efficiency in BTU per kWh. As you can see, the lower the radiator water temperature, the higher the performance and lower cost. The difference between operating at 120 °F and 100 °F is a coefficient-of-performance (COP) difference of 2.6 vs 3.1, or a 20% loss. If the storage tank temperature is set to 125 °F for worst winter day, and most winter days can do with 95 °F water, then the difference is almost 33%!

In addition, by not using the tank, every cycle of the heat pump system begins with the radiator water having cooled down below 70 °F. So the first part of each cycle is actually operating even more efficiently, at even lower temperatures on the left side of the plot, with the most efficient upper left portion of the red curve putting more heat in the water at lower cost.

Fighting for a Tankless System

None of the HVAC contractors would consider a tankless system because "that's just not how we do it, a tank is required." Yet the installation manual from the manufacturer was less stringent — that is, "recommending" a storage tank in some paragraphs and saying it was "required" in others. Clearly, in my view the difference is between radiators and baseboards (though that's not mentioned). In a baseboard system with huge but thin fin surface areas and smaller pipes, there is very little thermal capacity in the system and only a few dozen gallons of water. In contrast, my 90-year-old cast iron radiator system with 3-inch piping holds more than 180 gallons of water and has huge thermal mass. None of the contractors even considered that!

After much frustration, I finally got to dig down deep into the manufacturer's technical service staff and reached an old fellow who understood what I was talking about. He agreed with me about efficient operation at lower operating temperatures and concurred that with the huge thermal mass of my system I did not need the tank at all. In fact, the system would be more efficient without it. The lesson is to buy from engineers, not from salesmen.

Radiator Fans

My plan to improve the efficiency of the radiators and the efficiency of the heat pump to operate with a smaller 6-ton system and lower water temperature was to use fans where practical to improve convection across the radiators as shown in **Figure 12.12**. In the upper left is a typical vertical squirrel cage fan with the base and top cut off and mounted between two end boards to lie on the floor. At the lower right is a similar fan blowing air into a plenum box to distribute the air into a baseboard radiator. The upper right shows an ugly fan hidden behind my wife's indoor winter plants, and at the lower left is a yard-sale double-wide window fan against another radiator. Turns out, I could put fans in front of about half the radiators in the house more or less out of sight.

Not only do the fans improve the convection heating efficiency, but they also give us free zone control. That is, we just turn on the fan in the room where we are if we want it to be warmer, or turn it off if the room is unused

Figure 12.12 — Fans on radiators improve heat pump efficiency by bringing more heat into the room and keeping circulating water temperature into the heat pump lower, where it is more efficient.

and we want to waste less heat there. In unoccupied kids' rooms (they are long gone out into the world), we further reduce waste heat with a towel or blanket tossed over the unused radiators. None of the ancient water valves on the radiators worked anymore, so we had not been able to control flow anyway.

I ran a separate wiring circuit to all of these fans, so generally they only come on when the heating system is running. Using the fans puts more heat into the rooms and keeps the circulating water returning to the heat pump below about 105 °F during most winter days and no more than about 125 °F on the coldest days, again, improving the efficiency of the heat pump operating point.

Because heat pump efficiency goes down as the outdoor (or ground) source temperatures fall or output temperatures go up, all heat pump systems need some form of auxiliary heat to help when the temperature really gets cold. Usually it is resistance heat. But here again, I already have plenty of space heaters and big electric heaters from my earlier experiments (see Figure 5.3 in Chapter 5) and so an auxiliary system was not part of the contractor-installed system.

After more than four years with this system and with all our energy now coming from solar, we are very happy with the thermostat at 68 °F when we are home, 70 °F with guests, and no lower than 60 °F at night — a level of comfort we could not afford with oil.

Temperature Setback with a Heat Pump

In our system we can set higher and lower temperatures at will with the heat pump because we do not have the automatic auxiliary heat as do most other heat pump systems. Thus we do not pay a penalty by raising the thermostat more than 2 °F in a single step. In other systems, if you increase the heat by more than a couple degrees, the auxiliary heat will automatically kick in to raise the temperature more quickly and eat up most of the advantages of changing temperature set-points.

On the other hand, at our church, we must meet quicker response times and more critical comfort levels, and so the heat pumps have big 10 kW auxiliary strip heaters. The building is usually not occupied overnight or during the day and is only used in the evenings most of the time, so we want to have 8 °F setbacks at night. If we had just accepted the contractor settings, these setbacks would have forced triple-expensive auxiliary heat every single day when the thermostat prepared for evening meetings. But the fix was simple.

We got the contractor to tell us the access code to adjust factory settings and we changed the delta-temperature where the auxiliary heaters kick in to a 5 °F difference instead of the normal 2 °F industry standard. When the thermostat timers need to go from 60 °F overnight to 68 °F when the building is occupied, we set the thermostat timer to do it in two steps. First we go from 60 °F to 64 °F, and then an hour later to 68 °F. With this process, the auxiliary heaters never come on, and so we get maximum efficiency from the heat pump. If it cannot do the 4 °F rise in one hour, then when it bumps up again to 68 °F, the strip heaters will kick in and quickly bring up the temperature if needed.

A DIY Geothermal Heat Pump System

Prior to my major investment in solar and the geothermal heating system, for almost three decades I have been getting the equivalent of some geothermal boost to our home heating with a DIY "heat pump." I simply took a 10,000

BTU cast-off air conditioner and hung it from the floor joists in our unfinished basement right below the large central room in our first floor, similar to the arrangement shown in **Figure 12.13**. Its cold side was in the basement where it absorbed the nearly year-round 60 °F air temperatures and heat-pumped that to the hot coils, which were ducted up into the room above through a vent. This air conditioner acting like a heat pump was on a timer set to come on at 9 PM when the electric rates went down and run all night until the electric rates went back up in the morning. This was back when the electric cost was only 3 cents/kWh at night and more than 10 cents during the day.

That huge nighttime savings went away with utility deregulation, and now the day/night difference in time-of-use (TOU) rates is only about 20% instead of the 3-to-1 savings I enjoyed back then. Not only was this a simple system, but since the oil system thermostat was in that same central room, it also automatically kept the oil heat off most of the night with no other special controls. With the 3:1 higher efficiency of the heat pump and 1/3 cost of nighttime electricity, that heat was almost 10 times cheaper than electric heat. Oil was pretty cheap then too (maybe $1/gallon).

In addition to the 10,000 BTU of heat transfer through the refrigerant when acting as an air conditioner, when using it backwards as a heat pump it also dumps all the electric waste heat of the compressor and fan motor into

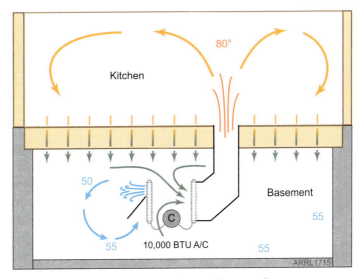

Figure 12.13 — An old window air conditioner unit can pump heat very efficiently from an unfinished basement into the room above, providing a poor-man's geothermal system.

the hot air stream on the other side as well. Perhaps the output is closer to 15,000 BTU of heat, while consuming only 1.5 kW of electricity when being operated as a heater.

Caution

One thing to consider is that an air conditioner unit is electrical, and when you hang it below the floor, there could be a potential fire hazard if it ever caught on fire. So the air conditioner unit's metal enclosure should be retained and the surroundings possibly covered in sheet metal in case of that eventuality.

Despite the fact that this DIY heat pump was pulling heat from the basement and dumping cold air down there for several months of the year, the basement temperature never really went down much (and my wife never noticed a difference) because the air was in contact with the large unfinished basement floor and four walls and adjacent crawl space. Those large surfaces brought in "geothermal heat" from the ground, and also, of course, waste heat from the laundry and from the oil boiler were also dumped there.

It was a great system that operated for about a decade each per old "found" air conditioner. Almost every air conditioner I ever found alongside the road had a good working refrigerant system and compressor. Almost always it had been discarded because the thermostat was broken or the fan was seized up and/or simply had never been oiled. A few drops of oil (if you could get to the shaft easily) usually restored these cast-off air conditioner units to good operation for years. And a bad thermostat didn't matter, as I bypassed the thermostat to run as a heat pump anyway.

DIY Defrosting

But here is the rub. If such a unit is going to run for hours, then it gets more complicated, because you have to have a way to defrost the cold coils that are now located in what was a humid basement. My first method was overly complex, with a wind vane opening a normally closed contact so that when air flow over the cold coils was reduced, the switch would close and turn on an old heating element from an electric oven hung in front of the cold coils. When the ice melted and the air flow improved, the switch opened and turned off the heating element. You can imagine how flaky this could be.

The better fix a few years later was simply to have the heating element unit on a timer to come on every hour or so for 15 minutes. Defrosting on a set schedule, whether it needed it or not, was not much of a concern because with oil up over $3 per gallon, the heating element for defrosting was adding heat to the house at no higher cost.

When the whole house geothermal heat pump was installed in 2014, we no longer needed the DIY repurposed air conditioner/heat pump system below the central downstairs room. However, since the original kitchen radiators were replaced with baseboard convectors decades ago, the lower temperature of the hot water circulating through the geothermal heat pump left the kitchen too cold for my wife's tastes. She would not let me put a full-size radiator back in the kitchen, so I solved it with another below-the-floor cast-off air conditioner unit to blow more than 15,000 BTU of heat into the kitchen from the 60 °F basement below it as shown in **Figure 12.14**. Since this could overheat the kitchen if left on, I simply wired it to a 60-minute timer switch on the kitchen wall. When it feels a bit chilly in the kitchen, we just crank the knob around to an hour and enjoy the heat. No defrost system was needed since this system does not run all night, and even if we are in the kitchen for hours the timer's auto shut off usually gives plenty of time for coil defrosting until we got around to dialing in another hour of supplementary heat.

Figure 12.14 — A castoff air conditioner mounted on the basement ceiling acts as DIY "heat pump" that blows hot side heat into the kitchen above while drawing "geothermal" heat from the basement walls and floor. The wooden deflector on the front keeps the cold air blowing out the top separate from the basement air rising from the floor.

House Fans

The use of house fans for efficient cooling is almost a lost art. Homes built for the last 60 years were designed to be tight boxes with the habitat maintained by energy-intensive heating and air conditioning. The art of using a fan to exchange cooler outside air overnight was not designed in. This is in contrast to the whole-house fan commonly used through the 1950s. (A whole-house fan is typically mounted in the ceiling in a central spot and turned on to draw cool outside air through open windows.)

Although a whole-house fan can be added with some expense, it is possible to enjoy good cooling with one or more window box fans. The key is to set the fan to exhaust. This removes hot air in hot rooms and draws in cool outside air into other occupied rooms. This also allows good flow control in any room of the house just by opening windows as needed in any occupied rooms where a fresh cooler incoming breeze is desired. This way, the breeze can be moved from room to room just by opening or closing windows or doors instead of having to move fans.

To maximize cooling, only turn on the exhaust fans in the evening, after the outside temperature goes below the inside temperature. Turn off the fans in the morning and close the doors and/or windows to retain the cool air most of the day. The nighttime low temperature in the summer is usually 20 to 30 degrees cooler than the daytime high in most areas, and so this can be considered taking advantage of free cooling instead of burning fossil fuels for the same energy transfer.

It should also be noted that as we clean up the daytime summer haze due to all that coal burning for air conditioning, the summer nighttime skies are clearer, and this leads to lower nighttime temperatures as the Earth is exposed to the near absolute zero radiated coldness of black sky at night.

Lawn and Garden Equipment

This is another area where we routinely face purchasing decisions, and often without thought, just buy another tool powered by a small gas engine. But the good old all-American lawnmower and other small power tool engines are the worst air polluters of almost all internal combustion engines.

Lawnmowers

The shocking truth is that switching to an electric corded or cordless lawnmower such as the one shown in **Figure 12.15** for a few hundred dollars can have the same personal effect in cleaner, less-toxic air as switching one's commuter car to an EV costing tens of thousands of dollars more.

Figure 12.15 — A gas mower emits about 10 times the toxic emissions of a car with catalytic converter. Plug-in or battery-operated electric mowers have no emissions and can store vertically in a small space, and some have lights for mowing quietly at night. [Rob Schedinger, photo]

Based on information from the EPA, the People-Powered-Machines web page concludes that the toxic emissions of a lawnmower used for one hour are about the same as two weeks of daily one-hour commuting in a modern gasoline powered automobile with a catalytic converter that conforms to all the latest EPA emissions rules — 1 mower = 11 cars. (See **www.peoplepoweredmachines.com/faq-environment.htm#pollutants**.) Although the net energy usage and contribution to carbon dioxide greenhouse gas emissions from gasoline-powered lawn and garden equipment are small compared to the number of cars (less than 1% of all emissions), their contribution to toxic air is an order of magnitude greater. (See "National Emissions from Lawn and Garden Equipment," available from **www.epa.gov/sites/production/files/2015-09/documents/banks.pdf**.)

About two-thirds of households in the US have lawnmowers, and those homes are usually in the suburbs where we are hitting the air with a double whammy, first from gas/diesel used in commuting to and from the 'burbs, and second from caring for our large lawns. In addition, lawn and garden tools are used within about three to six feet of the operator, who is inhaling this toxic brew, not to mention children, dogs, cats, and others in the vicinity.

I have long used corded electric mowers and put up with the hassle of the cords because in my very unevenly sloped yard, the thought of a very heavy battery-powered electric lawnmower using lead-acid batteries and nearly double the weight of a gas mower was an anathema to the concept of lightweight, easy mowing. But in 2017, when I needed a new mower immediately, the $350 corded electric push mower was not available at the local tool store. So I paid nearly double the price ($550) for a cordless lithium-ion battery-powered model that was self-propelled. Thinking I needed the exercise more than I needed to mow the lawn, I had always shunned the self-propelled types before, but it was the best decision I ever made.

The new technology of lithium-ion batteries cut the weight to a fifth of those with the old lead-acid batteries. The removable battery is no more cumbersome than a six-pound bag of flour, so I can leave the mower under a shed, pop out the battery, and bring it up the hill into the house to charge without having to take power from an outlet to the mower.

Small Lawn and Garden Tools

Although additional small, often overlooked, gasoline engines are only used a few hours a month, their net contribution to air pollution according to the EPA "National Emissions from Lawn and Garden Equipment" study cited above is 17 percent of all volatile organic compounds, 29 percent of the deadly carbon monoxide, and 12 percent of all nitrogen oxides. The smaller the gasoline engine, the worse the emissions.

These smaller engine applications have had electric alternatives for decades. Two-cycle leaf blowers, snow blowers, chain saws, trimmers, edgers, and cutters accounted for almost half of all emissions of lawn and garden gasoline tools, despite their being used much less than larger four-cycle lawnmowers. All of these alternative electric tools are practical, too, as they are most often reachable with an extension cord from your own source of clean renewable solar or grid energy.

The latest tools, such as the string trimmer shown in **Figure 12.16**, use modern lightweight rechargeable, high-capacity lithium-ion batteries for the ultimate in hand-operated convenience.

Figure 12.16 — A rechargeable battery-operated string trimmer can be used anywhere in the yard without noise or toxic emissions. [Rob Schedinger, photo]

Chain Saw

Of all the home and garden tools, the chain saw can find use beyond the home, especially among DIY community and ham radio operators who volunteer to help in a public service capacity, such as providing communications during disasters. It is also a very useful tool for cutting limbs and debris at the church or a neighbor's house, or clearing roads and other areas after storms. For this reason most people assume the portability of a gasoline powered chain saw is essential.

There are a couple of alternatives, as shown in **Figure 12.17**. A plug-in electric chain saw can be used in the yard around the house with an extension cord to a convenient outlet. Away from home, an inexpensive inverter connected to a car, EV, or hybrid 12 V battery can provide enough electricity to easily power an electric chain saw anytime, anywhere.

As with many other applications, high-voltage, high-capacity rechargeable lithium-ion batteries are revolutionizing portable power equipment. Available from some of the best names in the business, today's battery operated chainsaws offer excellent cutting power and long life between charges.

I remember when a tree fell across our dead-end street and all the neighbors were out hand wringing over calling the county road crew to come remove it, ignoring the fact that there were thousands of similar trees blocking

Figure 12.17 — Plug-in electric chainsaws can be used with an extension cord going to any convenient outlet, or even an inverter in a car for use anywhere. Today's rechargeable battery-operated chainsaws offer plenty of power and long battery life. [Rob Schedinger, photo]

thousands of similar neighborhoods, and it would be several days before they got to us. A few guys had their gas-powered chain saws, but some would not start, and others did not have gas or oil, and so no cutting was taking place. I was coming home from work, so I stepped over the tree, walked to my house got my lightweight electric chain saw came back, plugged it into the inverter in the trunk of my Prius, and cut the tree. Compared to the messy, noisy, hazardous gasoline chainsaw, I love my electric saw every time I use it. Since I don't have to carry oil and gas, it is easy to keep in the back of the Prius (with an extension cord) to serve occasional cutting needs at home, or anywhere else along the road without any smells or leaks.

Snow Blowers

The winter tool producing noise and toxic emissions is the snow blower. The cacophony of snow blowers that start up after a heavy snow is deafening. Yet my tiny electric blower (**Figure 12.18**) takes up only 20% of the storage

Figure 12.18 — My neighbor and I doing the cul-de-sac with our electric snow blowers plugged into my EV charging outlet down by the street.

space of my old gas unit, and it runs every time I plug it in. With my old gas snow blower, it sometimes took half a day in the cold to get it running. Combined with my standard 120 V EV charging outlets in my driveway and on a pole down by the street, I can do my whole driveway and cul-de-sac with just a single extension cord. And even if there is no power, a common occurrence after a storm, my home solar or the inverter in my car trunk is always available.

Noise

The other major advantage of electric power tools is the significant reduction in noise. Almost every weekend, there is too much noise in my suburban neighborhood to enjoy the birds and breezes. Some neighbor within earshot is always powering up one of their tools, and when they are done, another one begins. It never ends. Not only do I have a lot of neighbors, but also the number of gasoline powered tools seems endless. One neighbor prides himself on having a gasoline power tool for everything — lawn mower, trimmer, edger, mulcher, chain saw, leaf blower, generator, and even a snow blower. Multiply that by a hundred neighbors, and there is no peace and quiet.

Do not think of switching to electric for tools, appliances, and garden equipment as isolated events, but part of your own personal steps toward electrification of everything and participation in the clean renewable energy economy that is right here before us now.

New Home

Of course, another major life milestone where energy choices can be considered is the average American job change or move about every 12 years. This is another time when energy choices can have a significant impact. Choices include: What climate?, What house?, What location?, What sun orientation?, What HVAC system?

These are all questions that can be considered for their energy impact. Is the home well insulated? Does it have energy-efficient appliances? What about heating and cooling and hot water? What are its solar potentials? Does it have passive solar features such as overhanging eaves to keep out summer sun? Are the windows easy to operate for controlling breezes and temperature?

For solar panels, as discussed in earlier chapters, a southern exposure is no longer a firm requirement. Any angle from east to south to west can work, and in fact, east/west facing roofs can often use both sides for solar panels to generate up to 170% of the ideal south-facing roof.

Cars and Transportation

Buying a new car is probably the most frequent major energy decision we have to make, and therefore the greatest immediate impact on our emissions footprint. A car bought today will, on average, still be running (through multiple owners) up to 18 years before it is finally scrapped. Those with a concern for clean energy can simply no longer afford to approach a car purchase without having at least considered the impact of that choice and the available alternatives.

As discussed in Chapter 7, electric vehicles (EVs) today are a whole new paradigm that opens up one of our biggest energy requirements to clean renewable possibilities. About one third of our personal energy use is in transportation, and more than 95% of that is local and less than 40 miles a day (see **www.solarjourneyusa.com/EVdistanceAnalysis.php**). On average, individual Americans make a car purchase or trade about every six years, and now it is important to consider not just the purchase price and number of cup holders, but also the long-term overall lifetime costs and environmental consequences.

As this was written in 2018, 10 years into the modern EV revolution, there is no doubt that local travel, commuting and daily transportation can be done cheaper, cleaner, better and more conveniently with EVs than continuing to use inefficient gasoline burning internal combustion engines and depending on gas stations and foreign oil. In 2018, global EV sales

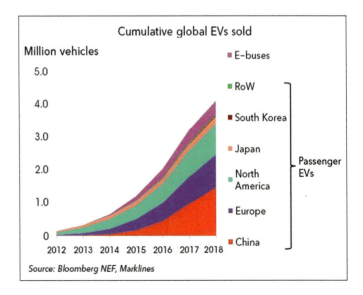

Figure 12.19 — Global EV sales passed 4 million in September 2018, with China leading the world. (See about.bnef.com/blog/cumulative-global-ev-sales-hit-4-million/.)

are exploding and exceeded 4 million as shown in **Figure 12.19**. There are at least 45 full-size electric or plug-in-hybrid cars on the market. (See Chapter 7 of this book and also **evadc.org/wp-content/uploads/2018/04/EVInfoSheet-20180403.pdf**.)

China started with EVs after the US, but in just four years China doubled the number of EV sales compared to the US. Most manufacturers have by now announced that all or most of their product line will consist of EVs or plug-in hybrids by 2025, totaling nearly 250 new models — all able to run on the clean, renewable electric energy sources we are developing. When we buy another gas car today without considering an EV, do we fully consider the impact of placing that fossil-fuel burner on the road for another 18 years?

Biking and Scooters

Another revolution that is shaping our energy future is the growth of electric bicycles and scooters. Electric bicycles such as the one shown in **Figure 12.20** have a battery that can provide a boost going up hills or while cruising to work.

There has also been a growth in commercial bike sharing systems that put bicycles where they are needed most. For a small fee, you use the bike to get from point A to point B and then leave it for someone else to use. These bikes provide great flexibility for people using public transportation to travel to city centers, and they remove many cars from our overcrowded downtowns.

Figure 12.20 — Electric bicycles use a battery and small motor to assist riders when needed, such as climbing a steep hill.

Near me, the Washington, DC, area bike share system — Capital Bikeshare — was launched in September 2010 (**Figure 12.21**). As of late 2018, they offered 4,300 bikes at 500+ locations in the greater Washington metro area. In late 2018, they added some electric bikes to the fleet. The city of Baltimore is launching a pilot program in 2018 as well, and it includes electric bicycles and scooters.

Making the Electric Choice

Figure 12.21 — Shared bicycles, such as those offered by Capital Bikeshare in the Washington, DC, area are a great urban transportation option. [Paul Wasneski, photo]

In this chapter you will notice a common thread: The switch to electricity as the common denominator of all of our energy systems. For some interesting reading on this topic, see "The Key to Tackling Climate Change: Electrify Everything," available online at **www.vox.com/2016/9/19/12938086/electrify-everything**.

Once we switch to electricity, then we have the option to use *any* form of energy generation as the source interchangeably. We can, as individuals, choose to change our electricity source from coal, natural gas, or propane to clean renewable energy with a check in the box of a utility form to subscribe to wind electricity, the installation of solar panels, or the overnight charging of our electric car.

Not only does this switch to electric give us access to clean renewable energy, in almost all cases, it is also less costly in the long run. By 2015, solar and wind were cheaper than even coal fired electricity. And if we are lucky enough to have a sunny roof, we also gain the self-sufficiency and security of owning our own energy supply for the rest of our lives, and being independent of political and market fluctuations in oil, gas and coal which tend to go in boom and bust cycles while creeping ever upward.

13 Making the Switch to Clean Renewable Energy—Examples

In this chapter, I will describe some practical examples of steps that average Americans can take to increase their use of renewable energy and reduce dependence on fossil fuels.

Local Transportation Forever

Nothing can make a better case for clean renewable energy than the perfect marriage of EVs and solar, such as suggested in **Figure 13.1**. Just

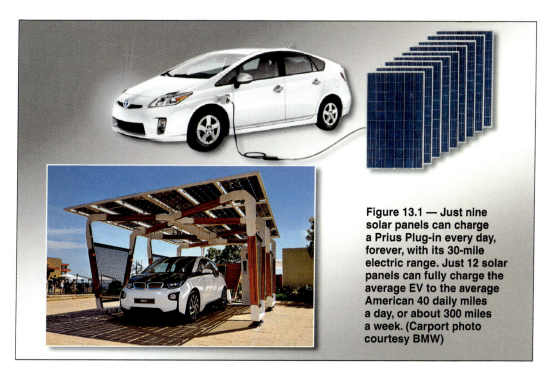

Figure 13.1 — Just nine solar panels can charge a Prius Plug-in every day, forever, with its 30-mile electric range. Just 12 solar panels can fully charge the average EV to the average American 40 daily miles a day, or about 300 miles a week. (Carport photo courtesy BMW)

covering a single parking spot with 12 solar panels can fully charge an EV every day forever on clean renewable energy from the sun to meet the American average 40 miles a day. And, each American car has multiple parking spaces somewhere — at home, at work, at church or school, at the mall or at the stadium, or on the street. Solar panel awnings also keep the car cool in the summer, and low winter sun angles can still get under them to provide warmth in the winter.

Just a few years ago, we anguished over the extraordinary 2 billion dollars a day cost of foreign oil and our dependence on it. Now, with a single investment of about $3000 for solar (the amount the average American used to spend in two years for gasoline), we can use free and clean energy from the sun to drive locally, every day, with zero emissions and without foreign oil dependence.

Charging at Work

The subtle paradigm change brought by EVs is that they charge conveniently while the car is parked and not in use. Cars typically spend more than 21 hours a day parked either at home or at work as shown in **Figure 13.2**, offering plenty of time for charging with no inconvenience to

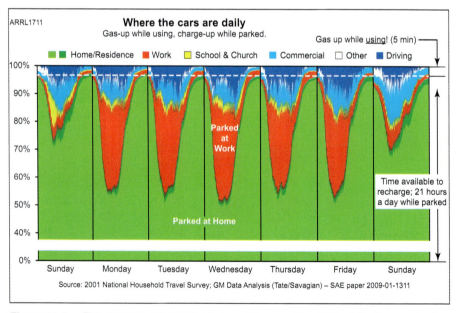

Figure 13.2 — The average American car spends more than 85% of its time parked either at home or work, providing ample time for daily charging.

the driver. For this reason, during 2013 to 2017 the Department of Energy led the Workplace Charging Challenge that encouraged employers to support EV charging at work. (Although this program is over, DOE offers information on charging at work online at **www.energy.gov/eere/vehicles/workplace-charging**.) Simply plugging into a standard 120 V outlet at home can maintain more than 40 miles of daily range, and also plugging in to an outlet at work can maintain nearly 80 miles a day, twice the national daily average.

Another useful conclusion can be seen across the top line in Figure 13.2. Notice that the car is actually only in use an hour or so a day for most people. All the rest of the time it is parked. Yet, for a gas car, this hour of use is the only time it can be refueled somewhere at a public gas station. That is an inconvenient time to refuel, because you are using the car for travel, or running errands, or whatever, and you have to take the time to drive to a gas station with nothing to do while it is being refueled but stand there and wait.

We are so familiar with this method of refueling that we think of the wasted five minutes as the ultimate in convenience. Yet in fact, it is the ultimate in inconvenience when you compare it to an EV. With an EV, refueling (charging) is out-of-sight-and out-of-mind convenience, simply requiring 5 seconds a day to plug in and 5 seconds to unplug, letting the car charge while parked.

A Family Example

My family's focus on renewable energy began in 2007 when news of the 2008 Tesla Roadster was coming out and Nissan and GM announced their plans for full size standard production EVs by 2011. Since my senior project at Georgia Tech 37 years earlier in 1970 was to build an EV from an old VW chassis, some batteries and an electric motor (shown back in Chapter 1 in Figure 1.1), an old flame was rekindled.

In 1970, the only way to get an EV was to build it yourself. This time, I eventually converted three salvage Priuses bought from junkyards at low prices to mild EVs. Since the range was short, and I was not allowed to plug in at work to recharge, I also added solar panels to the roof of two of them. Eight hours in the sun would add about eight miles of free electric range for the ride home.

When we bought our house in 1990, I had been interested in solar and the utility was offering time-of-use (TOU) metering that cut the daytime 10 cents per kWh to only 3 cents at night. With that 3:1 difference, I calculated that I could charge batteries cheaply at night for use in the day. Finally, with these batteries, I could have a real emergency ham station fully powered no matter what, and able to communicate independent of the utility power. But then I was shocked to find that the cost of battery replacement every five years would eat up any cost savings. The subtle lesson — one I carried for years — was that, even if electricity were almost free (such as solar), the cost of batteries and maintenance would eat up any benefit.

Solar Arrives

Solar kept getting cheaper. My epiphany came on the second Saturday in August 2010, when I realized that this modern revolution in home solar had nothing to do with batteries! Modern solar was grid-tie, meaning excess daily solar generation is stored in the grid by pushing the electric meter backward. When you need power at night, you get that power back as the meter goes forward. This revelation immediately upended my preconceived notion of home solar. Although our roof was surrounded by trees, we had a clear area at the back of our lot (**Figure 13.3**), and by spring of 2013 we were finally on line with an 8 kW array providing all of our annual electric needs and saving over $1400 a year with nearly zero electric bills. You can read more about this online at **www.aprs.org/my-solar.html**.

Heat Pump

Our biggest carbon footprint was not the coal-fired electricity we used, but the typical 1000 gallons a year of heating oil. At the time, home heating oil had risen to $3.50 per gallon — $3500 a year. Burning oil just for heat seemed

Figure 13.3 — My initial 8.5 kW arrays faced between southeast and almost south, each one pointed toward the center of its visible sky (140° for the two arrays on the left, 155° for the array in the center, and 170° for the array on the right).

unforgivable, so we switched to a geothermal (ground source) heat pump and by the fall of 2014 the ground-source heat pump system was installed and the nearly 80-year-old dirty, inefficient oil furnace and tanks were gone!

Because the heat pump is very efficient, generating two to three times the heat from the same amount of energy, it eliminated the $3500 annual home heating oil costs and added only about $1500 to our electric bill. We met this new demand for electricity by doubling our solar array to a new total of 16 kW on the garage, northwest roof, and floating pier as shown in **Figure 13.4**. After that, our worst electric bill (our total energy cost except gasoline) was $30 in February, with all the other months being only the $8 minimum utility account fee.

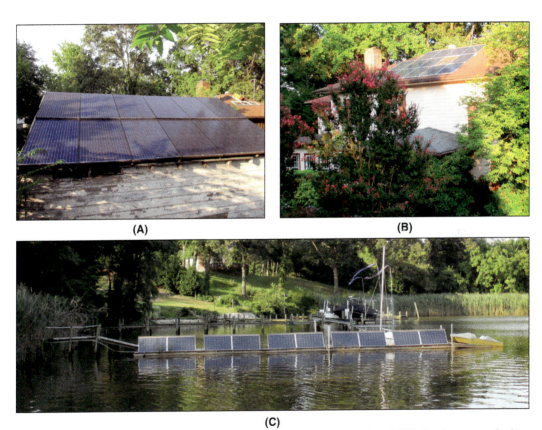

Figure 13.4 — To meet the added load of the heat pump, I added another 8 kW of solar arrays facing southwest on the garage (A), northwest on the roof of the house (B), and southwest on a floating pier (C). The northwest facing array on the roof gets afternoon sun and faces northwest at 295°. It is in parallel with the southeast array facing 155°.

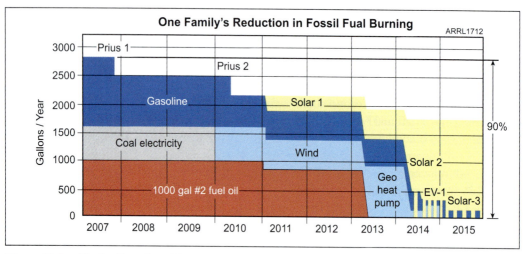

Figure 13.5 — My family reduced fossil fuel use by more than 90%, and we are spending less than when we were dependent on gas, oil, and electricity from the utility.

The plot in **Figure 13.5** shows the decline of our fossil fuel consumption from almost 3000 gallons a year (gasoline, coal equivalent electricity, and home heating oil) down to about 300 gallons a year by 2015. We achieved that by switching to the hybrid vehicles, replacing the oil boiler with the geothermal heat pump, and adding the solar panels for an overall 90% reduction in carbon emissions. By 2015, I found a low-cost EV to replace one of the Priuses, which further dropped our gasoline use to only a few hundred gallons a year for the other Prius and for trips.

This reduction in fossil fuels and emissions also reduced our total $6000 a year cost of electricity, heating oil, and gasoline down to the typical minimum $8 a month electric bill and $700 or so per year for gasoline for the other Prius.

Of course, nearly free energy for life from solar requires a substantial initial investment, as discussed in Chapter 3. The way to compare that investment to monthly utility costs is to amortize the investment over the next 20 years. In our case, this gave a comparable average retail equivalent of about 5 cents per kWh for electricity, about one third of what we would be paying per month if we had done nothing. Most importantly, this 5 cents should not only be compared to today's Maryland 14 cent rate, but to anticipated increases in the cost of electricity from the utility over the same 20 years. At an assumed annual rate increase of 3% per year, toward the end this would grow to 25 cents per kWh.

Reducing Fossil Fuel Use and Energy Costs at Our Church

Our small church was spending about $1500 a year on electricity and as much as $4000 a year on propane. Starting in 2011, we began to explore solar. By February 2014, Solar City installed a leased 9 kW system (see Figure 3.12 in Chapter 3) that we fully prepaid up front for a one-time $20,000 payment instead of monthly finance payments for the next 20 years. The amortized cost turns out to be about 6 cents per kWh, compared to the current utility power at 14 cents per kWh in 2015 (with expected increases over the next 20 years).

This is a huge savings in our church's operating budget. We chose the lease, because non-profits are not eligible for any of the many tax incentives available to homeowners and businesses that install solar arrays. But through a lease, the solar leasing company got to take all the local, state, and federal tax credits adding up to almost 50% and pass the savings on to us. The comparable purchase price of $53,000 only cost us the initial $20,000 prepaid lease, and our net monthly electric bills went to the minimum for an account ($8/month).

By 2014, propane had nearly doubled to $4 a gallon, so we replaced our fossil fuel heating system with a heat pump. Our total heating cost dropped from $4000 for propane down to about $1200 a year in the form of added electricity. The church then approved the purchase of additional solar panels to offset that new energy need to bring us back to 100% clean renewable solar for our building. As shown in **Figure 13.6** we were able to add another

Figure 13.6 — Our church reduced its net use of electricity from the utility to near zero with solar. The original array at our church was shown in Figure 3.12 in Chapter 3. In this photo, we have added another 3 kW row of panels across the bottom to make up for the heat pump we installed to replaced our propane-fired furnace.

13 panels to the same array by digging down a few inches into the dirt and adding the new panels in a vertical format. Since we already had our net meter and leased array (Figure 3.12) it was easy to just lean this new row of solar panels along the bottom and add a new inverter to make up for the added heating load. Of course these new panels will be covered in snow after a storm, as the snow now slides down the upper panels and piles up on the ground. But that is only a few days a year in Maryland, and the loss of a few days compared to the added 3 kW for the other 362 days is worth the effort to shovel them.

Geothermal Tradeoff

We had planned to go geothermal for the heat pump because of its efficiency, but then realized that we have no day school, nor any permanent office staff, and the church is unoccupied overnight and most daytime hours. Most usage is in the evenings, and the thermostat was set back overnight and mornings. Thus, the primary benefit of a geothermal HVAC system — to pump heat from the ground at 50 °F instead of the outside air at 20 °F or lower — was of little value to us.

Most of our heating (except Sunday) was in the afternoon, in preparation for evening meetings. Since the climate of Annapolis has an average outdoor temperature not much lower than 40 °F in the afternoons, even in January and February, we chose an air-source heat pump that was nearly as efficient as a geothermal system for us, but at half the initial cost. The result of switching from propane to electric (to be supplied by solar) saved us another $2500 a year in energy costs.

Classroom Heat Pump

In 2018, we added a full-time use of one of our classrooms for a private school organization. Rather than turning up the heat to the entire building, we simply installed a portable air conditioner in the kitchen, with its hot-air exhaust blowing through the wall into the classroom as shown in **Figure 13.7A**. This is three times better than typical resistance space heaters because the heat pump can make heat three times more efficiently for the same electric use. Also, the air in the kitchen is at least at 62 °F (the set-back temperature for the rest of the unoccupied building), so the air conditioner (working as a heat pump) is sourcing heat from 62 °F air and not the colder temperatures outside.

There is nothing wrong with this double pumping of heat. The whole building heat pump simply continues to maintain the 62 °F efficiently and this portable air conditioner (heat pump) boosts it to the warmth needed

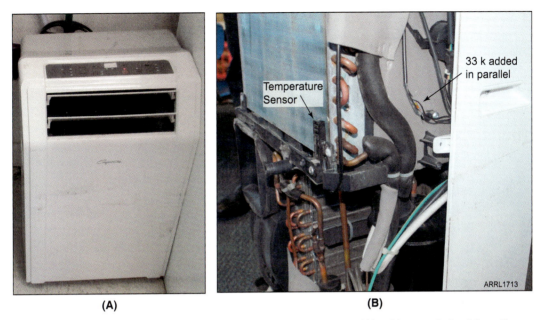

Figure 13.7 — A portable air conditioner unit used as a heat pump (A), taking waste heat from the kitchen at 62 °F and pumping it into the classroom on the other side of the wall at 100 °F. At (B), it's necessary to fool the thermistor into thinking the room is warmer so that the thermostat control will not turn off the air conditioner, but will let it keep providing heat independent of how cold the source temperature gets.

just for the classroom in the morning. As the outdoor heat rises around midday, the whole building heat pump schedule begins to raise the building temperature because it can do it more efficiently then.

When an air conditioner unit is used like this as a heat pump to provide intentional heat, its internal thermostat (designed for cooling use) might turn the unit off when the source side gets below about 62 °F, the lowest temperature setting on this unit. So I opened it up to find the thermostat to bias it a bit higher to allow it to work with source temperatures that are lower than its lowest AC setting. In Figure 13.7B, you can see the original thermostat in front of the indoor coil. I traced the wires and measured it with an ohmmeter to be about 5 kΩ at 62 °F and resistance goes down as the temperature rises. So I paralleled a 33 kΩ resistor to make it think it is a bit hotter than 62 °F so that it would keep running independent of how cold the source temperature was and still provide heat on its output hose to the other room. Of course at temperatures below, say, 40 °F it is doubtful that this air conditioner will still be producing usable heat. And long-term continuous operation may lead to frost collecting on the cold coils since there is no defrost cycle in an air conditioner unit.

For more information on the work we have done at our church, see the Annapolis Friends Meeting Environmental web page at **www.aprs.org/ AFM/environment.html**.

The EV Charging Sign Initiative

Another initiative that our church undertook was to enhance the visibility of electric vehicles. Although many people believe that public charging infrastructure is required before widespread adoption of EVs can become a reality, that's not the case. Every EV comes with a charging cord that can plug into a standard 120 V, 15 A ac outlet, and outlets are everywhere.

As discussed in Chapter 7, a significant portion of the value-promise of EVs is the convenience of charging at home or at work while the car is parked, and never having to go to a public charging station and having to "wait" for a charge. Since virtually every home and garage and most parking lots already have electricity, and all have the same standard 120 V outlet, we wanted to help educate the public that perhaps 95% of all daily charging needs can be met by simply plugging into a standard 120 V outlet while the car is parked. In Maryland, new laws encourage even multifamily dwellings, apartments, and condos to allow EV charging for residents where practical. (More information about Maryland's efforts can be found in the "Final Report to the Governor and Maryland General Assembly by the Electric

Figure 13.8 — Just putting up charging signs on our 120 V outdoor outlets has inspired about ¼ of our church members to switch to electric cars.

Vehicle Infrastructure Council," available online at **dlslibrary.state.md.us/publications/Exec/MDOT/SB176Ch400HB167Ch401_2011(2).pdf**.)

In 2011, our church put up simple EV CHARGING signs over two of our existing outlets on light poles in the parking lot as shown in **Figure 13.8**. This has been a beacon of change and visibility to the progress of renewable energy in our community, and a number of our church members now drive EVs. With the high visibility of our solar array in the front yard, we are seeing more rentals of our building and classrooms by environmental and energy groups looking for meeting rooms in facilities that are powered by 100% renewable energy. To meet this growing demand, we added three more EV outlets in 2016, including a Level 2 (faster) 240 V charging outlet on a pole next to the street. We keep the 240 V charge cord in the office for anyone to use.

Visibility and Ubiquity of EV Charging

It is important to understand that the value of these charging signs was not for the 1% that might actually use them, but for the other 99% to see and realize that EVs can actually charge everywhere. In the first several years the signs were up, we could probably count on one hand the number of times they were actually used. But seeing the signs on every visit had an effect and by 2016 more than 12% or our members were either driving EVs or considering one on their next car transition. In 2018, however, we had 12 EVs every Sunday. Two of them have 20-mile commutes in cars with 30-mile plug-in hybrid ranges, and these two will usually plug in on every visit so they can also return home on electricity instead of burning gas. The success of this simple "put up a sign" action inspired our establishment of a local initiative that grew to involve almost 20 other churches, schools, or businesses that had existing outlets and now have signs. (For more on this, see **www.aprs.org/EV-charging-signs.html**.)

We even demonstrated a solution to simple charging for those without driveways who have to park in the street. Just bending a piece of conduit seven feet high to reach out over the sidewalk can bring an EV charging cord to a car parked in the street without causing a trip hazard on the sidewalk as shown in **Figure 13.9**. In that photo you can also see our church's grid-tied solar array in the background.

This simple charging sign initiative is a great idea for groups seeking ways they can move forward on clean renewable energy by looking for outdoor outlets and approaching the owner to educate them about EV charging. All they have to do is decide what signage is appropriate for the user of their outlet and how they are going to ask for a contribution to the

Figure 13.9 — The conduit swings the charge cord over the sidewalk for easy and safe access to EV charging.

cost of the electricity. In Maryland, the cost to plug in an EV to 120 V is only about 20 cents an hour, which is probably not worth worrying about for occasional visitors.

For daily, all-day charging, the cost turns out to be about $1 per month per daily mile traveled. For example, a 15-mile commuter would pay $15/month for the privilege of plugging in every day. For employees or visitors who drive EVs on a long commute, this charging-while-parked is an everyday benefit, and well worth the few dollars a month for the privilege. If they can plug in at work, they can effectively double the car's EV range without the need to pay for an EV with greater battery capacity.

Federal Employee Commuter Charging

Even the federal government, in the Congressional FAST Act of 2015 and refined in the Office of Federal Sustainability Guidance of 2016, allows federal employees to plug into any available outlet or to use new outlets installed for the purpose at modest cost. Used on a daily basis, it's a monthly allotment of about $6 per bi-weekly pay period. This covers not only the cost of the electricity, but includes about $1.50 per pay period to amortize the costs of maintenance and the addition of new outlets as needed. This figure is the result of an assumed average 12 cents per kWh cost of electricity and an average federal employee commute distance of 15 miles a day.

Solar Investment Better than a Pension

Investing in solar for our own home or community is very encouraging on several fronts. First, it gets us clean energy at lower cost than fossil fuel such as coal or natural gas/propane. Second, it shifts some focus back on the common good for all of us when we tie our solar array system into the grid to help bolster the energy needs of our neighbors during the peak sun and peak loads of the day. Third, it offers us some sense of personal security as well as national security, through independence from global conflicts over oil.

It is often said that there is "nothing certain in life other than death and taxes," but this misses the third certainty which is *utilities*. We only evolved beyond hunter-gatherers due to our exploitation of external sources of energy to make us thrive, grow, and prosper, and so modern humans are dependent on external energy to live. So now, paying our energy bills is as fundamental to our lives as death and taxes have always been.

Fortunately, for the first time, with home (or community) solar energy, we are in the position to actually solve, here and now, our life-long need for energy with the simple investment in our own solar energy systems. As observed by Greg Baker, who was Minister of State for Energy and Climate Change in the UK from 2010 to 2015, putting retirement investment into one's own solar system will provide a better financial return than a pension. (See the story in The Telegraph, **www.telegraph.co.uk/finance/personalfinance/pensions/10615852/Solar-panels-better-than-a-pension-says-minister.html**.)

The costs of electricity are assumed to continue to go up in the future, but a solar system purchased now has no future costs other than maybe some occasional maintenance. The retiree with solar is immune to almost all future energy fluctuations and concerns. When married with an electric car to provide transportation that can run on this unlimited and clean power from the sun virtually forever, the retiree is fully independent of the oil industry as well.

14 Amateur Satellites and Thermal Energy Balance

With a parallel fascination with Amateur Radio satellites (AMSATs), and a job teaching aerospace engineering to undergraduates, I am continuously reminded of how much of the space industry is focused on Earth observation and sensors. While I am trying to figure out how I can get another amateur communication payload into space, many of the other competing missions are proposing all manner of Earth sensors to take stock of our planet. From space, you can look down almost anywhere on Earth from only 200 miles or so up and see how preciously thin is the atmosphere. For those who think we still have plenty of it, a glance at **Figure 14.1** reveals how very small our life-giving atmosphere actually is.

Take all the atmosphere on Earth and pull it into a ball and it barely even covers the western United States. The sphere of water is even smaller, and the fresh water sphere is smaller across than Texas. When seven billion of us on this planet (three times the planet's population when I was born) use this atmosphere as our dumping ground for everything we burn over two centuries, it is a scary proposition. Already it is estimated that the air in every breath we take has already passed through a fire or internal combustion engine at least once in the last few hundred years.

This is similar to the calculations used in a common problem for early chemistry students to calculate how many molecules of air that we breathe today were involved in Caesar's last breath more than 2000 years ago. The answer is about one. This is because the huge number of molecules in just one liter of air in Caesar's lungs is similar in scale to the huge number of liters of air in our atmosphere on Earth. So the probability that one of his molecules is in our liter of breath is about 100%. And not only is our health dependent on that air — that atmosphere is all that protects us from the extremes of space. (For some interesting reading, see *Caesar's Last Breath: Decoding the Secrets of the Air Around Us*, by Sam Kean.)

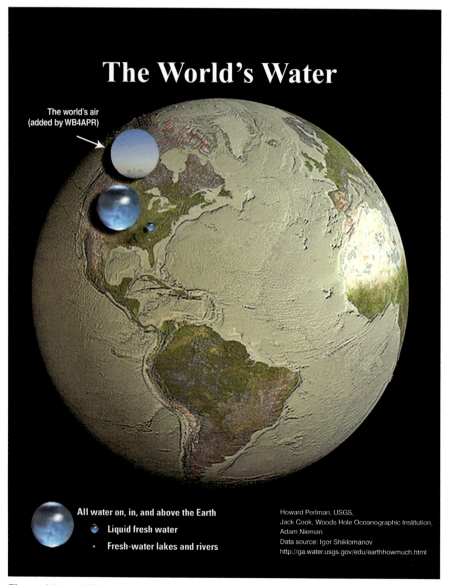

Figure 14.1 — All the air and all the water on Earth is not as much as we might think. For more information on this topic, see the US Geological Survey Water Science School web page at water.usgs.gov/edu/earthhowmuch.html.

Thermal Balance

Another fascinating revelation to me in aerospace technology comes from the routine design of amateur satellites for operation in space. The temperature extremes on the sunny side of any object in space can reach hundreds of degrees Fahrenheit, while on the shadow side temperatures can get to the minus hundreds of degrees. It is a very precarious balance to design a small satellite to operate in a survivable range.

Luckily the design of our amateur satellite PCSAT (NO-44) shown in **Figure 14.2** got it pretty close and stays in the range from about 0 °F on the

Figure 14.2 — PCSAT (NO-44), built by students at the US Naval Academy, was the first dedicated APRS satellite (see www.aprs.org/pcsat.html). Like all satellites, it achieves thermal equilibrium in space based entirely on the color of its surfaces. I was thrilled to show PCSAT to astronaut and US Senator John Glenn during Space Day 2002 at the National Air and space Museum. [Photo courtesy Art Feller, W4ART]

dark side of Earth and about 90 °F on the sunny side. This is quite tolerable for our electronics. After 17 years in space as of 2018, and still semi-operational, it is considered one of the longest surviving student satellites in space. A nice median temperature inside the space frame seems to be around a cool 40 °F or so, and a nice support for its APRS transponder.

What defines these temperatures is the very simple balance between the absorption of sunlight on all surfaces, and at the same time the emission of heat radiation from the satellite parts to the near absolute zero –454 °F of black space. So in effect, you can achieve almost any balance you need by simply choosing surfaces that have a certain absorption to sunlight and a separate emission coefficient to infrared radiation as heat. You can read much more about this in "Appendix A: The Thermal Behavior of Objects in Space" from *Countermeasures*, available online at **pdfs.semanticscholar.org/13ea/3 d02e5f0e0f7e2732012ae37119d4b2e3f11.pdf.**

For example, take three identical aluminum basketballs and place them in space about the same distance from the sun as we are on Earth. One student paints his ball black to absorb sunlight. Another one paints his ball white to reflect sunlight, and the third student does nothing and leaves his ball a shiny aluminum surface. The results are surprising to most students, as shown in **Figure 14.3A**. The white sphere will reach equilibrium at a

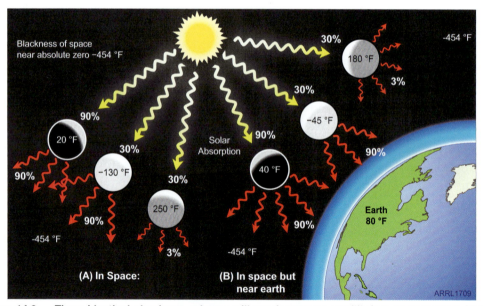

Figure 14.3 — Three identical aluminum spheres will reach extreme equilibrium temperatures based solely on the color (black, white, or shiny aluminum) and material of their surfaces and nearness to Earth.

very cold – 130 °F, while the black sphere will stabilize at about 20 °F. But the aluminum sphere will heat up to 250 °F — well above boiling. These drastic temperature extremes arise partly because black absorbs about 90% of sunlight, whereas white and aluminum might only absorb about 30% of sunlight and reflect the rest. No surprises here.

Black

But when it comes to getting rid of heat through radiation, both black and white are equally efficient at about 90%. That's why black reaches a modest 20 °F, reradiating almost equally 1:1 most of the heat gain from the sun to the black coldness near absolute zero of space. It is no coincidence that when you go underground into a cave, you find that our Earth has also reached equilibrium at a similar temperature, plus some warming from the core to around 55 °F at this same place in space, 93 million miles from the sun. Looking at Earth from afar, the colors are about right, and the heat gained from the sun is balanced by the emission of heat back to the near absolute zero of space through the exact balance of our surfaces and atmosphere.

White

White and most other colors radiate heat in the infrared almost equally as well as black, but the high reflectivity of white allows it to only absorb a third of the visible radiated energy from the sun. It gets rid of heat three times better than it absorbs it from the sun and will get very cold before it reaches equilibrium. This is why we always paint all our outdoor electronics white to avoid heat buildup. Of course, air convection in our atmosphere mitigates the difference quite a bit on Earth.

As a side note, while looking back at Earth from space, remember that this reflection of white (such as from winter snow and polar ice) has also been a significant contributor to not only weather, but our Earth's steady state thermal balance for millions of years. Any change of that balance, such as less ice and snow, will have a rising temperature effect.

Aluminum

Aluminum is the real surprise. It reflects and only absorbs the same one-third of the energy from the sun as white, but it has an amazingly low heat emission coefficient of only 3%. Thus it gains heat 10 times more efficiently than it can get rid of it, and so it gets very hot before it reaches thermal equilibrium.

It is this low heat radiating property of aluminum that makes it a good wrapper for a baked potato. Although aluminum is one of the best heat conductors (worst insulators), its inability to radiate heat can keep the heat inside and the potato quite warm. While not radiating as much heat as other objects at the same temperature, this fools the infrared heat sensors in your hand to think that it is not so hot because you don't feel as much radiant heat as you would expect. Hence the term "hot-potato" when you pick it up and find it is a lot hotter than your hand infrared sensors "see."

In Earth Orbit

The three examples in Figure 14.3A are in free space. But when these same three spheres are in orbit around Earth, the temperatures are not so extreme. This is because they only see about half of the blackness of space at near absolute zero, and the other half of their view is mother Earth. With Earth generally at a tepid average 61 °F on the surface (or perhaps 80 degrees in summer), then the infrared radiation from Earth is another source of heat to the spacecraft. It warms these satellites to the slightly more moderate temperatures shown in Figure 14.3B.

Of course, all of these extremes are further mitigated here on the surface of the Earth where we are surrounded by an atmosphere and most of our heat transfer is through air convection, not just infrared thermal radiation. But still, a piece of shiny aluminum can get quite hot in the sun and white will always be coolest.

Surface Effects

For these reasons, it is very important to pay attention to the exact surfaces when trying to make these calculations. If the aluminum is polished, it gives the results mentioned here. If it is dull or dirty, the effect can be quite different. We tried for years in the lab to get the wide theoretical temperature separations of the three surfaces, but never could get aluminum much hotter than black. Then one year while preparing aluminum in the lab, just before putting it into the vacuum chamber, I noticed that the aluminum was covered with my fingerprints! So we were not getting the aluminum effect, but the thermal balance of greasy finger oils. When we cleaned the surface with alcohol to remove all the surface contaminants, then we finally got the hot results expected for aluminum.

Along the same vein, we found some thermal tapes given to us from a space lab. Both appeared to be shiny aluminum, but one was a bit duller. On looking them up, the shiny one was labeled as low emissivity and would cause something to not radiate heat very well and it would get hot as in the above example. The other was coated with a thin layer of some kind of transparent film that had high emissivity. This one would do the opposite and be good for covering a surface you wanted to not get very hot very fast from the sun because it would cool quickly by radiating heat away in the dark.

Cast Iron Radiators in the Home

Bringing this experience back to Earth, but before learning all the nuances of surface effects on temperature, I had wanted to paint all the old cast iron radiators in the house black to improve their heat radiation into the room. My wife said no. Turns out, as noted above, white paint or almost any other color of paint radiates about the same. Also, most of the heat transfer is air convection anyway. But there is another take-away from the above discussion. In some houses you might find some thin shiny aluminum flashing stuck to the wall behind radiators. This takes advantage of the only 3% infrared emissivity so that the aluminum absorbs very little of the infrared heat but reflects the other 97% back into the room.

Thermal Heat Gun Tricks

Another tidbit for the energy DIY experimenter is to not be too enamored with the output of the plethora of easy-to-use thermal infrared heat guns available. Just point and click and it is supposed to tell you the surface temperature of anything you point at — but only in the hand of a knowledgeable person. The gun does not measure temperature at all. It can only measure infrared thermal heat radiation. Then the temperature is calculated from the degree of IR radiation converted to temperature by an assumed emissivity factor of the surface. The default value is about 0.9, which is true for almost all normal surfaces and paints as noted before.

But there are many tricky surfaces too, not only due to the differences in emissivity, but also due to reflection. Shine it at a modern classroom white board, which is really a white surface on a metal background, and you will not get the temperature of the wall, but what the white board "sees." Again, I learned this in the classroom. Pointing it at the students gave the expected 37 °C body temperature. Pointing it at other stuff in the room gave the expected 25 °C nominal room temperature, but pointing it at the white board gave the same 37 °C as the students. This confusion was resolved later when looking at the white board with a thermal camera. The white board was a perfect reflection of the infrared image of all the students in the room.

Pointing at a baked potato in aluminum foil can give all kinds of results. It could show just the temperature of the room if the aluminum is highly polished and reflecting the IR signature of the room and not emitting but 3% of the heat from the potato. Or it could read 100 °F, the temperature of the potato itself if the aluminum is all covered with the greasy handprints of the cook.

Another trick with the heat gun is to take it outdoors on a hot day even in the summer and point it off into the sky, away from the sun. It will read off-scale low (too low to measure) because the IR coming from space at –454 °F is just too low for any IR sensor to read.

Thermal Cameras

This is a real toy for the DIY energy experimenter. Now costing only a few hundred dollars, these are great tools for looking around the house for thermal leaks and hot spots. In the winter, windows of course look quite hot compared to the insulated walls. This image is used to sell a lot of very expensive thermal windows to homeowners.

But what is the IR sensor looking at? Could it be showing a huge thermal leak? Or could it be looking *through* the window and seeing just the expected warm temperature inside the room? Is the window made for solar or for IR transparency? Is it low-E or high-E glass? How much of that apparent high temperature leakage is actual IR (measured by the camera)? Most of the heat loss through a window is either leaking air or convection across the window by air (neither measured by a thermal imager). I still do not know the answers to these very subtle but important distinctions. And in most cases neither does the salesman trying to sell you the expensive windows.

Thermal Imaging of Walls

The thermal imager really does give an excellent picture of walls and ceilings and floors. On my house I could see the radiator pipes through the walls, and I could see sections of the studs with poor and good insulation.

As an example, to hang the propeller shown back in Chapter 1 in Figure 1.2 on the wall, I had to install lag screws through plaster-and-lath walls and be sure to hit the studs. With the lath and almost 1/2 inch of plaster, you cannot tap the walls to hear the studs. So I got a bunch of 500 W spotlights and directed them at the other side of the wall for an hour or so to make the back wall very warm. Then I went to the side where I wanted to hang the propeller and took a look through a thermal imager. I could see the studs perfectly. Then to mark the spots, I had my wife move her finger (bright white in the IR display) along the wall to where I could see the image of the stud was and mark it.

Figure 14.4 shows an example of a thermal image of a home exterior. Note that the window areas are warmest (red), while the ground and sky are coldest (blue).

The Hot Spot Tale

Once when poking around the basement looking at IR signatures of the floor above me for a while, I noticed about a 1 foot diameter, very bright

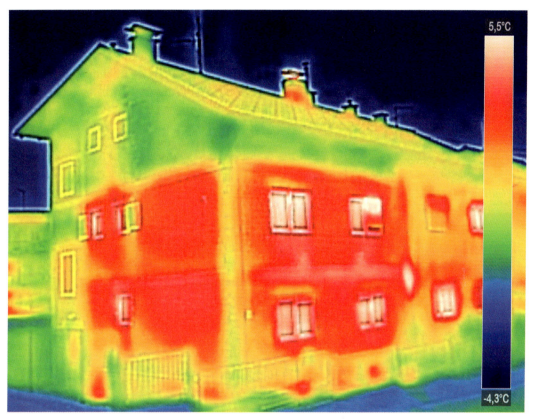

Figure 14.4 — Thermal camera images of a house are often used to look for heat loss. Note the red around the windows, indicating the warmest areas. [ivansmuk/iStock]

spot in a place I did not expect it. I realized it was near the stove and there is nothing it could be but something wrong — a fire or something? I dashed up the stairs to find the source of heat. It was a useless cat asleep on the rug by the stove. This was amazing to me. I was distinctly seeing a cat, through a solid ¾ inch wood subfloor, then another ¾ inch reconstruction underlayment, ¼ inch of mortar, then ceramic tile, then a ¾ inch thick braided rug. And finally a sleeping cat. With that kind of sensitivity, these cameras are invaluable for the energy enthusiast. You can even add a thermal imager to your phone or tablet.

Thermal Balance of the Earth

This aerospace background in space temperature gives me a special appreciation for our place here in the universe. This balance of energy that applies to small amateur satellites operating at comfortable temperatures also applies equally to something the size of our planet Earth. And Earth has arrived at equilibrium over billions of years at this spot in space with its present temperatures, its present weather, and its present flora and fauna. It's actually a very nice place to be. Not because we made it that way, but because we as a species found it comfortable as a place to evolve and thrive over the last tens of thousands of years to match the conditions that were here.

But just as we are here because of this nice balance of energy, we are also just as vulnerable to new equilibriums and temperatures when anything upsets this critical balance. Just look at Mars, which has lost 99% of its atmosphere and is cold — around –67 °F — and barren. Or look at Venus, which has captured all of its carbon dioxide and has a temperature over 870 °F. We need to remember that we only have one planet — spaceship Earth — to carry us through the cosmos, and we are now realizing we can no longer consume everything on it for immediate use and profit and ignore the long-term consequences to our thin atmosphere which defines the balance that supports life as we know it.

15 How Our Energy Use Shapes Our World Today

From tens of thousands of years ago, when humans were evolving, the feature that separated us from other creatures was our harnessing of external sources of energy to improve our existence. Our source of useful energy was almost always to burn something. First we burned fallen wood, then we harvested standing trees. When the trees were gone (**Figure 15.1**), we burned dung and peat and killed whales to burn their blubber. Then we mined coal,

Figure 15.1 — As the US population expanded, our thirst for energy decimated forests across the land. [Library of Congress, photo]

and finally we pumped oil and natural gas. All of these were consumed with vast inefficiency, and burning fuel released huge amounts of carbon dioxide into the air just for the heat we needed for warmth, cooking, and growth.

To our credit, humans have found ways to use some other forms of energy where practical. We used the power of falling water for centuries to pump water, grind grain, and eventually to smelt iron. Into the 20th century, we use it to generate electricity. Even at sea level, the Danes and Dutch developed windmills to pump water out of inundated land to create farms. Seafaring civilizations used wind to navigate the seas.

Moving to Renewable Energy

Only in the last century has man discovered a new form of renewable energy — the direct conversion of sunlight into electricity. And only in the last decade has that process become economical for everyone; and economical it is!

Figure 15.2 — Diesel trains deliver coal mined in the remote mountains of West Virginia to energy plants serving populated areas such as my home in Maryland. [John Mueller via WikiMedia Commons, photo]

But our current lifestyle is simply not sustainable in our conventional use of legacy fossil fuel energy sources. This is not so much a critique of the way we live today as it is simply the human condition. Ever since we transitioned from hunter-gatherers, mankind has simply taken what we need from mother Earth and, after the local resources are all gone, moved on to greener pastures to begin the process again. When we put down roots, we expanded into other places where the resources were still available and easier to get, exploiting them to devastation while transporting the resources back home (**Figure 15.2**).

For the few who think about going off grid and/or returning to an independent agrarian lifestyle, we need to consider that the agrarian lifestyle of our farms is not as energy independent as we might think. Some have even compared the relative energy sustainability of a horse to that of a Prius and can show that the horse comes in about double the energy efficiency. (See **fatknowledge.blogspot.com/2005/05/horses-vs-cars.html**.) This comparison uses the energy equivalency of horse grazing food per acre to a gasoline equivalence based on potential biofuel growth per acre. Not a bad approach, but it is simply dead wrong because it makes the wrong comparison based on a legacy of fossil-fuel/gas-tank thinking. It ignores where we are today, when only a single parking space of solar panels can power an electric car for over 40 miles a day forever. Or put into the same per-acre comparison, instead of powering one horse for a year, or one Prius for a year via grown biofuel, now the same one acre of solar panels could power 100 cars virtually forever at our current 40 miles a day of driving.

The simplicity of solar panels to provide energy to live trumps all previous lifestyle sources of energy by orders of magnitude. The sun has indirectly fueled our emergence as a species over tens of thousands of years, but only via consumable and limited resources with carbon stored up for us on this planet over millions of years. Now we are finally realizing that this is impossible to sustain, and this simple turn toward the direct conversion of sunlight into energy gives us plenty of hope for the future.

A Community Resource

A lot of people think that much of the talk about clean independent living involves stepping backward into a simpler and less energy intensive way of living. Similarly, some think of references to the future of solar energy as suggesting a hint of living "off the grid" through resilience and energy independence as isolated individuals.

Today, however, we understand the explosive growth of solar is not in off-grid systems (that are dependent on yet unrealized energy storage batteries), but in the progressive adoption begun over the last decade of net-metering policies that allow grid-connected personal solar systems to become economical and to bring the cost of solar electricity down below the cost of even the least expensive fossil fuel. In other words, the trend is not a withdrawal from the grid to isolated self-sufficient individuals, but a coming together in a web of distributed power of mutual support and benefit to our larger connected community.

Now as the huge economic benefits of grid-tie-solar are realized for the homeowner with good sun on their roofs, we are also just beginning to see the birth of community solar concepts that bring solar to everyone in any community independent of their roof, or shade, or housing mobility.

Growing Energy Demands

The past nature of human growth, expansion, exploitation, and consumption has worked for tens of thousands of years as humans expanded to every habitable corner of the planet. But just in my lifetime, the human population has tripled to over seven billion in 2015. The ability of our Earth to support this consumption is reaching its limits. What drives this engine of the human condition is the need for food, water, shelter, energy, and transportation.

In the United States, our thirst for energy is unparalleled. We individually consume four times more than the world average and until recently we have shown little appetite for reducing our lifestyle and consumption. However, we are turning the corner. Electricity consumption in the US peaked in 2005, and by 2014 was down to 1997 levels (see **data.worldbank.org/indicator/EG.USE.ELEC.KH.PC?locations=US**).

The long predicted peak of oil appears to have occurred or is occurring now, though there is little agreement other than it is "now" or "soon." But everyone seems to agree that it doesn't matter how much oil and coal is still in the ground. We will have serious consequences if we keep extracting and burning it at our previous rates. This new limit on "peak oil" is not based on how much we still have in the ground, but on how much of it we can actually burn without permanently unbalancing our environment. That's what makes the peak oil prediction so contentious.

The average American home consumes electricity equivalent to about four tons of coal a year to meet its energy demands (**Figure 15.3**). And the significance of that coal consumption in the eastern states is dwarfed by the unseen 80 tons of trees, habitat, flora, and fauna bulldozed into the valleys and streams of West Virginia to get those four tons of coal (**Figure 15.4**). This is the equivalent of four railroad cars of habitat lost per year per American home, an unseen travesty by any measure. Only from the air can

Figure 15.3 — The average American home consumes electricity equivalent to about four tons of coal a year to meet its energy demands. [Dr. Roy Winkelman via Florida Educational Technology Clearinghouse, photo]

(A)   (B)

Figure 15.4 — Trees are stripped and 80 tons of habitat bulldozed into nearby streams and valleys to get to my four tons of coal. The impoundment at (B) is designed to hold 5 billion gallons of slurry (liquid coal waste from mining). [Vivian Stockman, ohvec.org, photos]

Figure 15.5 — This aerial view shows the scale of mountaintop removal/valley fill coal mining in West Virginia. [Vivian Stockman, ohvec.org, photo]

we see the scale of 80 tons per American home of habitat loss as a volume of rock shown in the mountain top mining operation in **Figure 15.5**.

Land to Energy

An interesting exercise is to consider our energy consumption relative to the amount of land and nature we need to live. When our forefathers came to North America, it might have taken about four acres of forest to produce a sustainable yield of firewood to burn to meet the energy demand of a small family. And burn we did. Even the earliest photos from the 19th century show the clear-cutting of forests as we consumed our environment and pressed ever westward.

As we ran out of forests, we turned to coal, then petroleum, and then to natural gas to burn for our insatiable energy needs. Now in the 21st century we are reaping the downside of this consumption of fossil fuel that is releasing the millions of years of sequestered carbon back into the atmosphere in only a few hundred years and upsetting the balance of nature that makes our planet and climate habitable for human life.

Sun to Energy

Fortunately, along with this perilous growth in human consumption, the ability to convert solar power directly to usable energy has also been growing. In my middle school years in the 1960s and the beginning of our excursions into space, solar cells were new and essential to the space program as they were the only practical way to generate power in space for satellites.

The cost then was about $100 per watt. Although a $10 solar panel (100 milliwatts) could power a transistor radio, a $10,000 solar panel was needed to light just one 100 W light bulb. As our access to space has grown, so has the economy of scale in the development of solar cells. By 2011, the cost of large home solar panels was down to only about $4 per watt. By 2014, the cost was down to well under $1 per watt. In 2015, the cost of large-scale solar plants for electric utility production had dropped below even the cost of a new coal plant and had the advantage of no further costs for fuel!

As a result, the growth of solar systems in 2018 is increasing at nearly 120% per year and the death of coal is apparent with nearly 20% decline per year, the steepest decline since records began in 1949. (See **www.eia.gov/forecasts/steo/report/coal.cfm**.)

Living on the Land

Considering the phenomenal growth of solar energy, it is interesting to note the land required to support a solar array to sustainably power a small family in 2018 compared to the four acres of forest needed to support that family in the 18th century. There are two easy comparisons. The size of the solar array can usually be no larger than the roof of the typical house — about 0.5% of the land required 200 years ago. But what if you have shade? In that case, there is another useful comparison. That is, the area of one mature shade tree (about 400 square feet) is about the same area of solar panels needed to power a small house.

While it is disconcerting to cut down a shade tree to install solar panels, there is another important element at play. Studies have shown that each kilowatt (kW) of solar panels eliminates about the same carbon emissions as does the growth of six to eight mature trees. (See **newenglandcleanenergy.com/energymiser/2015/09/24/tree-math-2-solar-vs-trees-whats-the-carbon-trade-off/**.) Multiply this by the typical 7 kW of solar panels for a home, and putting up the solar array has the same carbon emission reduction advantage as planting an acre of trees! By another measure, removing one shade tree to install a solar array is about the same benefit as activating 50 trees relative to our overall CO_2 emissions reduction.

Trees

Trees have another value in addition to carbon absorption and making good antenna supports. They also generate at least half of the oxygen we breathe (the other half is from plankton in the oceans). In that case, it is a sobering statistic that each human on Earth needs seven to eight or so fully mature trees to live. (See **www.sciencefocus.com/qa/how-many-trees-are-needed-provide-enough-oxygen-one-person**.) From these statistics it is interesting to make a sketch of our individual sustainable footprint on Earth. We have already noted the vast reduction from four acres for firewood energy down to the size of a roof for solar. But we also need to sketch in the other requirements for human life, as shown in **Figure 15.6**.

The sketch suggests a small family might need about three acres of

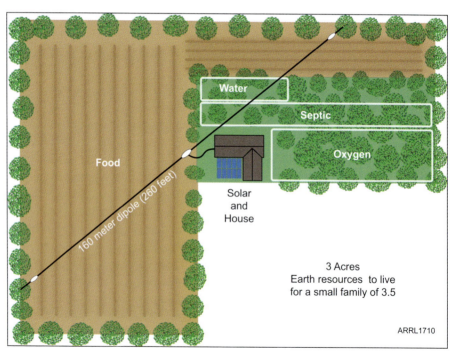

Figure 15.6 — It takes about three acres of resources to sustain a 3.5 person family and a full-size 160-meter dipole.

planet Earth to meet their sustainable resources. The area of our roof or one mature tree, as already discussed, can supply our electrical energy. Twenty tree areas can supply the oxygen, and 2+ acres of arable land can supply our food. Thirteen tree areas are needed for a conventional septic field (although this can overlap the oxygen and/or garden requirements). And a full-size 160-meter dipole can easily fit along the diagonal. Finally, four tree areas are needed for a typical house footprint. Water may come from wells below ground or from rain water on the roof. For 50 inches or so average rainfall a year such as in the eastern states, it would take about 3000 square feet, or eight tree areas, of rain water collection and storage to sustain the family.

These estimates are very approximate. For example, a common estimate of 1.25 acres per person for food can be improved nearly 7-to-1 by using intensive and well-honed farming methods. In our summary we chose two acres for crops for 3.5 people in a small family.

The purpose of this illustration is not to suggest we go back to the woods or small family farming unless we need more land for our antenna farm, but simply that we should be stewards of all of nature around us, not just the few square feet we might own or rent. A third of us live in urban environments, but there are still parks and trees as well as great rural forests and farms to protect. We can have oxygen to breathe as long as we protect eight trees somewhere for our air, and we can eat if we protect farmland somewhere from being paved over. We can also benefit from a few square feet in the community solar garden for our electric production, or a few gallons of water from the community water supply, and a few gallons of waste treatment in the community treatment plant.

Protect Nature Everywhere

If we multiply the three acres per family as a round number for our needs times the 324 million US population in 2016, we get a number that is about the same as the sum of the 750 million acres of forest and the 280 million acres of prime farmland in the US. This suggests that we are getting close to being full. We need to protect these millions of acres of forests and grasslands and farmlands to sustain our living, energy, and breathing needs — but we can only do this as a society if we collectively have the will to protect those acres. To achieve this, we must battle the calamity of the human condition, that is, the greed of the few to exploit for personal gain at the expense of all. For this reason, each of us, even if we do not own a foot of land, can work toward the common good and contribute to the protection of our forests, trees and arable lands. Find a cause, contribute, and preserve your acres somewhere. And do this all while reducing our emissions and switching to clean renewable energy where we can.

16 Conclusion

My life-long journey through the hobby of Amateur Radio provides a real cross-section between my use of energy and my interest in the use of Amateur Radio for public service. But what inspired me to write this book was the realization that we procrastinate with things that are new and are put off by the need to get around to making changes even if we know in the long run it might be the right thing to do.

When I realized that most of us end up facing major energy-changing decisions every few years as detailed in the Chapter 12, Life's Major Energy Milestones, that became the real focus of this book. That is, to help fellow hams and DIY friends to be prepared for the inevitable major energy decisions in life that they are going to have to face every few years anyway. I wanted to help them be prepared to make the right choice for a sustainable future and to improve their own financial well-being as well as being prepared for power outages and emergency communications where possible.

Looking at these energy decisions one at a time, we realize, for example, that we only get one chance every 15 years or so to change a home heating system. It would be a travesty to replace an old fossil fuel burner with a new fossil fuel burner that will continue to degrade our environment and is forever tied to a dwindling source of fuel. Instead, our home heating can be powered by sunshine forever in the future.

Similarly, we probably stumble into a possible new car decision on the American average of every six years. But each car we buy remains on the road for an average 18 years before it is finally scrapped. Again, it is a travesty to buy a pure gasoline-powered car today due to lack of thoughtful preparation. That gas-powered car will still be on the road, consuming fuel and spewing toxic emissions, in 2036. Instead, we could buy any one of the

45 EVs now on the market, and with a few solar panels have transportation energy for life.

Switching from plastic to paper, replacing meat with vegetables, and planting a tomato are great, but the sum of all the *little things* are just *little* — a pittance compared to the three major things we each need to do now, which are big. We need to stop using coal-fired electricity (switch to solar and wind), stop burning gasoline for local travel (EV or plug-in hybrid), and stop burning heating oil and propane for heat when a heat pump can do it cleaner and cheaper and with 100% renewable clean energy.

For power generation, natural gas is twice as clean as coal, and on parity with the cost of renewables, but it is still burning toxins into our air and still fuels a dependence on centralized big corporations, and exploitation of natural resources, and divisive politics. So even natural gas should be replaced and phased out when we have the opportunity.

What could be better for our communities and financial well-being, than the independence and security we get from solar energy and the electrification of transportation which uses an energy source 99% originated in the United States? This gives us freedom from international sources of oil and all other fossil fuels, while preserving those resources for the special uses where they are actually needed.

And who better to help bring about this change than the DIY ham radio operator with a long tradition of self-sufficiency through non-infrastructure-based communications and reliable portable and emergency power? The changes needed for the future depend on us all as individuals to make the next steps. And the talents of the cadre of DIY hams are a good place to start.

Your Solar Energy Choice

As you are reading this book, it is important to be thinking about all these rapidly changing technologies as summarized in **Figure 16.1**. Since economic breakeven with solar came in 2012 or so, everyone is still riding the exciting leading wave of solar implementation everywhere. Anyone who installed solar during this decade easily recouped their investment quickly and will likely be grandfathered in for the rest of their lives no matter how the grid and associated politics develop.

But in California and Hawaii, the value of solar (without storage) as evident in the Duck's Back curve (see Chapter 11, Figure 11.3) is starting to go down as more solar over-supply is coming on line. It is still a good deal, but the best deals are declining in California and Hawaii, while in other states the value of solar is still rising. Fortunately, the possible concern in

Figure 16.1 —It's a whole new world of power and energy, and DIY hams are in a great position to lead the transition.

Hawaii and California will soon be mitigated by the arrival of cost-effective home storage batteries, which are a spin-off of the EV revolution. Clearly the utilities can also invest in batteries — at large scale and cheaper than the homeowner. So like anything else, the early bird gets the worm.

By now, 46 of the 50 states are mostly on board with supporting net metering for solar to customers. This is up from only 17 or so back around 2012. Some provide much better deals than others. And now some states —

my home state of Maryland, for example — have moved on to the next wave by offering tax credits for home battery storage.

The questions to answer over the next year or so are:

1) When are you going to stop throwing away dollars to a monthly utility bill when solar is cheaper?

2) When do you need a replacement car, and how many daily miles does it need to meet your needs? If you buy a gas car, what will be the resale value in a few years when most new cars are all electric?

3) Should you consider a heat pump water heater for triple the efficiency when your existing one fails?

4) When the furnace or air conditioner unit fails, are you going to throw more money at outdated fossil fuel replacement or go with a heat pump that can run on clean renewable energy and do both heating and cooling at higher efficiency?

5) What kind of backup emergency power system do you need and for how long? Could your hybrid or EV provide the hours/days needed?

Who can deny that a source of power that is now cheaper than even coal, and that you can own yourself, is not a good investment? The only question is, who gets the benefit? You, the utility, the fossil fuel lobby, the solar leasing company, or the politicians? Even if you can't go solar due to your current situation, consider fighting back these negative forces for the benefit of your fellow neighbors, as your contribution to our future of clean renewable energy.

Finally, don't overlook the perfect marriage of home solar and EVs for perpetual free local transportation energy for life. The ultimate security in life is running your own solar energy system that can power your car and provide heat pump heating and cooling, along with having a huge battery either in your car or in your garage for perpetual energy storage under all conditions.

Appendix
References and Bibliography

Listed here are a number of resources that were helpful in the preparation of this book and may be useful for those interested in learning more about alternative energy.

General Resources

Websites

Bob Bruninga, WB4APR — **www.aprs.org**
    Updates to this book — **www.aprs.org/ARRL-power.html**
CleanTechnica — **cleantechnica.com**
Environmental Protection Agency — **www.epa.gov**
International Energy Agency — **www.iea.org**
Lawrence Livermore National Laboratory — **www.llnl.gov**
National Renewable Energy Laboratory (NREL) — **www.nrel.gov**
Princeton Laboratory for Energy Systems — **energysystems.princeton.edu**
US Department of Energy — **www.energy.gov**
US Geological Survey — **www.usgs.gov**

Automatic Packet Reporting System (APRS)

Website
Bob Bruninga, WB4APR — **www.aprs.org**

Articles
Bruninga, Robert, WB4APR, "Universal Ham Radio Text Messaging Initiative," *QST*, Sep. 2009, pp. 72 – 74.

Bruninga, Robert, WB4APR, "Maximizing the Mobile Motorist Mission," *QST*, Sep. 2008, pp 30 – 33.

Backup and Emergency Power

Websites
Bob Wilson — **hiwaay.net/~bzwilson/prius/priups.html**
PriUPS (Richard Factor, WA2IKL) — **www.priups.com**

Books and Articles
Allison, Bob, WB1GCM, "A Look at Gasoline Powered Inverter Generators," Product Review, *QST*, June 2012, pp 49 – 53.

Bryce, Mike, WB8VGE, *Emergency Power for Radio Communications*, 2nd ed., ARRL: 2012.

Cadex Electronics, Batteries in a Portable World, 4th ed., Cadex: 2016 (available from ARRL)

Gruber, Mike, W1MG, "Your Portable Generator to the Rescue," *QST*, Nov. 2013, pp. 44 – 49.

Hallas, Joel, W1ZR, "Storage Battery Planning for Public Service," *QST*, Sep. 2012, p. 43.

Hallas, Joel, W1ZR, "Velleman SOL8 Solar Panel and SOL4UCN2 Charge Controller," Short Takes, *QST*, Feb. 2011, p. 66.

Kleinschmidt, Kirk, NTØZ, "Modern Portable Power Generators — Small, Sleek and Super Stable!," *QST*, June 2008, pp 45 – 48.

Kutzko, Sean, KX9X, "Goal Zero Sherpa 50 Solar Battery and Portable Panel," Short Takes, *QST*, June 2011, p 50.

Nellis, Mert, WØUFO, "A Battery Monitor for 12 V Systems," *QST*, June 2013, pp 43 – 44.

Palm, Rick, K1CE, "Aspect Solar EnergyBar 250 and EP-55 Solar Panel Charger," Product Review, *QST*, May 2015, pp. 54 – 56.

Palm, Rick, K1CE, "Add an Inverter to Your Field Operations Kit," Public Service, *QST*, Jan. 2018, pp. 85 – 86.

Palm, Rick, K1CE, "Goal Zero Yeti 400 Lithium Portable Power Station," Product Review, *QST*, Sep. 2018, pp. 40 – 42. (Feedback, Nov. 2018 *QST*, p 35.)

Palm, Rick, K1CE, "West Mountain Radio Epic PWRgate DC Power Manager/Charge Controller," Product Review, *QST*, Dec. 2018, pp. 44 – 46.

Paquette, Jerry, WB8IOW, "Overvoltage Protection for AC Generators — Revisited," *QST*, Apr. 2013, pp. 43 – 46. (Feedback, June 2013 *QST*, p. 33)

Robins, Howard, W1HSR, "DC to AC Power Inverters," Product Review, *QST*, Apr. 2009, pp. 44 – 49.

Salas, Phil, AD5X, "West Mountain Radio CBA-IV Battery Analyzer," Product Review, *QST*, Nov. 2013, pp. 59 – 61.

Talens, Jim, N3JT, "An Emergency Backup Solar Power System," *QST*, May 2011, pp. 37 – 40. (Also see additional information in response to this article from Mike Bryce, WB8VGE; Gary Meyn, K1YAN; Jim Talens, N3JT; and Bob Bruninga, WB4APR in Technical Correspondence, *QST*, Sep. 2011, p. 53 – 55.)

Wilson, Mark, K1RO, "Bioenno Power 12 V LiFePO4 Batteries," Product Review, *QST*, Sep. 2017, pp. 50 – 52.

EVs and Hybrid Vehicles

Websites

Clean Vehicle Rebate Project — **cleanvehiclerebate.org**
Electric Vehicle Association of Greater Washington, DC — **evadc.org**
Electric Auto Association — **www.electricauto.org**
Green Car Reports — **www.greencarreports.com**
OpenEVSE — **www.openevse.com**
Solar Journey USA — **www.solarjourneyusa.com**

Articles

Danzer, Paul, N1II, "Going Mobile in an All-Electric Vehicle," *QST*, May 2014, p. 50. (Also see "Going Mobile in All-Electric Vehicles: More Tips" by Tom Tcimpidis, K6TGT, in Correspondence, July 2014 *QST*, p. 24.)

Smith, Stephen, WA8LMF, "Mobile Installation in a 2005 Toyota Prius," **wa8lmf.net/mobile/prius/index.htm**

Treharne, David, N8HKU, "Using Plug-in Hybrid Power for Amateur Radio Operation," *QST*, June 2018, pp. 66 – 68.

Solar Power and Home Energy

Websites

California Independent System Operator (CAISO) — **www.caiso.com**
Electric Choice — **www.electricchoice.com**
Green Building Advisor — **www.greenbuildingadvisor.com**
Solar Energy Industries Association (SEIA) — **www.seia.org**
US Energy Information Administration — **www.eia.gov**

Articles

Brock-Fisher, Tony, K1KP, "Can Home Solar Power and Ham Radio Coexist?," *QST*, Apr. 2016, pp. 33 – 37. (Feedback, June 2016 *QST*, p 70)

Bruninga, Robert, WB4APR, "Solar Power," Technical Correspondence, *QST*, July 2012, p 51.

Bruninga, Robert, WB4APR, "Rethinking Electrical Power for the Ham," *QST*, Aug. 2012, pp 41 – 43.

Bruninga, Robert, WB4APR, "Solar Can Be Simple and Quiet," Technical Correspondence, *QST*, Sep. 2016, pp. 61 – 62.

Factor, Richard, WA2IKL, "Solar Power and Amateur Radio," Correspondence, *QST*, July 2016, p. 24.

Haeberlin, Heinrich, HB9AZO, "Solar Power Optimizer RFI," Technical Correspondence, *QST*, Jan. 2017, p. 78

Johnson, Glenn, WØGJ, and Johnson, Vivien, KL7YL, "Solar Power and Amateur Radio," Correspondence, *QST*, July 2016, p. 24.

Nellis, Mert, WØUFO, "Characterizing Solar Panels for Amateur Radio Applications," *QST*, Feb. 2012, pp 33 – 36.

Zimmermann, Fred, N7PJN; Ryan, James, KE7GRV; Olberg, Carl, AD7LA, "Some Thoughts on Solar Trackers," *QST*, Nov. 2008, p 78.

About the Author
Bob Bruninga, WB4APR

My career in electronics, communications, and space, plus a 49-year career in the Navy (20 on active duty), began in 1955 with the building of little telegraphs from images in the encyclopedia in 2nd grade. By 4th grade, all kids within three blocks were networked with wires spliced together from the short pieces found in the Bell Telephone dumpster. I still remember the feeble glow of a flashlight bulb trying to send CW at 1 WPM because of the slowness of the orange filament to heat up after going through a neighborhood of #24 AWG hookup wire. We moved up to voice when we found some carbon mics and ear pieces from the same source, and eventually to speaker/intercoms when my FBI father brought home an obsolete "bug" microphone and its shoe-box size amplifier. The "secret mic" was the size of hockey puck! It was ancient — hence a throw-away to the government.

The author holding the RAFT cubesat at the 2004 AMSAT symposium.

My 6th grade science project was based on a CK722 transistor amplifier following a crystal radio. By middle school (1957) the space race was on, and by high school we had ham radio licenses and could communicate great distances using WWII surplus radios. To power these toys during scout camping we followed a *QST* article to rewind an old car generator to produce 110 V from a discarded lawnmower motor.

This early interest in energy evolved to my senior project at Georgia Tech in 1970, which was to electrify an old VW to participate in the first MIT/CalTech Cross-Country Clean Air Car Race (**aprs.org/my-EVs.html**). The car made it to the Mississippi. After Georgia Tech, which I had attended on an ROTC scholarship, I was shipped across country to Navy graduate school in Monterey, California. There, I got on 2-meter FM with a club buy of Motorola surplus "dispatcher" radios. At my next duty station in Pearl Harbor, I configured a suitcase-sized VHF FM transceiver in the trunk of my car and used an old telephone dial to make phone calls through the ham radio repeater on Diamond Head in 1971.

During this time, the University of Hawaii had experimented with similar radios to interconnect remote teletypes from the other islands to access the central computer on Oahu with modems. This shared use of a data channel was called the Aloha protocol and can be considered the beginnings of packet radio and eventually what evolved into things like the internet. By 1975, and while stationed in the Washington, DC area, our local radio club developed similar teletype links to one of the first microcomputers (a 6800 CPU) in my basement. We spun off teletype support into one of the first dial-up TTY networks for the deaf. For faster speed, our local club (AMRAD) developed the AX.25 protocol for data over radio and the FCC made it legal in 1978. It is viable to this day.

During a sea tour in Japan I began to experiment with this data channel for plotting the location of ships using a knock-off Apple-II type motherboard and by the mid 1980s had developed a protocol called the Connectionless Emergency Traffic System (CETS) which was demonstrated at the National Disaster Medical Exercise (NDMS) in 1986 to facilitate ham radio support of emergency communications. By 1992, I combined the position info with the traffic data and called it the Automatic Packet Reporting System (APRS) to match my call sign, WB4APR. Since that time, APRS has grown worldwide with many tens of thousands of users and is accessible to anyone via the APRS Internet system and such access sites as **FINDU.COM** and **aprs.fi**. More information about the history of APRS may be found at **www.aprs.org/APRS-docs/ARTICLES.TXT**.

By 2001, I was teaching at the Naval Academy and married to a lovely astrophysicist (so I could get access to her observatory roof for my antennas). There, I mentored our first student satellite, PCSAT (NO-44), to carry this protocol into space. This was followed by 10 other such spacecraft, including PSAT (NO-84) and other experiments paralleling the 2007 timeframe when I had my energy epiphany chronicled in this book and began my remaining lifelong journey, working to change the world to renewable energy as described in these chapters.

Index

The letters "ff" after a page number indicate coverage of the indexed topic on succeeding pages.

A

Air (world's supply): 14.2
Air conditioner and heat pump: 12.11
    DIY project to heat a classroom: 13.8
Amateur Radio
    ARRL Field Day power sources: 5.3, 9.12ff
    Author's experiences: 1.1ff
    Automatic Packet Reporting System (APRS): 1.9ff
    Backup/emergency power system: 9.1ff
    Bulletin board system (BBS): 1.8
    Golden Packet APRS event portable power: 10.8ff
    Home solar system radio frequency interference (RFI): 6.8ff
    LED lighting radio frequency interference (RFI): 6.4ff
    Mobile installation in EV: 7.10
    Mobile operation RF interference: 6.2
    Radio frequency interference (RFI) from new energy systems: 6.1ff
    Satellites: 14.1ff
    Solar power for the ham shack: 5.22
    Space needed for 160 meter dipole: 15.8
Amateur Radio Research and Development (AMRAD): 1.8
Amateur satellite: 14.1ff
    PCSAT (NO-44): 14.3
    Thermal balance: 14.3ff
Arc-flash: 1.6

ARRL Field Day
    Solar power: 9.12
    Using power from a plug-in hybrid: 9.14
Automatic Packet Reporting System (APRS): 1.9ff
    Energy objects: 1.13
    Frequency Format: 1.13
    Golden Packet event portable operation: 10.8ff
    Repeater objects: 1.13
    Voice Alert: 1.12

B

Backup power: 9.1ff
    Battery system: 5.2, 5.23, 9.1ff
    Battery system for minimal needs: 9.11
    Estimating power needs: 9.5
    High-voltage dc systems: 10.1ff
    Hybrid battery capacity: 9.16
    Inverter in 12 V vehicle: 9.18
    Jim Talens (N3JT) battery system: 9.1ff
    Lighting: 9.6
    Plug-in hybrid example: 9.14
    Portable generator: 9.8ff
    Prius battery capacity: 9.23
    Refrigerator/freezer requirements: 9.7
    Tesla Powerwall: 11.8
    Uninterruptible power supply (UPS) in Prius: 9.20
    Using a hybrid or EV: 9.12
    Using power from a Prius: 9.18
    Vehicle-to-Home: 9.13, 9.25
Battery
    Backup power system: 5.2, 5.23, 9.1ff, 11.8
    Backup power system for minimal needs: 9.11
    Electric vehicle (EV) capacity: 7.2
    Home power storage: 3.6
    Not a fuel tank: 7.2
    Overcharging safety: 1.16
    Storage: 11.1ff
    Storage for afternoon utility peak: 11.6

Battery swap technology: 7.17
Bicycle
    Electric: 12.31
    Sharing: 12.31

C

Chain saw: 12.27
Charging
    At work for federal employees: 7.7, 13.12
    DIY electric vehicle (EV): 5.18
    DIY J1772 EVSE design: 8.8
    Electric vehicle (EV): 7.2ff
    Electric vehicle (EV) charging speed: 7.20
    Electric vehicle (EV) cost: 7.3, 7.24
    Electric vehicle (EV) grid load: 7.4
    Electric vehicle (EV) signs: 13.10
    Electric vehicle (EV) while parked: 13.1ff
    EVgo public charging station: 7.22
    EVSE Level 1: 7.19
    EVSE Level 2: 7.20
    EVSE Level 3: 7.21
    J1772 EVSE connector: 7.19, 8.6
    Retractable L1 EVSE cable: 8.10
    Triangle (options available): 7.23
Chevy Volt: 1.23, 7.13
    Inverter installation: 9.21
Coal
    Burning for power: 15.1
    Mining: 1.22, 15.4
Community solar: 12.7, 15.3
Cubesat: 3.5

D

Duck's Back curve: 11.4

E

Elect-Reck EV project: 1.3
Electric boat (DIY): 1.20, 5.21
Electric vehicle (EV) (*see also* Hybrid vehicle): 7.1ff
    Battery capacity: 7.2
    Charging at work: 13.2, 13.12
    Charging at work for federal employees: 7.7
    Charging cost: 7.3, 7.25
    Charging from solar panels: 13.1
    Charging signs: 13.10
    Charging types: 7.19ff
    Charging while parked: 13.1ff
    Chevy Volt: 1.23, 7.13
    Civic Truck-E conversion: 8.18
    Conversion from gas engine: 8.12ff
    Cost (new and used): 7.8
    Dealership concerns: 7.25
    DIY charging: 5.18
    DIY J1772 EVSE design: 8.8
    DIY projects: 8.1ff
    During power outages: 9.24
    Elect-Reck project: 1.3
    Extending Prius range (DIY): 8.13
    For home backup power: 9.12
    Ham radio installation: 6.2, 7.10
    J1772 EVSE operation: 8.6
    Local travel and commuting: 7.5ff
    Long distance travel: 7.18
    Maintenance: 7.10
    Mild EV project: 8.1
    MPGe: 7.14
    Nissan Leaf: 7.13
    Pickup truck: 7.13
    Pre-heating hacks: 8.2
    Public charging: 7.21, 13.11
    Radio frequency interference (RFI) 6.2
    Range: 7.14
    Range vs cost: 7.3
    Replacing gas cars: 12.30

    Retractable L1 EVSE cable: 8.10
    Sales history: 12.30
    Sebring Vanguard Electric City Car: 1.8
    Solar carport: 13.1
    Steering wheel heater: 8.5
    THINK City Car: 1.22
    Transmission adapter plate: 8.16
Emergency power (*see* Backup Power)
Energy losses in gas or diesel car: 7.11
Energy milestones: 12.1ff
    Summary: 16.1ff
Energy sources
    Coal: 15.1
    History of: 15.1
    Move to renewables: 12.1ff, 13.1ff, 15.2
    Wood: 15.1
Energy sources and consumption in the US: 3.1
Energy supplier choices: 12.1
Energy use past and present: 15.4
EV Supply Equipment (EVSE): 7.19ff
    Level 1: 7.19
    Level 2: 7.20
    Level 3: 7.21
EVgo public charging station: 7.22

F

Fans
    Radiator: 12.18
    Whole house: 12.24
Fossil fuel use reduction: 13.6ff

G

Generator (portable): 9.8ff
    Energy production per gallon of gas: 9.19
Geothermal HVAC heat pump (*see* heat pump)
Grid storage: 3.4
Grid-tie inverter: 3.7, 4.1ff

H

Heat pump: 1.21, 12.11ff
    Cost vs oil heat: 13.4
    DIY geothermal system: 12.20ff
    Efficient operation: 12.16
    Geothermal HVAC: 12.14ff
    Hot water: 5.13, 12.8
    HVAC units: 12.11
    Portable air conditioner: 12.11
    Radiator fans: 12.18
    Solar powered: 12.12
    Storage tank: 12.17
    Temperature setback: 12.20
    Using portable air conditioner (DIY): 13.8
    Window or portable: 5.16
Heating project
    DIY radiator-based hot water: 5.6
    DIY resistance coils: 5.6
Heating-ventilation-air conditioning (HVAC): 12.10ff
High-voltage dc
    Arc-flash: 1.6
    dc/dc converter: 2.7
    Disconnect: 5.9
    Distribution: 2.6
    Emergency and backup power: 10.1ff
    EV charging: 7.21
    Long distance power distribution: 10.8ff
    Power connectors (DIY): 10.6
    Power cords: 10.7
    RC snubber: 1.7, 10.2
    Safety: 1.6, 2.6, 10.2
    Single wire earth return (SWER): 10.8ff
    Solar array taps: 2.8
    Solar backup power system: 9.28
    Uninterruptible power supply (UPS) input from Prius: 9.17, 9.20
    Universal power supply: 2.3
    Used with 12-V input inverter: 10.4

Hot water
- DIY project: 5.10
- Heat pump: 5.13, 12.8
- Solar thermal system: 5.11

Hybrid vehicle (see also Electric vehicle (EV)): 1.14ff, 7.11ff
- Battery overcharging: 1.16
- Cost (new and used): 7.12
- Extending Prius range (DIY): 8.13
- For home backup power: 9.12
- Mobile operation RF interference: 6.2
- MPGe: 7.14
- Plug-in: 7.11
- Prius Hotel: 1.17
- Prius Inn: 1.17
- Range: 7.14
- Salvage Prius: 1.15
- Woodie Prius: 1.15

Hydrogen fuel cell vehicle (FCEV): 7.16

I

Infrared heat gun: 14.7

Inverter
- Converting from 12 V to higher-voltage dc input: 10.4
- For 12 V vehicle: 9.18
- Grid-tie: 3.7, 4.1ff
- Maintenance: 4.8
- Microinverter: 4.4
- Optimizer: 4.7
- Over-rating with additional panels: 3.20
- Radio frequency interference (RFI): 6.9
- Secure power outlet for grid-down use: 9.27
- String inverter: 4.3

Inverter generator: 9.8

J

J1772 EVSE connector: 7.19, 8.6
- DIY charge tester: 8.9
- DIY design: 8.8
- Retractable L1 cable: 8.10

L

Land
- Resources needed for a family: 15.8
- Sustainable power requirement: 15.7ff

Lawn and garden equipment: 12.24ff
- Chain saw: 12.27
- Electric vs gas powered: 12.24
- Lawnmower: 12.24
- Noise: 12.29
- Snow blower: 12.28
- String trimmer: 12.26

LED lighting: 9.6, 12.8
- Radio frequency interference (RFI): 6.4ff

M

Maximum Power Point Tracking (MPPT): 3.10
Microinverter: 4.4
MPGe: 7.14

N

Net metering: 3.8, 4.13, 5.18
Nissan Leaf: 7.13
- DIY EVSE charging box: 8.11

O

Optimizer: 4.7
- Radio frequency interference (RFI): 6.9
Orientation of solar panels: 3.15ff

P

Plug-in hybrid: 7.11
Power cords: 10.7
Power supply: 2.1ff
- Dual-voltage 120/240 V: 2.4
- High-voltage dc input: 2.3
- Safety: 2.6
- Universal: 2.2

Powerwall: 11.1ff
Prius: 1.15, 7.13
    Backup power with high-voltage dc UPS: 9.20
    DIY instrumentation: 8.12
    For home backup power: 9.18
    Standalone battery capacity (for backup power): 9.23
PVwatts calculator: 3.11ff

R

Radio frequency interference (RFI): 6.1ff
    LED lighting: 6.4ff
    Mobile operation in a hybrid: 6.2
    Solar system mitigation: 6.16ff
RC snubber: 1.7, 10.2
Roof replacement: 12.4

S

Safety
    DIY geothermal system: 12.22
    DIY heating project: 5.7
    DIY hot water heating: 5.11
    EV battery overcharging: 1.16
    High-voltage dc: 1.6, 2.6, 10.2
    Hot water systems: 5.13
    Power cord ratings: 10.8
    Single wire earth return (SWER): 10.11
    Spooled power cords: 8.11
Sebring Vanguard Electric City Car: 1.8
Secure power outlet (SMA inverter): 9.27
Shading considerations
    Solar panel 3.22ff
    Tree removal: 12.6
Single wire earth return (SWER): 10.8ff
    Soil resistance: 10.11
Snow blower: 12.28
Soil resistance: 10.11

Solar cell: 3.9ff
    Current vs voltage (I-V) curve: 3.9
    Efficiency: 3.2
    Illumination: 3.10
    Maximum Power Point Tracking (MPPT): 3.10
    Price history: 3.3
Solar panel
    Azimuth angle: 3.16
    Cleaning: 5.26
    In parallel - facing different directions: 3.18
    Orientation: 3.15ff
    Shading (effects of): 3.22ff
    Sun tracking arrays: 3.20
    Tilt angle: 3.16
    Vertical or horizontal placement: 3.23
Solar Pathfinder tool: 3.24ff
Solar power: 1.18ff, 3.1ff
    Array azimuth angle: 3.16
    Array tilt angle: 3.16
    Battery storage: 3.6, 11.1ff
    Breakeven cost ($ per watt): 3.14
    Carport for EV charging: 13.1
    Cleaning panels: 5.26
    Community solar: 12.7, 15.3
    DIY car charging: 5.18
    DIY heating project: 5.6
    DIY projects: 5.1ff
    DIY system vs contractor installed: 5.24
    Electric boat (DIY): 1.20, 5.21
    Electricity pricing: 4.14
    Financing options: 4.9ff
    Floating deck: 5.22
    Grid storage: 3.4
    Grid-down EV charging: 9.27
    Grid-tie inverter types: 4.1ff
    Grid-tie system DIY projects: 5.19
    Heat pump: 12.12
    Heat pump hot water: 5.13
    High-voltage dc taps: 2.8
    Home solar systems: 4.1ff

Illuminance map: 3.13
　　Inverter secure power outlet: 9.27
　　Leased system: 4.9
　　Maximum Power Point Tracking (MPPT): 3.10
　　Net metering: 3.8, 4.13, 5.18
　　Off-grid system: 5.1ff, 5.25
　　Panel orientation: 3.15ff
　　Paralleling different facing solar panels: 3.18
　　Peak power value: 4.13
　　Performance estimates: 3.11ff
　　Plugging in extra panels: 5.20
　　Purchased system: 4.11
　　PVwatts calculator: 3.11ff
　　Radio frequency interference (RFI): 6.8ff
　　Rooftop system: 12.4
　　Shading considerations: 3.22ff
　　Single panel for minimum loads: 5.14
　　Solar cell efficiency: 3.2
　　Solar cell price history: 3.3
　　Solar cell technology: 3.9ff
　　Solar Pathfinder tool: 3.24ff
　　Solar pier: 1.20
　　Summary: 16.2
　　Sun tracking arrays: 3.20
　　Sundicator tool: 3.23
　　Thermal hot water system: 5.11
　　Tree removal: 15.7
　　Without net metering: 5.14
String inverter: 4.3
String trimmer: 12.26
Sun path: 3.26
Sundicator tool: 3.23
Switching to clean renewable energy (examples): 12.1ff, 13.1ff

T

Tesla
　　Powerwall: 11.1ff
　　Powerwall cost: 11.6
　　Supercharger network: 7.21

Index　11

Thermal balance
    Effect of color: 14.4ff
    Objects in space: 14.1ff
    Of Earth: 14.10
    Surface effects: 14.6
Thermal imaging: 14.8
THINK City Car: 1.22
Transient suppressor: 4.7

U

Uninterruptible power supply (UPS)
    High-voltage dc input: 9.17
    High-voltage dc input in Prius: 9.20
Universal power supply: 2.2
    High-voltage dc input: 10.3
Utility power
    Cost fluctuations: 11.1
    Cost vs solar system: 4.11, 13.4
    Demand vs time of day: 11.3
    Duck's Back curve: 11.4

V

Vehicle-to-Home
    Nissan Leaf: 9.13
    Toyota Prius: 9.25

W

Water (world's supply): 14.2
Wind power
    Home system: 1.4
    Large-scale utility installation: 12.3

Notes

Notes

Notes